Legality, Morality, and Ethics in Criminal Justice

edited by
Nicholas N. Kittrie
Jackwell Susman

Published in cooperation with the
American Society of Criminology

LEGALITY, MORALITY, AND ETHICS IN CRIMINAL JUSTICE

PRAEGER PUBLISHERS
Praeger Special Studies

New York   •   London   •   Sydney   •   Toronto

Library of Congress Cataloging in Publication Data

Main entry under title:

Legality, morality, and ethics in criminal justice.

   1. Criminal justice, Administration of--United
States--Addresses, essays, lectures. 2. United
States--Moral conditions--Addresses, essays, lectures.
3. Ethics--Addresses, essays, lectures. I. Kittrie,
Nicholas N., 1928-   II. Susman, Jackwell.
HV8138.L352   364'.973   78-11537

PRAEGER PUBLISHERS
PRAEGER SPECIAL STUDIES
383 Madison Avenue, New York, N.Y. 10017, U.S.A.

Published in the United States of America in 1979
by Praeger Publishers,
A Division of Holt, Rinehart and Winston, CBS, Inc.

9   038   987654321

ACKNOWLEDGMENTS

Most of the papers that form the basis of this book were read at the 1975 and 1976 annual meetings of the American Society of Criminology. Many writers graciously accepted the invitation of the editors and made changes in their manuscripts for purposes of publication. We wish to thank the authors.

Burton Atkins, Associate Professor, Department of Government, The Florida State University

Richard A. Ball, Professor, Department of Sociology, West Virginia University

Nancy J. Beran, Associate Professor of Sociology and LaVelle Professor of Criminal Justice, Ohio Dominican College and Assistant Professor, School of Public Administration, Ohio State University

Scott Decker, Assistant Professor, Administration of Justice, University of Missouri-St. Louis

Richard Dembo, Associate Professor, Department of Social Sciences, Clarkson College

Dennis D. Dorin, Assistant Professor, Department of Political Science, The University of North Carolina at Charlotte

John Hagan, Associate Professor, Department of Sociology, School of Graduate Studies, Centre of Criminology, University of Toronto

Marshall J. Hartman, Executive Director, Criminal Defense Consortium of Cook County, Inc., Illinois

Jerome Himelhoch, Professor, Department of Sociology, University of Missouri-St. Louis

Leonard J. Hippchen, Professor, Administration of Justice and Public Safety, Virginia Commonwealth University

Alphonso Jackson, Director, Department of Public Safety, City of St. Louis, Missouri

Lawrence Kielich, Assistant Professor, Department of Sociology, Aquinas College

Jack B. Kamerman, Kean College of New Jersey and Graduate Student, Department of Sociology, New York University

Marianna Koval, Undergraduate Student, Department of Politics, Princeton University

John C. Meyer, Jr., Associate Professor, School of
Justice. The American University

Raymond J. Michalowski, Associate Professor, Department of Sociology, University of North Carolina at
Charlotte

Harold E. Pepinsky, Associate Professor, Department
of Forensic Studies, Indiana University

Mark Pogrebin, Associate Professor, Graduate School
of Public Affairs, University of Colorado at Denver

Jeffrey Reiman, Professor, School of Justice, The
American University

Rosalind Reiman, Probation Officer, U.S. District
Court, Washington, D.C.

Peter Scharf, Assistant Professor, Program of Social
Ecology, The University of California at Irvine

John C. Watkins, Jr., Professor and Chairman, Criminal Justice Program, The University of Alabama

Vergil L. Williams, Associate Professor, Criminal
Justice Program, The University of Alabama

L. Thomas Winfree, Assistant Professor, Department
of Sociology, East Texas State University

The editors also wish to thank Jill Berman Wilson for her editorial assistance. A word of thanks is also due to Patricia Marshall
for her persistence and assistance in tying up loose ends.

CONTENTS

Page

LIST OF TABLES AND FIGURES

INTRODUCTION
Nicholas N. Kittrie and Jackwell Susman

Watergate and Vietnam have raised questions of moral and
ethical values for our system of justice that have not yet been resolved. Civil disorder by political protesters, the criminal prosecution of those challenging the legality of America's foreign involve-
ments, violations of the law by government officials in the name of
national security, the unauthorized release of classified official
documents, the granting of the Nixon pardon and the impact of the
Vietnam amnesty—all these are mere random samples of the host of
issues raised in recent years. Yet the questions of values have been
skirted, by and large, by both scholars and practitioners, even though
the answers are central to an understanding of the working of the
criminal justice system.

This book offers a new and uncommon contribution to the growing field of criminal justice evaluation. It seeks to deal with the
evaluation of the goals and values of the system rather than the evaluation of processes and operations. The systems analysis approach,
long in vogue as an evaluation technique, has focused on the effectiveness of justice system operations and has been concerned with
measuring goal attainment. But no matter how sophisticated or complex, systems analysis is basically technocratic in orientation. From
its particular perspective the goals and values of the criminal justice
system are assumed or, perhaps, taken for granted. Yet the greatest
understanding of the raison d'etre and the dynamics of institutions
(as well as of individuals) is contained in the very values that we take
for granted.

Our approach differs from most efforts by being holistic; that
is, we view legality, morality, and ethics as three autonomous yet
interrelated scales for the analysis of our system of justice. Each
measure provides us with a standard for evaluating both the criminal
justice system and its actors. To look at criminal justice in terms
of the goals and values of both the system and the actors is more difficult than trying to measure effectiveness, but it is essential if we

1

are to measure the quality of justice. Recent interest in the quality of life and its measurement through social indicators suggests the applicability of these approaches to the field of justice.

By and large, most of the evaluation that is conducted of criminal justice utilizes the systems approach. As important as the knowledge gained through this method may be for operative and managerial purposes, it is insufficient to reflect the deeper concerns and conflicts in contemporary life in the United States. Much of the writing that has been done recently with regard to justice goals and values tends to be limited in meaningfulness and impact. The literature has often been abstract and nonoperational in approach; frequently, it has overlooked the actors while concentrating on the system. The work of John Rawls, for example, for all its stirring impact, has had limited practical and policy implications. The efforts of others to articulate standards and goals for criminal justice has likewise suffered from the failure to offer tools for the evaluation of goals. In this volume, we seek to advocate a comprehensive evaluation effort with a balanced mix of both systems analysis and goals analysis.

The goals analysis approach to criminal justice evaluation begins with the premise that the distinctive character of an institution (as well as of its actors) is in great part determined by its goals. At times, the goals of a criminal justice system are specifically articulated in the law or in some other formal pronouncement. However, such formal goal manifestations are often lacking, or otherwise, must be amplified or modified in light of actual practice. Generally speaking, however, the goals of a society, institution, or actor are evidenced by both their stated values and their behavior. In our attention to goals evaluation we seek to explore, in particular, a values approach.

We suggest that there are three clusters of values that underlie the goals of criminal justice and those of its actors: legality, morality, and ethics. In any consideration of the relationship of legality, morality, and ethics to the criminal justice system, it is important to indicate how we use these terms. By legality we mean the rule of law. Legality imposes an environment of constraint, of tests to be met, of standards to be observed, and of ideals to be fulfilled (Selznick 1966). The internal logic of legality may be found in two distinct and sometimes conflicting traditions, those of natural law and positive law. The former sees the rule of law as drawing its authority from a supreme lawgiver (or from some equally binding social or psychological or other compelling forces); accordingly, the reason why men and women abide by the rule of law is because it purports to sanction the natural law which has been written into every man's and woman's makeup. Positive law sees the rule of law as drawing its authority from state sovereignty and power. The resultant rule of law is thus based upon a sliding scale of force ranging from education and social pressure to criminal sanctions and terror in all forms.

Ethics, as used here, refers to the general, at times abstract yet comprehensive principles (for example, justice as fairness), which underlie human systems. Ethical principles are not rules of conduct, but rather formulas for testing legal and moral rules. The role of ethical principles is not to tell us what to do in particular cases (which is the function of a legal or moral rule system) but to provide us with standards of relevance or reasonableness when the appraisal of rules is desired or required. With regard to ethical principles, and to rules of law as well, it is possible to see their sources in either positive ethics or natural ethics.

Morality is used here to specify those rules of conduct, applicable to both the system and its actors, which go beyond the legal rules. The moral level is where operational questions are being asked and given: What ought I to do in such and such a situation? At this level, there appear a problem of conduct and a problem for appraisal and ultimate decision. When we operate at the moral level we normally operate within tacit group norms, trying to apply these ethical rules to concrete situations (Aiken 1962: 65-87). As Thomas Hobbes has noted, the moral level refers to "decency of behavior as how one should salute another, or how a man should wash his mouth, or pick his teeth before company and such other points of small morals" (Hobbes 1946: 63). But moral rules encompass also a host of more complex questions of conduct which seriously affect both individual and communal life.

One of the purposes of this volume is to help define and clarify legality, morality, and ethics as they affect both the goals and the functioning of the criminal justice system and of the diverse actors within it. No effective evaluation of a criminal justice system can take place without such scrutiny of its goals. Equally important is our suggestion that the values and goals of both the system and the actors must be separately identified and examined. Although the values of the actors and of the system may be in harmony, we cannot overlook the possibility of disagreement or conflict which might impact on the functioning, or produce a disfunctioning, of the system.

We content further that the study of legality, morality, and ethics furnishes important insights into the exercise of discretion by criminal justice actors. The exercise of discretion has received increasing attention in recent years, with the police, prosecutors, and judges becoming subjects for study. Discretion, as we identify it here, refers to certain categories of decision making by actors in the system. Indeed, one of the major functions of discretion might involve the resolution of conflicts between clusters of values: the

legal, the moral, and the ethical. A central issue in the new concern
with discretion might not be merely the fear of partiality, but the
awareness of potential conflicts produced by these diverse value
clusters.

The exercise of discretion, we suggest, may be conceptualized
in three distinct ways, each utilizing a different model. The first
model of discretion may be described as mixed. Discretion, from
the point of view of the actors in the system, involves in this case
choosing between societal legality, morality, and ethics as the basis
for the decision. We suggest also another—the ethical or moral—
model of discretion, in which the choice might be between the actor's
and society's differing ethical or moral requirements. Finally, there
is the legal model of discretion, which involves, from the actor's
perspective, a choice between legality and illegality in the making of
a decision.

Legality, morality, and ethics, with their differing roots, offer many potentials for conflict within the criminal justice system.
These conflicts may make it impossible to describe the goals of the
criminal justice system in a logical and consistent manner. The conflicts may make it impossible to harmonize the personal goals of the
actors with the goals of the system. Finally, these conflicts may
make the achievement of specified societal goals difficult or even
impossible.

Thus, beyond its concern with goal evaluation, a major thrust
of this book is to provide a fresh look at discretion from the perspective of the actor. The papers in this volume make it clear that we
cannot readily predict how actors will behave without understanding
the nature of the value conflicts. Only through increased attention to
these conflict areas may we gain the necessary insights into criminal
justice evaluation and be better able to understand why the goals of
the system may or may not be effectuated.

Before proceeding to a detailed discussion of the papers included in this book, several general matters should be kept in mind.
To begin with, many of these papers deal with moral issues that proceed on more than one level. In part, this occurs because the context
of moral discussion tends to be a shifting one. Second, the moral
issues raised in these papers tend to be practical in intention and in
effect. This ties in very well with the nature of the analyses; they
are primarily pragmatic rather than logical. Third, the individual
feelings or aspirations of the authors are often quite obvious. This
is not to say that the justification for their arguments is absent.
Rather, our point is that some of the arguments are "objective" and
some of the arguments are more "subjective," as we shall see in
more detail later. The editors of this collection assume responsibility
for the decision to assign a paper to a particular section. It has

sometimes been a difficult decision, and we do not doubt that other ways of categorizing a paper are possible.

The first section of the book includes papers that examine aspects of the <u>Linkages Between Legality, Morality, and Ethics</u>. Ideally, there should be a congruence between legality and the moral rules and ethical principles that support laws. Law-abiding behavior would follow as a matter of course. Hippchen argues in the first paper in this section that delinquent behavior is expressive of a lack of moral values. Applying Maslow's metamotivational theory, Hippchen goes further. He claims that delinquent behavior is produced as a result of the deprivation of intrinsic values. Furthermore, according to Maslow, the primary sources of value deprivation are the materialistic environment and "inner ambivalence and countervalues." Hippchen finds that he and his co-workers have had great success in treating delinquents by teaching selected delinquents the meaning of certain values. The next paper in this section takes another tack; Dorin looks at the moral outrage generated by Watergate and its aftermath and wonders about the long-term effect this may have upon the public's support for the criminal justice system. He suggests two basic alternative futures: support for the system may decline or support for the system may actually increase. The crucial difference seems to be whether the public's perception is fixed upon the crimes of Watergate, on the one hand, or their resolution in Congress and the courts, on the other. In either case we see more concretely how inner ambivalence and countervalues are generated.

The role of personal commitments, organizational constraints, and community standards are to some extent discussed by Pogrebin and Atkins in their review of perspectives on police corruption. They note that the values of legislators and interest groups as embodied in legislation may differ from the values of police who are drawn from a different social class and who tend to isolate themselves from other occupational groups. Community attitudes toward the police are ambivalent; the community wants honest policemen but also wants to bribe them. Furthermore, there is no community consensus on the enforcement of moralistic laws. This situation creates many opportunities for corruption.

In the next paper, Hartman and Koval consider plea bargaining immoral, although it is legal. They make basically two pragmatic arguments to support their contention about its morality. Plea bargaining is costly, and defendants are penalized for exercising their constitutional right to trial. Generally, we determine the morality of a rule by appeal to a higher-order principle. We have no such principle here for at least two reasons.

On the one hand, there would have to be widespread agreement about the factual status of bargaining. That is, there would have to be some kind of consensus that, for purposes of achieving justice, the method of plea bargaining is not appropriate because it violates some of the rules (such as discussed by Hartman and Koval) that express our valuation of justice as an ideal. In addition, there would have to be a consensus about what rules manifest the ethical ideal of justice. Insofar as plea bargaining is concerned, neither of these two conditions exist; there is precious little consensus about justice and very little consensus about how to achieve justice. Put another way, there is some consensus to support the notion that justice may be achieved through plea bargaining. For example, in a recent issue of Psychology Today a prosecutor presented a picture of the moral anguish he felt before reaching a bargaining decision (Phillips 1977: 70-75, 85-88). We do not get a sense of whether his feelings represented public or private anguish; however, he does convey the feeling that justice was well served.

Hagan looks at the linkages between legality, morality, and ethics from a different perspective. He asks why all upperworld citizens are not criminals. Hagan suggests that a combination of inner moral controls and external situational controls keep most people from acting illegally or immorally. But, on the one hand, upperworld morality is ill-defined, rendering inner controls problematic. On the other hand, situational controls depend upon perceived risks and benefits, and the perception of risk seems to be decreasing. As this perception becomes widespread the social pressures that have restrained criminal behavior may become pressures that encourage criminal behavior. As a result, violations of public and financial trust and other forces of upperworld crime may become more commonplace. This type of analysis could be (and to some extent has been) used to explain ordinary, lower-class crime, just as Hippchen's approach has been used to explain upper-class crime. What needs further study and analysis is the relationship between upperworld crime and lowerworld crime.

Beran's paper, the last in this section, makes an argument somewhat similar to Hagan's, but she more specifically directs herself to one elite, criminologists. She claims that the absolutism of the social order is disintegrating; there are no longer any absolute definitions of crime or morality. Even value-free science is a myth. There is a crisis in social theory, social thought, and in society itself. The structural inducements to behave morally in society are disappearing. In addition, she argues that we are grossly confused about values, and until some clarification is achieved the activities of criminologists will continue to be arbitrary at best and inimical to the elusive concept of morality at the worst. She hopes for a restructuring of the total society, although it is not clear what this restructuring may mean. The moral absolutism that Beran implies to have existed in the past is as mythical as a unicorn; moreover, we would not be very happy if such a system were to be imposed upon us. We are facing real dangers—a moral relativism tending toward nihilism, a pragmatism tending toward an amoral instrumentalism, a realism tending toward cynicism, an individualism tending toward atomism, and a faith in reason and democratic processes tending toward more credulity and idolotry—but they will not be solved with the romantic imagery of the past. The future is likely to be similar to the present and the past, full of conflicts, perils, and changes, and we shall have to find ways to deal with them. For example, some people sense in many middle-class environmentalists an asceticism which the latter would like to impose on everybody: less meat, fewer cars, durable denim, recycling, smaller homes, humbler forms of recreation—a return to the "simple" life. But the labor movement and working-class people may have other priorities (Baldwin 1976: 7-11). At the same time, moral outrage and criminal behavior may reflect the confusion or the absence of values which result from conflict, among other causes. Conflict may undermine morals and ethics, or their structural foundations, but it is doubtful that we can or should eliminate conflicts. The feelings of these authors are authentic, but we need other perspectives to help us understand and deal with the many questions that the relationship between legality, morality, and ethics raise for us.

To other theorists, apparently concerned with similar problems, ethics have suggested a biological basis for ethics. Maslow (1970: 75-95), whose theory was utilized to some extent by Hippchen as a basis for his work, argues that the need for basic values is "instinctoid," as we noted above. Somewhat less definite in this regard is Kohlberg, whose theory forms the basis of Scharf's study (discussed below). Kohlberg argues that individual moral development proceeds in a universal sequence of distinct stages from what he refers to as the preconventional level, through the conventional level, to the postconventional level (see, for example, Tapp and Kohlberg 1974: 62-83). This developmental process apparently occurs in all cultures, although not all people in a culture develop fully or reach the highest stage of moral development. Kohlberg's system (and that of Piaget upon which it is, in part, based) is remarkably similar, we note, to the Hindu description of levels of consciousness. This system involves "climbing the ladder" of seven chakras or stages (Dass 1974: 28-30, 82-85). The process is to move from the first chakra—a concern with survival as an individual—to the seventh chakra—full consciousness of the unity of all. Every higher chakra is a more total organization of the universe and a more cosmic way of perceiving, understanding, and living with it. However, the ethical imperatives found in Kohlberg are absent in the Hindu system.

It is also worth noting that both Kohlberg and Maslow provide us with theories concerning the origin and nature of individual morality. Wilson (1975), extrapolating from animal studies, has given us a new conception of sociobiology and group ethics. According to Wilson, altruism is genetic; people are altruistic as a result of "kin selection." They will sacrifice themselves in favor of the survival and reproduction of relatives who possess the same genes by common descent. Finally, we note Selznick's position regarding natural law (1966: 154-93). Natural law searches for and incorporates enduring truths regarding the nature and requirements of a legal order. He implies that there is a tendency toward legality that may be an inherent characteristic of human society. These theorists need and deserve further study for the knowledge and insight they may provide concerning legality, morality, and ethics in criminal justice today. Failure to follow all possible lines of thought in searching for answers to our dilemmas leads back to Phillip Rieff's now famous epigram: Can unbelieving man be civilized? It recalls also Sorokin's (1941) early and insightful analysis of our sensate culture in which "Everyone becomes his own lawgiver and judge, deeming his own standard just as good as anybody else's," and force and violence settle moral questions that once were answerable by faith and community (Nisbet 1975).

In the second section of the book, Insights into Criminalization, the papers range from abstract arguments to empirical investigation of why and how ethics and morals are translated into laws and the extent to which change takes place.

It is curious that John Rawls apparently did not consider whether punishment was consistent with his conception of justice and, if it were, what form it must take to be consistent with his two principles of justice. Decker's article, the first in this section, considers these matters and concludes that punishment can be justified even in a just society! He feels, for what it is worth, that only "rehabilitative punishment" is consistent with Rawls' conception of justice.

In the next paper, however, Williams and Watkins seem to believe that it is possible for society to legislate "good" laws, eliminate conflicts, and adopt ethical principles that will increase liberty and avoid suffering and injustice. They argue that criminal behavior causing injustice, suffering, and limiting liberty is the result of obsolete criminal laws. These laws institutionalize a value system derived from a secularized, puritan moral code. They argue that social science rather than theology should be used to revise the criminal code; it is a body of knowledge which includes knowledge of crime prevention. They also propose an organization of scholars to disseminate knowledge of social research to legislators. While we might agree that legislators should be more familiar with the work of social scientists, we dissent from the arguments of Williams and Watkins on two grounds. First, the relationship between the results of social research and law making is not isometric (Lazarsfeld and Reitz 1975). Increased direct involvement in the legislative process is more likely to result in increased politicalization of social research rather than a decrease in the politicalization of policy. In addition, researchers who produce the social research are themselves the products of their society, and its morals and ethics influence in a serious and important fashion the kinds of questions they ask and, therefore, the kinds of answers that result, as will be clearer in the last section of this book. Finally, there is no reason to think that social science is in some sense better suited to produce criminal laws that will reduce undesirable behavior than other belief systems.

Jeffrey Reiman states the issue more directly and baldly than our previous authors; all laws contain moral judgments, regardless of the ideological bases of the legislation. Reiman, like Williams and Watkins, is interested in decriminalization. He argues that a broad moral belief in liberty and prevention of suffering are at the core of our legal tradition and support the legitimacy of the system. If behavior imposes no harm that limits liberty or causes suffering, then to make such behavior a crime is to violate the very moral values that make for legitimacy. This argument, which Reiman uses to support decriminalization, does not rest on the belief in a value-free social science but frankly acknowledges its moral position vis-a-vis the morality of the present law. Unfortunately, Reiman's argument is, as presented here, too concise and too general not to raise serious questions. We are particularly concerned here with the meanings that should be assigned to harm, liberty, and suffering. Clearly, Reiman refers to individual liberty and harm to individuals in his argument. As important as this position is, its implications for the problem of the limits of human behavior are vague and uncertain if we consider a society or a collectivity as more than the sum of its individual members (for a related argument see Smith 1975: 384–409). From this perspective the rampant individualism of Reiman's argument becomes destructive (Van den Haag 1976: D1, D26). It provides us with no contemporary standards of relevance or reasonableness when we are required to appraise lower-order moral rules. President Carter, for one, seemed to be aware of this problem but not its potential for paradox when he observed:

> I don't ever want to do anything as President that would
> be a contravention of the moral and ethical standards that
> I would exemplify in my own life as an individual or that
> would violate the principles or character of the American
> people (Sheer 1976: 74).

Reiman's formulation requires some very troublesome assumptions about human nature. His approach does not take sufficient account of the demonic side of human nature, that is, people's insatiable appetites. Finally, it says nothing that will aid us in confronting the major social forces in our lives, bureaucracy (Berger et al. 1973) and technology (see Boorstin 1977: 36-38).

Criminal justice today is a mammoth bureaucracy into which technology is being dumped with bewildering and uncontrolled rapidity. But the technological revolution lacks any moral foundation. Harnessing technology to the agencies of legitimate force in society without providing help for this impartial giant to select its goals is to allow it to be used as it is by other segments of society. In the business and industrial world the main governing force of technology is the desire for private gain. Many calculated small decisions are made that often escalate into unexpectedly large ones as our problems with pollution and diminishing resources indicate. The new nature of our acting through technology and bureaucracy calls for a new ethics of long-range responsibility, coextensive with the range of our powers. One of the writers who sees this need warns of the "apocalyptic pregnancy of our actions" (Jonas 1973: 31-54). The contemporary critical stance toward technology is typically based upon a reinterpretation of our moral heritage. Jewish commentators on the Tower of Babel story in the Torah have perceived its relevance to this contemporary problem. The story warns us that technology is good but, if it is not linked with morality and responsibility, it is potentially and actively destructive. Technology without responsibility is sin. But the real and growing problem is that technology is a counterculture with its own definitions of good and evil and with the desire to supplant older myths and symbols. Most of the moral issues raised by the authors of papers in the subsequent section stem from these facts, although they are often not too clear or explicit in this regard.

In the next paper, Himelhoch makes the important point that our notions of legality and morality are elastic and that the same acts may be evaluated differently due to exigencies of the moment. Thus "post-Watergate morality" represents a redefinition of the meaning of some of the moral and legal rules applied to political and economic elites as well as to radicals and dissidents. Our ethical principles do not necessarily change; they stretch and contract. Two examples will illustrate this fact. First, we note that the number of indictments of public officials by grand juries has climbed steadily from 63 in 1970 to 337 in 1976. The head of the United States Department of Justice Criminal Division explained that the increases do "not mean that there is more corruption now than in years past, just that some prosecutors are making more attempts to prosecute official corruption" (Rawls 1977: A1, A15). Secondly, the Superintendent of the

United States Military Academy at West Point, discussing the recent and most extensive cheating scandal, observed: "There has been great discussion about integrity in the army itself, most of it arising out of My Lai. Frankly, this is a terribly difficult time for the academy" (Time 1976: 18-29). But even now there is some movement toward redefining again the meaning of the rules and laws; Irving Kristol (1976) asks, in the New York Times, "Post-Watergate Morality: Too Good For Our Good?" One important issue that neither Himelhoch nor Kristol addresses is the relationship between elastic public morality and elastic private morality.

In the last paper in this section, Meyer provides a different example of public morality. He claims as do others that the media's conception of crime and official actions will influence the public's conception of the moral order. Furthermore, he argues that the public's conception will differ depending upon the style and content of the media's language. He applies content analysis to a sample of news stories in the New York Times and the New York Daily News to test for quantitative differences in style between them. Meyer finds no really important differences between them except a slight tendency for the Times to print more information regarding the actions of agents of the system than does the Daily News. It is not clear what this difference means, if anything. We know very little about how perceptions of crime and justice are shaped. For example, we have no way of understanding the relationship between the reporting of crime and justice in the media and its impact on the people who read it. Studies that link the media and deterrence (Geerkin and Gove 1975: 497-513) and the media and violence (Goldstein 1975: 32-43) with other knowledge about human behavior have not been developed to provide us with a fuller picture. Such knowledge would allow us to better judge the impact of the media on our senses of legality and morality.

The third section of the book, The System of Justice and Its Actors, deals with linkages between legality, morality, and ethics as they affect the behavior of the actors. There is no question that guilt must be punished; but who are the guilty and what should be their punishment? Whatever values inform criminal law, they are never sufficiently clear so as to rule out questions of fact; for example, What kind of person and what kind of behavior are to be included within its ambit? Winfree and Kielich studies the factors used by the professional staff of a prosecuting attorney's office in defining what constitute a crime and a criminal and examined the influence of these factors on the decision to prosecute. The attorneys knew they had to exercise discretion and were well aware of the impact of their decisions upon the persons who stood accused. In their interviews with Winfree and Kielich, the attorneys emphasized the importance of the accused person's character and background, the nature of the alleged offense, and the community's feeling about crime. The attorneys also seem rather emphatic about their need to be convinced that the accused is guilty before they will take the case to trial. Although the authors couch their study in the language of labeling and discretion, it should be clear that we are also dealing with the relationship between private morality and public morality. This becomes clearer, perhaps, in an area such as pornography. Larry Parrish, the U.S. Attorney in Memphis, Tennessee, who won the "Deep Throat" case, claims that his personal inclinations are much more strict than the law. Furthermore, he argues: "It's not that I'm prosecuting because of my personal inclinations, it's that prosecutors have no right not to prosecute because of their personal inclinations. It's the two-edged blade, and the side that slices most often is the refusal to prosecute" (Morgan 1977: 16-17, 26-37). We would suggest that conceptualizing these issues as matters of discretion allows writers to pretermit the moral issue involved. Thinking about discretion in terms of morality invites us to consider issues that we might otherwise overlook, among them being the pressures toward separating public and private morality and the meaning of this separation for society. We may also want to look at the impact of this situation on the lives of judges, prosecutors, and others in terms of the stresses that it may induce. Conceptualizing issues in terms of morality rather than discretion also invites comparisons. For example, two physicists at the Stanford Research Institute recently wrote a book on experiments that were favorable to psychic ability; an anonymous reviewer in The Journal of Electrical and Electronic Engineers wrote: "This is the kind of thing I wouldn't believe in even if it were true."

The ambiguity and conflict found in rules of conduct and their relationship to discretion concerns others in the system. Rosalind Reiman examines the probation officer's moral dilemma. She argues that moral conflicts confront probation officers because each of their roles (law enforcer and social worker) are subject to distinctive and conflicting laws and rules of conduct. Since the community and the criminal justice system both seem to want probation officers to play these two roles, Reiman is pessimistic about the possibilities of the moral conflicts. She acknowledges that these cross-pressures are not the constant companion of the probation officer; they confront some probation officers some of the time but are not any the less anguishing. Reiman tries to resolve the dilemma by invoking another set of rules based on the issue of whose interests the probation officer should represent, the probationer or the community. Although she opts for the latter, she does not feel that this resolves conflicts so much as creates additional dilemmas. What is not clear from Reiman's analysis is whether she would locate the source of concern for the interest of probationers in the probation officers' professionalism or in the officers' personal commitment to their charges—two sources of moral rules that she does not discuss.

Pepinsky, in the next paper, is quite critical of the use of social science in criminal justice. Social science, he contends, is used as authoritative bases for decisions by officials; these officials abdicate any personal responsibility for their decisions. This abdication of personal responsibility allows criminal justice officials to inflict suffering on others in the name of science. Contrary to the implications of the paper by Williams and Watkins, discussed above, Pepinsky does not see the canon of social science as being intrinsically better able to reduce undesirable behavior. But Pepinsky is optimistic; he believes it is possible and desirable for social science to encourage officials to accept personal responsibility and to be compassionate in their decisions.

Among the preceding articles in this section, the focus was, in varying degree, upon conflicting moral rules and those sources of conflicts that could be identified. If the authors attempted to suggest a way in which the dilemmas could be resolved, it was usually by arbitrarily favoring one source of conduct rules (for example, professional standards over organizational norms) instead of another. Jackson's article, the next in this section indicates that the institution of law has established a hierarchy of rules and norms that in many situations will resolve conflicts. Furthermore, the legal system recognizes general principles, some of them founded in the Constitution, that are not in themselves rules of conduct, but rather embody criteria that may be used to judge the adequacy of the lower-order rules, just as ethical principles may be used to assess lower-order moral rules and laws. Jackson examines the use of consent decrees in juvenile courts to involuntarily commit juveniles to state mental health commissions. Consent decrees developed in response to the judicial need for swift disposition of certain juveniles without a hearing. While these decrees raise moral issues and many questions such as the rights of children versus the rights of parents, Jackson concludes that consent decree commitments are improper (1) under statutory interpretations, (2) under principles of general fairness, and finally (3) under the constitutional principle of due process of law.

Ball's articles and Scharf's article, the last two in this section, explicitly examine the relationship between bureaucracy and justice. Ball argues that the implementation of justice through law is the key to its realization. Although law is a balance of power and ethics, it is implemented through organizations that are concentrations of power but are without a tradition of ethics. The lack of an ethical tradition of bureaucracies is attributable to the fact that ethics have developed in terms of personal behavior. Thus, all of the organs of the administration of justice manifest an inherent tendency toward authoritarianism and tend toward the corruption of justice. Scharf, on the other hand, believes that organizations have a "justice structure" and moral atmosphere and that it is possible to empirically assess them. He argues that there is a direct relationship between the "justice structure" and the moral atmosphere of prisons and their rehabilitative potential. He applies his approach to three male prison settings and describes procedures by which it appears possible both to change prisons in the direction of making them more "just" and to change prisoners. His most successful experiment involves a kind of therapeutic community. Whether this provides a new synthesis of ethics and power, which Ball believes is the only way to interrupt the inevitable corruption of justice in bureaucracy, is not clear from Scharf's discussion. We should also bear in mind as we ponder these papers, the series of studies leading up to Milgram's (1975) disquieting investigations into the nature and extent of obedience. The integration of sociological, psychological, and historical insights would greatly enhance our understanding and perhaps show us more clearly the mountains that lie ahead, even if failing to show the way through. Surely the recurrent problems of business ethics and integrity remind us that no easy solution will be found to the antinomy of technology, bureaucracy, and the habits of obedience.

The last section of the book deals with Legality, Morality, Ethics and Criminological Research. The first paper by Michalowski examines criminological research in an effort to determine what criteria criminologists employ in selecting research topics. He concludes that values, not empirical criteria, play a major role in the criminologist's decision to study criminal homicide rather than traffic accidents. Michalowski is not pleased with this state of affairs since he believes traffic accidents are as worthy of study as homicides. But he does point to some of the structural conditions that influence the values of criminologists. In effect, then, he seems to be saying that when people are acting as criminologists, they assess "variable" facts in terms of quite similar and unquestioned moral rules. This habit of thought is shared by criminologists with prosecutors and probation officers, among others, as the papers in the previous section seem to indicate.

Dembo, in the next article, seems to see the moral dilemmas of researchers working in corrections as the result of a potential three-sided tug-of-war between the ethical norms embodied, respectively, in standards of professionalism, the demands of the organization, and the personal commitments of the researcher. He argues that there are organizational pressures to adopt an uncritical stance in research which is further constrained by funding and employment directed toward the study of system efficiency. He believes that

professional standards legitimate the questioning of assumptions and
the free flow of research reports. Yet another set of rules of conduct
grows out of the social commitments of the researcher. Dembo suggests that a code of ethics for the criminology profession might ease
the burdens of making decisions touched by these conflicting norms.
We are not as optimistic as Dembo about the possibility of resolving
these conflicts. Similar types of conflicts have existed in the past.
In China, for example, beginning in about the fourteenth century, a
source of conflict between the monarchy and those of the elite who
"make a living by plowing with the pen" was the personal, as distinct
from the public, interests of the latter (Wakeman 1972: 35-70). The
solutions attempted then included organizing the elite into tangs or
factions which were often not acceptable to the monarchy. But ultimately, it appears, the separation of public and private life was
tolerated, giving rise to the aphorism: "Confucian in office, Taoist
without."

Dembo raises, as does Rosalind Reiman in the preceding section, a related issue. Given a conflict, which source and which set
of rules has priority and should be followed by an actor in the criminal
justice system? We wonder also about community standards and expectations; their meaning with regard to pornography is anything but
clear—are they likely to be clearer with regard to criminology or
probation work? What, furthermore, should be the role of a professional organization in criminology or in probation work? And given
the degree of polarization that exists in the field of criminology and
criminal justice (Miller 1973: 141-62), what could be the role of a
professional organization? We would ask whether or not (or under
what circumstances) an employing organization (for example, a correctional institution) should have the right to require that its employees
follow its rules of conduct. Finally, what should be the role of personal commitments in criminological research?

Kamerman, in the last article, pursues the concept of "profession" as applied in research on criminals. He notes that this conception not only buttresses the ideological claims of thieves as ranking
highest in the criminal hierarchy but also normalizes criminal activity, that is, that criminals are just like everybody else. Kamerman
locates the roots of such attitudes and behavior among criminology
researchers in their puritanism which is simultaneously repulsed
and attracted by sin. Thus, personal moral ambivalence is translated into questionable professional moral judgments. Recently,
President Carter took great care to inform some of the electorate
(in Playboy Magazine) before his election that he would separate his
private morality from his official actions (Sheer 1976: 63-86). But
his choice of a forum and his revelations in it raises questions in our
minds about the unknown, possibly morally ambivalent nature of his
puritanism and its effects on public policy.

Unfortunately, none of the papers in this collection deals specifically with the question of the utility of a value-free science in addressing ethical issues. We see this relation as problematic in at least two ways. First, there is a problem that grows out of the formal structure of social science language, a language foreign to moral considerations. Secondly, and not unrelated to the first point, there is a serious methodological problem. This problem revolves, in part, around the relationship of a deterministic social science to the notion of free will implicit in ethical discourse. We would suggest, further, that these issues are in great need of extended discussion and even debate in the criminology community as they have been in other scholarly circles (see, for example, Bendix and Roth 1971).

In conclusion, we wonder, now that Watergate sensationalism has peaked, what faculties of law, criminal justice, and criminology are doing to further our knowledge of the relationship between legality, morality, and ethics, what governmental and private agencies are doing to support studies of these matters, and what students are learning about these issues.

REFERENCES

Aiken, H. D. 1962. Reason and Conduct. New York: Knopf.

Baldwin, D. 1976. They said it couldn't be done. Environmental Action 8 (May 22).

Bendix, R. and G. Roth. 1971. Scholarship and Partisanship. Berkeley and Los Angeles: University of California Press.

Berger. P. L., B. Berger, and H. Kellner. 1973. The Homeless Mind. New York: Random House.

Boorstin, D. J. 1977. Tomorrow: the republic of technology. Time, Jan. 17.

Dass, R. 1974. The Only Dance There Is. New York: Doubleday (Anchor).

Geerkin, M. R. and W. R. Gove. 1975. Deterrence: some theoretical considerations. Law and Society Review 9.

Goldstein, J. H. 1975. Aggression and Crimes of Violence. New York: Oxford University Press.

Hobbes, T. 1946. Of the difference of manners. In Leviathan, ed. M. Oakeshott. Oxford: Basil Blackwell.

Jonas, H. 1973. Technology and responsibility: reflections on the new tasks of ethics. Social Research 40 (Spring).

Kristol, I. 1976. Post-Watergate morality: too good for our good? The New York Times, November 14.

Lazarsfeld, P. F. and J. G. Reitz. 1975. Introduction to Applied Sociology. New York: Elsevier.

Maslow, A. H. 1970. Motivation and Personality, 2d ed. New York: Random House.

Milgram, S. 1975. Obedience to Authority. New York: Harper Colophon Books.

Miller, W. B. 1973. Ideology and criminal justice policy: some current issues. Journal of Criminal Law and Criminology 64 (June).

Morgan, T. 1977. United States versus the princes of porn. The New York Times Magazine, March 6.

Nisbet, R. A. 1975. Twilight of Authority. New York: Oxford University Press.

Phillips, S. 1977. Justice for whom? Psychology Today, March.

Rawls, W., Jr. 1977. Indictments on rise for public officials. The New York Times, February 11.

Selznick, P. 1966. Natural law and sociology. In Natural Law and Modern Society, eds. J. Cogley et al. Cleveland: World Publishing Co.

Sheer, R. 1976. Playboy interview: Jimmy Carter. Playboy, November.

Smith, M. B. E. 1975. Is there a prima facie obligation to obey the law? In Today's Moral Problems, ed. R. Wasserstrom. New York: Macmillan Publishing Co.

Sorokin, P. A. 1941. The Crisis of Our Age. New York: Dutton and Company.

Tapp, J. L. and L. Kohlberg. 1974. Developing senses of law and legal justice. In Crime and Justice, ed. J. Susman. New York: AMS Press.

Time, Inc. 1976. What price honor? Time, June 7.

Van den Haag, E. 1976. What is a civil libertarian to do when pornography becomes so bold? The New York Times, November 11.

Wakeman, F., Jr. 1972. The price of autonomy: intellectuals in Ming and Ch'ing politics. Daedalus, Spring.

Wilson, E. O. 1975. Sociobiology: The New Synthesis. Cambridge: Harvard University Press.

PART

I

LINKAGES BETWEEN LEGALITY, MORALITY, AND ETHICS

1

CAN WE HAVE AN EMPIRICAL SCIENCE OF VALUES?

Leonard J. Hippchen

INTRODUCTION

Before his death in 1970, Abraham H. Maslow had spent 40 years as a behavioral scientist, attempting to develop a theoretical basis for an empirical science of values. Maslow was convinced that the value-free model of science, inherited from the physical sciences, was not appropriate for the study of human life. His theory was that the social and behavioral sciences should be based upon a view of humankind which he termed "holistic"—one encompassing the full range of biological and psychosocial aspects of life.

Further, Maslow felt that with our ever increasing social problems, scientists were neglecting their duty to mankind by not facing the value question:

> The classical philosophy of science as morally neutral, value-neutral is not only wrong, but is extremely dangerous as well. It is not only amoral; it may be antimoral as well. It may put us into great jeopardy (Maslow 1972: 21).

Maslow called upon his fellow scientists to solve what he called the "big problems" of our time—big in the sense of being important research questions begging to be investigated. He said that the first and foremost big problem of our time is to make the Good Person. He deplored science's tendency to study "sick" or "underdeveloped" persons; he urged that we study physically and psychologically healthy persons, and that we discover how to help people become "self-actualized" and highly evolved. Maslow felt that this task was imperative to our survival.

> This Good Person can equally be called the self-evolving person, the responsible-for-himself-and-his-own-evolution

person, the fully illuminated or awakened or perspicacious man, the fully human person, the self-actualizing person, etc. In any case it is quite clear that no social reforms, no beautiful constitutions or beautiful programs or laws will be of any consequence unless people are healthy enough, evolved enough, strong enough, good enough to understand them and to want to put them into practice in the right way (ibid.: 19).

Maslow stressed that the other big problem of our time is to make the Good Society. By Good Society, Maslow meant one species, one world. The Good Society is based upon the Oneness of Mankind, the recognition of the same source of life for all members of the human world, the recognition of the interdependence and interrelatedness of all humans on the planet. He emphasized that the Good Person and the Good Society need each other. They tend to help each other. Maslow, in fact, felt that it would be impossible to achieve either one without the other.

Maslow confessed that his review of the predictive literature of what the world will be like in the year 2000 frightened him. This reaction, he said, was based upon his observation that "95 percent of this literature deals entirely with purely technological changes, leaving aside completely the question of good and bad, right and wrong (ibid.: 23)

The problem of the Good Person and the Good Society has special relevance to today's criminologists and criminal justice practitioners. Never before in modern times have we had to face the current extent and severity of criminal and social problems. The crime rates continue to rise unabated. Drug and alcohol addiction and a wide range of other vices continue to spread. Our jails and prisons are overcrowded. White collar crime, at every level of society, eats at the heart of our social institutions. Meanwhile, criminologists continue to use concepts of man and criminal behavior which ignore the value question. Thus, their contributions to our understanding and control of this behavior are no further advanced today than they were 200 years ago. Likewise, criminal justice practitioners continue to handle the criminal throughout the system as though they were dealing with some sort of wild animal which merely needs to be caged and punished. Here, too, the question of the value aspects of human potential are overlooked. The result is an almost complete helplessness in accomplishing the important task of correction of the criminal. The ultimate defeat is seen in the current trend to build massive prisons for so-called "incorrigibles."

Maslow's ideas relating to an empirical science of values are contained in his posthumous work, The Farther Reaches of Human Nature. In this book, he outlines what he calls a "theory of metamotivation."

The theory includes a set of 28 hypotheses, which he presents as scientifically testable propositions. He recommends that these hypotheses be tested by observational and applied methods.

The main purpose of this writing is to present the results of an application of these concepts in the criminal justice system, especially as they relate to the correction of criminal behavior in applied settings. The first section will consist of a review and brief discussion of nine key concepts of Maslow's metamotivation theory. These concepts illustrate his attempt to show why and how an empirical science of values can be developed. The implications of these concepts for criminologists will be discussed. The second section will present and review the findings of six correctional projects in which metamotivational theory was used. The implications of these outcomes for modern-day criminal justice approaches to the handling of juvenile delinquents and criminals will then be discussed.

KEY CONCEPTS OF METAMOTIVATION THEORY

1. The full definition of the person or of human nature must include intrinsic values as part of human nature.

From his studies of "self-actualized" persons, Maslow concluded that, in order to have an effective science of values, we must study the most mature and psychologically healthy specimens of the human race. He referred to these researches as studies of the "good specimen" and the "growing tip." He said that this was similar to the study of any species: If we want to know the qualities and characteristics of various forms of life, we tend to study the more evolved, developed forms of this life in order to understand its full range of potentialities.

For criminologists, this concept would seem to imply that our entire approach to the study of criminal behavior should be modified. Certainly, if we are to understand people, we should not base our theories on studies of animals. Also, we should not attempt to derive our theories from studies of criminal behavior exclusively. Rather, we should concentrate more in our studies on contrasting criminal behavior with psychologically healthy behavior and look for the causal links from the viewpoint of higher-evolved versus lower-evolved behavior.

Maslow also found that self-actualizing people seem to be primarily motivated by intrinsic or ultimate values. He also found that the average individuals had so-called "peak experiences" during which they had sensory contact with ultimate values, although most of their other time was devoted more to gratification of their lower basic needs, such as, physical needs, safety needs, needs of love, belonging, and self-esteem. On the basis of these studies, Maslow concluded that "to be comprehensive we must include not only the person's constitution and temperament, not only anatomy, physiology, neurology, and endocrinology, not only his capacities, his biological style, not only his basic instinctoid needs, but also the Being Values, which also are his Being values" (ibid.: 311). Maslow stressed that not only were these Being values the primary distinguishing factors of humanity from other species, but that it is in the area of these Being values that the true individuality of each person is found.

For criminologists, this concept implies that not only should we be directing our studies to the total range of human physical and psychosocial qualities, but also that we should seek to identify those distinguishing and individualistic qualities of the individual, even among our studies of delinquents and criminals.

2. These intrinsic values are instinctoid in nature, that is, they are needed (a) to avoid illness and (b) to achieve fullest humanness or growth. "Illnesses" resulting from deprivation of intrinsic values (metaneeds) we may call metapathologies. The "highest" values, the spiritual life, the highest aspirations of mankind are therefore proper subjects for scientific study and research. They are in the world of nature.

Maslow's studies found evidence that Being values are instinctively related to life preservation and growth. His findings suggest that criminal behavior may be special cases of B-value deprivation, that the "illness" personified by this behavior has its roots in the deprivation of these important B values in the person.

Table 1 includes a representative list of 15 Being values. Next to each, Maslow lists a description of the related pathogenic deprivation and also some more specific metapathologies which may result from the deprivation. It is well known that criminals tend to exhibit a large number of the specific metapathologies listed, and it is logical that contributing causes to these pathologies could be B-value deprivation such as those for truth, goodness, beauty, uniqueness, justice, order, richness, and meaningfulness.

The listing in Table 1 was derived by Maslow from study of what he terms "good choosers" and "bad choosers." He found that self-actualizing subjects were more accurate perceivers and that they tended to make choices that enhanced both their physical and psychosocial growth and well-being. Conversely, he found that persons with various pathologies tended to be poorer perceivers and to make choices that tended to increase their pathology.

Maslow found from these studies that these pathologies are indicative of a diminution of full humanness and that gratification of the

B values enhances human potentials. Therefore, he concluded that these ultimate values may be taken as instinctoid needs. As instinctoid needs, he claimed, they fall properly within the realm of nature and thus, are susceptible to investigation by social and behavioral scientists.

3. The metapathologies of the affluent and indulged young come partly from deprivation of intrinsic values, frustrated "idealism," and disillusionment with a society they see (mistakenly) as motivated only by lower or animal or material needs!

Maslow's concept of metamotivation deprivation and the resultant metapathologies raise important theoretical questions for criminologists and criminal justice practitioners. To what extent, for example, are our deviant or delinquent youth the result of inadequate performance on the part of families and religious and educational institutions? If these persons are suffering from Being-value deprivation, who has failed to provide this basic nurturing and guidance? Why has this occurred and what can be done to rectify the problem? To what extent can the blame be laid at the feed of materialistically motivated business, government, and political institutions? How much of the delinquent or deviant forms of behavior are the result of an affluence which allows a materialistic indulgence of the young and which deprives them of B-value instruction and models to use as a guide?

In addition to such research questions as these, what are we, in society and in the criminal justice system, to do with these "misfits," these nonproductive persons, these dangerous and violent young people. How is social order and peace to be maintained? How can justice be done? How can we control these people? How can they be corrected and be allowed to function freely in society? What are we to do about the increasing costs of processing, adjudicating, and incarcerating these persons? When do we stop building more prisons with which to hold the increasing numbers of dangerous and incorrigible persons?

Also, what can be done to restore the socializing influence of families, religious institutions, and schools? What agencies can be devised to divert these youth from the criminal justice system, and what kinds of programs and staff are needed by these agencies to solve these problems through early intervention?

Finally, what can be done to restore honesty, integrity, an attitude of service, and trustworthiness among our political, business and social leaders? How can vice and corruption in high places be made unpopular and, much more, a thing to be avoided as a poison? How can local, state, and national pride be instilled? How can pride in the human race be developed? How can justice and peace on a world-wide scale be achieved?

TABLE 1

Being Values and Specific Metapathologies

Being Value	Pathogenic Deprivation	Specific Metapathologies
1. Truth	Dishonesty	Disbelief; mistrust; cynicism; skepticism; suspicion
2. Goodness	Evil	Utter selfishness; Hatred, repulsion, disgust; Reliance only upon self and for self; Nihilism; Cynicism
3. Beauty	Ugliness	Vulgarity; Specific unhappiness, restlessness, loss of taste, tension, fatigue; Philistinism; Bleakness
4. Unity; Wholeness	Chaos; Atomism, loss of connectedness	Disintegration, "the world is falling apart"; Arbitrariness
4a. Dichotomy-Transcendence	Black and white dichotomies; Loss of gradations; of degree; Forced polarization; Forced choices	Black and white thinking, either/or thinking; Seeing everything as a duel, war, or conflict; Low synergy; Simplistic view of life
5. Aliveness; Process	Deadness; Mechanizing of life	Deadness; Robotizing; Feeling oneself to be totally determined; Loss of emotion; Boredom, loss of zest in life; Experiential emptiness
6. Uniqueness	Sameness, uniformity, interchangeability	Loss of feeling of self and of individuality; Feeling oneself to be interchangeable, anonymous, not really needed
7. Perfection	Imperfection, sloppiness, poor workmanship, shoddiness	Discouragement, hopelessness, nothing to work for

7a. Necessity	Accident; occasionalism; inconsistency	Chaos, unpredictability; Loss of safety; Vigilance
8. Completion; Finality	Incompleteness	Feelings of incompleteness with perseveration; Hopelessness; Cessation of striving and coping; No use trying
9. Justice	Injustice	Insecurity, anger, cynicism, mistrust, lawlessness, jungle world view, total selfishness
9a. Order	Lawlessness; Chaos, Breakdown of authority	Insecurity; Wariness; Loss of safety, of predictability; Necessity for vigilance, alertness, tension, being on guard
10. Simplicity	Confusing complexity; Disconnectedness; Disintegration	Overcomplexity; Confusion, bewilderment, conflict, loss of orientation
11. Richness; Totality; Comprehensiveness	Proverty; Coarctation	Depression, uneasiness, loss of interest in world
12. Effortlessness	Effortfulness	Fatigue, strain, striving, clumsiness, awkwardness, gracelessness, stiffness
13. Playfulness	Humorlessness	Grimness, depression, paranoid humorlessness, loss of zest in life; Cheerlessness; Loss of ability to enjoy
14. Self-sufficiency	Contingency, accident, occasionalism	Dependence upon the perceiver; it becomes perceiver's responsibility
15. Meaningfulness	Meaninglessness	Meaninglessness; Despair; Senselessness of life

Source: From Maslow (1971).

All of these questions seem to be relevant to the problem of a generation of depraved, deprived youth—youth without a strong anchor in Being values, which would help provide a basis for meaning and direction in their lives while forming a measuring rod with which to assess the performance of our social institutions.

4. This value starvation and value hunger come from both external deprivation and from our inner ambivalence and counter values.

Maslow contended that the primary value deprivation comes from our materialistically oriented environment; however, we also tend to have an inner fear of these higher values as they seek to emerge into a conscious influence on behavior. Further, certain counter values tend to work against exploration of Being values.

Materialism places high prominence and high premium upon power and the wealth that can buy power and influence. Materialism tends to scoff at the concept of Being values, belittling attempts to manifest these values in the marketplace, government, and politics. Materialism tends to devalue humanity to the level of animals, admitting only that man is a higher form of animal species rather than a separate and superior species.

The materialistic climate tends also to discourage the inner development and expression of Being values. Children who may begin to express these innate values in small ways in their daily lives are told that they are silly or crazy; they may feel that these expressions are something to fear or that they are strange and unusual feelings. Thus, children may develop defense mechanisms to help control and cope with these strange inner feelings and urgings at a very early age. They may easily become blocked and distorted.

5. The hierarchy of basic needs is prepotent to the metaneeds.

Maslow has observed that both the basic needs (physiological, safety, belonging and love, self-esteem) and the metaneeds (Being values, aesthetics) can be withheld from humans. However, he feels that the basic needs are stronger while the metaneeds appear to be weaker and less demanding. Thus, deviance or delinquency may result from deprivation of either the basic or metaneeds, but since the basic needs are stronger they are more apt to lead to obvious and open types of pathology. We can easily recognize when a child is deprived of food, clothing, and housing, but deprivation of the metaneeds is more subtle, less easily seen, and less suspected. Thus, the basic needs appear to take precedence over the metaneeds.

However, if we consider that the most distinguishing feature of what it means to be a human being relates to the manifestation of the Being values and aesthetic needs, deprivation in these areas can be seen to be an even more important source of explanation for certain pathologies. It may well be that a very important causal factor in much present deviance will be found to relate to metadeficiency needs in these youth. This is an extremely important research question for criminologists.

6. The value life (spiritual, religious, philosophical, axiological, etc.) is an aspect of human biology and is on the same continuum with "lower" animal life (rather than being in separated, mutually exclusive realms). It is probably, therefore, species-wide and supercultural, even though it must be actualized by culture in order to exist.

Here Maslow emphasizes his view that what has been called "spiritual" life is a natural part of the human essence. In past times, this aspect of human behavior, largely undeveloped in an evolutionary sense, was thought to be supernatural or outside of the human natural experience.

Maslow sees the spiritual life as a defining characteristic of human nature without which it is not complete. He holds that the spiritual life is within the normal jurisdiction of human thought and is attainable, in principle, by human efforts. Thus, the spiritual life should be open to investigation, description, analysis, and control in the same way that the biological plane is studied.

If criminologists were to study the spiritual aspects and potentialities of deviants, delinquents, and criminals, it might be discovered that these persons have higher levels of potentialities for the spiritual life than the noncriminal. They even may find that their behavior, in part, may be explained as a deprivation of opportunity to develop and manifest these aspects of their lives. If so, a whole new era of discovery may be opened. Undoubtedly, this is one of Maslow's main challenging thoughts to the field. It is especially important in the area of cross-cultural studies. Rather than merely studying the differences among various cultures, criminologists should be exploring the underlying, unifying aspects of culture, the universal principles of civilization. Through these studies criminologists could make significant contributions to the establishment of world order, justice, and peace.

7. Since the spiritual life is instinctoid, all the techniques of "subjective biology" apply to its education.

By this Maslow means that the "Real Self" has "inner signals" which, although weaker than basic need signals, can be "heard," and measured. Thus he feels, in principle, that all the exercise which help to develop sensory awareness of our body can be studied and applied to our metaneeds, that is, to the education of our yearnings for beauty, truth, justice, perfection, etc.

Likewise, Maslow contends that just as the physical body has been shown to have an innate "body wisdom" leading to its own health and development, so does the Real Self have an "inner voice of widdom" which can be cultivated and used toward development and protection of the Real Self.

Thus, criminologists should be able to use the "subject biology" of the Real Self as a means of measuring the state and growth of this aspect of the human being. Criminal justice practitioners, on the other hand, can concentrate on the development of those techniques of subjective biology which can aid in the development of the Real Self in delinquents and criminals which will lead to the true correction of this behavior. This aspect of corrections has long been ignored and, this, possibly, is the major reason for the ineffectiveness of the system in correcting criminal behavior.

8. Being values seem to be the same as Being facts. Reality, then, is fact values or value facts.

Maslow's study of self-actualizing persons showed that the B values of these persons were actualized as B facts. That is, the attitudes and behavior of these persons were empirically consistent with their value systems. He also found that the B values of the average person were actualized as B facts during "peak experiences." It is upon these kinds of observations that Maslow felt, an empirical science of values could be based—that is, through descriptive studies of self-actualizing persons, and of the average person during their "peak experience" periods. It is not possible to empirically establish values through studies of non-actualized persons, since it is only in the self-actualized person (or in the "peak experience" of the average person) that values manifest themselves as facts to be measured. Maslow's contribution in this area explains one of the "mysteries" of why science has never considered it possible to establish a science of values—the subjects for measurement had not been defined and could not be measured.

9. "Intrinsic conscience" and "intrinsic guilt" are ultimately biologically rooted.

Maslow contended that intrinsic conscience was a biologically innate faculty of the Real Self. Not to be confused with "social conscience," which is learned from our sociocultural environment, the function of intrinsic conscience is to guide the human with an "inner voice" or "inner wisdom" into behavior which is growth enhancing and which will lead to development of full humanness. "Instrinsic guilt," also instinctoid, is a warning that the individual's behavior is moving in a direction opposed to the full development of individual and species-wide evolutionary behavior.

This hypothesized mechanism should be studied by criminologists, since its empirical verification would add important knowledge to our understanding of criminals. Also, criminal justice practitioners should use and test this hypothesis in the correction of criminal behavior, since the use of such a mechanism would be highly useful as a means of internal control by the criminal.

SOME APPLIED CORRECTIONAL PROJECTS
USING METAMOTIVATIONAL CONCEPTS

This section reports on the use of metamotivational concepts in six applied correctional pilot projects. These have been largely exploratory studies, but several have used control and experimental groups with appropriate before-and-after measurements, and, in some instances, follow-up of the subjects.

These projects have been conducted in a variety of settings: a maximum-security prison, a county juvenile and adult court, a metropolitan residential treatment center for offenders, a Marine brig, a medium-security prison, and a training school for girls (Hippchen 1973). These correctional settings are located in Georgia, Florida, and Texas.

Each of these projects has been described in detail in earlier professional publications. On the average, the results have indicated significant behavioral improvement for about 70 percent of all offenders volunteering for the instructional program. The limited follow-up on these projects to date suggests a recidivism rate for those completing instruction of less than 10 percent. With juvenile delinquents and maximum-security criminals alike, and regardless of severity or chronicity of offense, successful restoration to the community without subsequent offensive behavior has been in the range of 90 to 96 percent.

The basic assumptions behind the approach used in the projects can be identified in reference to the following metamotivational concepts of Maslow:

1. Delinquents and criminals are suffering primarily from B value deprivation. The roots of the disorder can be traced to early childhood and later years of their development during which their innate strivings for B-value expression were blocked or distorted by a denying environment. It is assumed that these persons had unusually strong innate drives for B-value development and that this blockage, in conjunction with constitutional and temperament factors of an acting-out type, manifested themselves in antisocial forms of behavior.

Once identified and labeled as antisocial by the environment, the behavior tended to receive additional reinforcement to insure continuance of the behavior, since the basic cause was neither identified nor effectively dealt with by the environment.

2. Regardless of the degree of behavior distortion experienced by a criminal, it is possible to correct the error by aiding the person in the development of B values. As innate potentials, they exist from birth and, even though later severely blocked or distorted, they can be brought out with proper education and practice. This is comparable to persons who did not learn to read as children, but as adults quickly learned to read up to the level of their innate capacity.

3. It is assumed that V-value development, as a capacity which is species-wide, is possible for all human beings regardless of race, class, or culture. Thus, the approach should be applicable with offender groups in any part of the world. Of course, as in other areas of human potentials, some variations in degree of capacity can be expected to be found. Some of these variations can be assumed to be innate differences between people; other variations can be attributed to cultural influences.

4. Being values can be understood to manifest themselves in the realm of human behavior in terms of certain psychological (spiritual) laws or principles. These laws define the difference between "right" and "wrong" behavior. When a person follows the guidelines of these natural laws, behavior is produced which is seen to be "social"; when these laws are violated, the resultant behavior may be seen as "deviant," "antisocial," "delinquent," or "criminal." Basically, these B values, expressed as natural laws of human behavior, are assumed to serve the needs of evolution. If followed, the individual behavior aids preservation of life and development of civilization; if not, various forms of disorder tend to appear which disrupt and retard social advancement.

5. If the laws relating to B-value development can be learned and made an intrinsic part of the being of any person, criminal or otherwise, the individual's behavior will become productive both to him or herself and society. Once learned and made fully manifest, this new behavior tends, with practice, to become crystallized into a new set of habit patterns which resist regression to their former state. Thus, even the worst criminal behavior, once developed to the level of B-value functioning, will have its own set of positive reinforcement experiences to insure maintenance of the new behavior.

6. The learning and adoption of B values by criminals does not constitute a form of brainwashing, since ideology is not involved. It is assumed that the individual is merely developing innate capacities according to universal, natural laws of human behavior. Further, it is assumed that the individual has intrinsic and innate mechanisms

of "conscience" and "guilt" which can provide some guidance not only about the "rightness" of the laws which are being applied, but also to guard against any attempt at ideological proselytizing to which one may be exposed. In any event, individuals must be free to explore and make up their own minds concerning the appropriateness of the universal laws proposed as well as the behavior which ensues from their following or not following these laws. It should be assumed that the criminal's "inner voice" and "inner wisdom" can be brought forth and used as the basis for decisions whether or not to continue the proposed program of development.

7. It is assumed that the most accurate and precise statement concerning the B-value laws as a guide to human behavior can be gleaned from an examination of the sacred scriptures of the world's great religions—Buddhism, Hinduism, Judaism, Zoroastrianism, Christianity, Islam, and Baha'i. All of these scriptures have been demonstrated to be capable of contributing to the development of B values. Thus, a synthesis of these revealed laws—those which are found to be in agreement in all of these texts—can be assumed to represent a valid source of axiomatic principles.

Also, it is assumed that persons, with innate senses of "conscience" and "guilt," can verify within themselves the validity of these laws.

The procedures used in these projects can be summarized as follows:

1. An instructional method is utilized, including use of two instructors, one a beginner and the other advanced. This instructional team works intensively with five offenders over a twelve-week period. Separate training classes are held weekly both for beginning and advanced instructors. The instructors also meet once each week with the five offenders as a group for a two-hour session.

2. Initially, offenders are assessed in terms of their basic attitude sets through use of two tests—the Minnesota Multiphasic Personality Inventory and the Social Concept Quiz. The Social Concept Quiz consists of 159 questions designed to determine the degree that students understand certain key words used in the psychological laws, for example, love, forgiveness, humility, justice. The first two or three sessions, in addition to obtaining motivational information, are spent reviewing with the students what these tests revealed about their attitudes in general and in helping them gain a clear definition of the key concepts which they did not understand in the test. Some time in these early classes is spent helping students understand the way the mind and body function together to produce behavior, and how positive and negative attitudes influence the self and social relations.

3. One or two classes are used to discuss the concept and function of laws—physical laws, psychological (spiritual) laws, and

the laws of society. Then, a process is begun in which the student is challenged to test the application of the psychological laws on his own behavior. The student is introduced to such laws as love for the Creator, love for Real Self, and love for neighbor, the law of humility or of right action toward others, the law of forgiveness, the law of severance, of benevolence, and of sacrifice. Then, each week, he is given a specific set of experiential exercises to help him act out each of the specific laws. He is given selected materials from various of the world's religious scriptures to read and meditate upon. He is given universal, nonsectarian types of prayers which he can recite several times during the day. The purpose of these exercises and aids is to provide an immersion into these writings so that the words and their deeper meanings can permeate and penetrate his Real Self and release his B-value potentials. The student is free to use or not to use the materials and exercises given, but he understands that there will be no progress or way to measure progress unless an attempt is made. The student is encouraged to make an assessment of his feelings concerning the laws he is testing and how his behavior is being affected by following or not following the laws.

4. Later exercises are devoted to the development of simple life goals and working toward those goals on a daily basis. This encourages development of will power. Written records are kept by the student of all progress on these and earlier exercises.

5. Each week's two-hour session is devoted, first, to a discussion by all of successes and failures in applying the previous week's assigned exercises, and second, to receiving instructions and materials for the next week's assignment. Learning and motivation is enhanced by the exchange of information on progress among the students, while the instructors are able to clarify any problems which may have arisen in regard to the technique or results to be expected from the exercises. A student can drop from the class at any time. Also, if a particular student falls too far behind in his progress in relation to the group of students, he will be asked to drop back to a new group which has been formed more recently.

6. About every four weeks, the students are retested with the MMPI and the Social Concept Quiz. This gives an opportunity for each student to reassess his learning of the key concepts and to identify attitudes which continue to be problem areas for future work. The attitudes can be related to the specific laws which have not yet found their place in the behavior of the student. The test also indicates the degree to which instruction is succeeding, and points out to the instructors specific areas which need their attention in the class sessions.

7. Following the twelve weeks of class each student is tested and finally evaluated in terms of progress: the amount of learning is

measured, attitude changes are recorded; peer assessments are made, and staff ratings of behavior change are utilized. Students who successfully complete the course are given the opportunity either to work with one other volunteer offender to help him to use the materials or to be trained as a beginning instructor.

Students who accept this offer not only further their own development, but also provide a means to assist other volunteer offenders. Most students tend to welcome this opportunity, and, when they do, they further develop and crystallize the B values within themselves. Students are encouraged to continue their own study and development upon leaving the institution, and, if possible, to find some way to help other offender groups through use of this method.

SUMMARY AND CONCLUSIONS

Maslow has presented us with the challenging proposition that our civilization will be seriously hampered in its evolution unless we find ways of developing the Good Person and the Good Society. His contribution to this task is his metamotivational theory of human development. He proposes this as a stimulus to an empirical science of values.

It is urged that criminologists give serious consideration to the testing of the hypotheses which Maslow presents in his theory. Criminologists need a broader concept of human nature and potentials for development to aid in their understanding of deviant and criminal types of behavior. This understanding would enable criminologists to make important contributions to society in its attempt to prevent, control, and treat these dangerous forms of behavior. The challenge is even more significant today because of the rapid increase in the amount of violent crime.

It is urged further that criminologists broaden their scientific task to the world scene and assist in identifying those universal values which could aid in realization of world order, justice, and peace. It is not enough to study social disorder, wars, and crime. It is not enough to study these phenomena on a local, state, national, or cross-cultural, comparative basis. To make a positive contribution to world order, criminologists should concentrate on identifying and testing the universal, unifying value systems. A world torn by disunity and disorder sorely needs the cement of unifying ideas, and criminologists can make an important contribution to world peace through a concerted effort to discover and aid in the implementation of these unifying values.

For the criminal justice practioner, Maslow's metamotivational theory represents an astounding challenge for change. Most of the present practices in the system—law enforcement, criminal law, the courts, and corrections—have been established on the basis of a concept of humanity that is far below its potentials. The system tends to deal with people as though they were animals to be tamed through punishment. How much more befitting of humanity's true station it would be if the system were organized to deal with persons in terms of their Being-value potential. All present-day practices would have to be modified from a punishment approach to a corrections approach. More diversion from the system would be attempted and used effectively. Recidivism rates would decrease greatly. To render the justice due to individuals as creatures of B-value potential would indeed require modification of the entire system.

In society as a whole, order could be restored and work on the Good Society could begin. Family life could be restored, the schools could revitalize their curriculum to emphasize B-value development, and religion could be unified around the common goal of spiritual development under one creator of all. The unifying force resulting from these efforts would not only restore order, and reduce lawlessness and crime, but it would also allow the cultural advancement of every community, state, and nation. The task, as Maslow has stated, is as basic and simple as that of first developing the Good Person. Then, these Good Persons will undoubtedly give themselves to the more difficult and lengthy task of developing the Good Society.

REFERENCES

Hippchen, L. J. 1973. Effects of EMI on delinquents at a training school for girls. Proceedings of the Southwestern Sociological Association.

MacDougald, D. 1971. Judicial service agency: statistical effect on juvenile crime. Albany, Ga.: Dougherty County Juvenile Court.

McCarty, W. D. 1969. New approaches to moral rehabilitation. Proceedings of the American Correctional Congress.

———. 1972. Results of emotional maturity instruction at Sumter Correctional Institution. Proceedings of the American Correctional Congress.

Maslow, A. H. 1971. The Farther Reaches of Human Nature. New York: Viking Press.

Warren, D. C. 1969. A promising new approach to rehabilitation. Proceedings of the American Correctional Congress.

2

WATERGATE'S IMPACT UPON SUPPORT FOR THE CRIMINAL JUSTICE SYSTEM: A CRIMINOLOGIST'S DILEMMA

Dennis D. Dorin

One of the significant contributions of modern criminology[1] has been its conceptualization of the persons and institutions with the primary responsibility for deterring criminal behavior as constituting a system.[2] From this perspective, crime is an input to which presidents, governors and mayors, legislatures, law-enforcement agencies, courts, and correctional institutions must respond. These subsystems of the criminal justice system engage in the conversion processes (decision making and policy making), which produce outputs (public policies) whose objectives include the prevention or, at least, deterrence of criminality. The society's reaction to their successes or failures is then reflected as feedback (for example, a reduction, stabilization, or increase in the crime rate) communicated to the system as a new source of input (Monsma 1973: 11-20).

Systems theorists maintain, however, that an analysis of the input-conversion process-output-feedback cycle provides only a partial understanding of a governmental system. Attention must be directed not only to the system's formal institutions, but also to the political culture or environment in which it functions (Easton 1965: 59-75).

A crucial part of this milieu is the support[3] which the system receives from the elites and the public.[4] Support, for example, is a critical factor in the effectiveness of the criminal justice system. Political elites must be willing to fulfill their responsibilities under the law in a way which will not alienate large segments of the populace. The public must assist the police if they are to identify and apprehend appreciable numbers of criminals (Walker 1973: 2). The courts will maintain their legitimacy only as long as they are supported by the people. "Public support for jails and prisons . . . may have an impact on . . . whether the philosophy of corrections will be rehavilitative or punitive" (ibid.). Ultimately, the stability, and even the survival, of a criminal justice system depends upon the level of support it obtains from the citizenry (Monsma 1973: 12).

From this perspective, the scandals permeating and transcending the Nixon administration[5] raise a particularly significant question for criminologists: What will be the impact of Watergate upon support for American political institutions in general and the criminal justice system in particular?

This question might well pose a dilemma for criminologists. On the one hand, they confront strong pressures to provide an answer through "instant analysis." On the other, is the social science imperative to suspend judgment in the absence of empirically verifiable data.[6]

Watergate, like the Martin Luther King and Robert Kennedy assassinations and urban riots of the late 1960s, has deeply concerned the American people.[7] In its wake, as with these previous phenomena, has come intense demands for on-the-spot assessments of its implications. Politicians, journalists, and academics of seemingly endless ideological persuasions have been only too happy to respond to this need by "shooting from the hip" about Watergate's legacy.[8] Witness the deluge of speeches, electronic and print news analyses, professional articles, and books on the subject.[9]

Is the criminologist, with expertise in this area, to remain silent in the face of such an outpouring of commentary? Or should he or she be in the front lines of the raging debates about Watergate in the media?

Arnold Trebach has predicted accurately that Watergate would be followed by a period of nationwide concern about corruption in government during which far-reaching reforms would be politically attainable—an analog to the movement for civil rights legislation in the aftermath of Martin Luther King's marches, the assassination of John F. Kennedy, and the ascendancy of Lyndon Johnson (Trebach 1974). The Campaign Reform Act, the movement to reform the nation's intelligence agencies, among so many similar developments, demonstrates that such an interlude has followed the Watergate disclosures.

At such a crucial juncture in the nation's policy making, can the criminologist afford to expend the time and energy necessary for the incremental development of empirically based conclusions relating to Watergate's possible implications for the criminal justice system? Can he or she run the risk of finally presenting findings when the society no longer cares about Watergate-related issues?

But what about the other horn of the dilemma—the possibility that students of criminal justice might cast aside the raison d'etre of their discipline as they rush to disseminate their speculations about Watergate.[10] Why continue the pretense of a social science if the criminologist reacts to an event such as Watergate with a role conception indistinguishable from that of the politician or journalist?

Is not the discipline's detached, critical scrutiny of such events its unique contribution to society?[11]

This chapter assumes that there is more to be gained by criminologists' approaching the implications of Watergate as social scientists. It asserts that they can add much to the debates about Watergate if they reveal the speculative nature of conclusions based upon impressions, interpretations, and predictions not grounded upon empirical analysis. It invites criminologists to attempt to transform current hunches about Watergate's impact into support for the criminal justice system based upon empirically verifiable hypotheses.

As an initial step in this direction, three plausible scenarios concerning Watergate's implications for public trust and confidence in the criminal justice system are distilled from the popular and professional literature—the apocalyptic, the some-more-equal-than-others, and the system-vindicated visions. Criminologists are then called upon to test inferences suggested by these and similar models through recourse to behavioral methodologies developed and employed on an interdisciplinary basis.

THE FIRST SCENARIO: THE APOCALYPTIC VISION

This scenario depicts Watergate as a profound threat to support for the entire governmental system. It is premised upon the assumption that, up to the present time, the dominant American ideology has been constitutionalism. Americans have always demonstrated high levels of agreement with the view that public officials may take only lawful actions and that their exercise of power should be held in check by constitutional and statutory restrictions (Hartz 1962, Devine 1972). The American ethos demands, no matter how fiercely the game of politics is played, that politicians stay "within the rules." At least within the United States, the end cannot possibly justify every conceivable means.[12]

Nevertheless, according to this scenario, the American people have suddenly found themselves confronted with the realization that leaders at the very pinnacle of their government, as well as hundreds if not thousands of their subordinates, ran roughshod over these major tenets or constitutionalism. Seemingly routine violations of the criminal laws relating to campaign activities, bribery, breaking and entering, electronic surveillance, unauthorized opening of mail, perjury, obstruction of justice; the spectre of a C. Gordon Liddy's discussing blackmailing, kidnapping, and assassination of political opponents as possible options with high officials of the Justice Department; the spectacle of the president himself caught with "the smoking howitzer" (Time 1974b)—the revelation of these events, as well as an apparently interminable list of similar ones,[13] could not help but shake the American people's confidence and trust in the integrity of their governmental system.

Moreover, the justifications offered for their actions by Richard Nixon and his operatives have ominous implications for constitutional principles. Nixon was the President and, as such, a "sovereign" who was above the nation's criminal laws when he dealt with matters he found to involve "national security" (Harrock 1976: 15). The national security appeared threatened in the Ellsberg affair. A White House-ordered burglary, or even armed robbery, of Ellsberg's psychiatrist's office was thus legally permissible (New York Times 1973: 511-19, 531-33). Indeed, any violation the Bill of Rights or penal code would be excusable if committed by officials following the president's orders in such instances.

In accordance with the apocalyptic vision, the revelation that such views dominated the White House cannot help but create a crisis in Americans' confidence in their political institutions. An already diminishing trust in government will be further dissipated by a profound increase in alienation and cynicism, with awesome implications for the maintenance of law and order.[14]

"In a government of laws," Justice Brandeis warned in Olmstead v. United States (1928),

> The existence of the government will be imperiled if it
> fails to observe the law scrupulously. Our government is
> the potent, the omnipresent teacher. For good or evil, it
> teaches the whole people by its example. Crime is con-
> tagious. If the government becomes a lawbreaker, it
> breeds contempt for law; it invites every man to become
> a law unto himself; it invites anarchy.

In the context of such a precipitous drop in support for the governmental system, discontented groups will make much of the fact that the White House, CIA, FBI, and many other agencies flagrantly violated the law. Such a government, they will maintain, is so corrupt and repressive that any assault upon it, even one outside the law, is justifiable.[15]

Such appeals, this scenario warns, could be particularly dangerous in the light of studies which suggest that American children tend to personalize, and become introduced to, the political institutions of their country through their image of the president (Easton and Dennis 1969: 206-07). Criminologists might well wonder about the future of a generation whose early impressions of the political process are dominated by the spectacle of a president's resigning from office in the face of evidence suggesting strongly that he was a "crook."

Indeed, the apocalyptic perspective suggests that Watergate might well encourage juveniles—the group in society most prone to commit "street crimes"—to view a Patricia Hearst not as, in the phrase of a former Attorney General, a "common criminal," but as a rebel with a cause. In such a context, the criminal justice system might well face an insurmountable challenge.[16]

THE SECOND SCENARIO: SOME MORE EQUAL THAN OTHERS

In accordance with this scenario, Watergate will lead to a substantial drop in support for the criminal justice system. "Equal justice under law" is a widely supported precept of the American constitutional system. Nevertheless, a theme long current in both social science and popular literature concerning the prosecutorial process is that its scales are tipped decisively in favor of the defendant who has money and influence.[17] Individuals from the upper socioeconomic classes, with their access to high-priced legal talent, can either avoid the consequences of their criminal behavior entirely or, at the worst, suffer only a "slap on the wrist." On the contrary, persons of the lower strata, particularly if they are members of unpopular racial, ethnic, or political groups, can be expected to have the "book thrown at them."

The investigations and prosecutions of alleged Watergate conspirators, as depicted in this scenario, can only give a great deal more credibility to this view. The full explosion of the Watergate scandal was preceded by the spectacle of the Vice-President of the United States "copping a plea" through which he bartered away his high office in exchange for a markedly lenient sentence. This episode was followed by the "cooperation" of John Dean, through which he deftly avoided being "the fall guy" for the administration, as well as a severe criminal sanction. The latter's early release from prison leaves no doubt as to whom the American system of justice allocates its advantages. Finally, Richard Nixon's pardon, in the context of strong evidence that he might well have committed at least one felony, will be seen as the penultimate case study of the machinations through which a powerful man can shield himself from prosecution.[18]

With the illusion of impartial justice totally destroyed, this scenario concludes that trust and confidence in the criminal justice system will plummet. Large segments of the population will not expect justice in the courts. In such an atmosphere crime might well be expected to increase dramatically.

THE THIRD SCENARIO: THE SYSTEM VINDICATED

This scenario is far more optimistic. In the wake of Watergate, it predicts that support for law enforcement, the courts, and corrections will not decline. Indeed, it may even increase. Americans, this interpretation goes, have always shown an ambivalence toward the political process. They register high levels of respect toward their political institutions. They revere governmental service in the abstract, with strong support for positions such as president or Supreme Court justice. They expect morally upright conduct on the part of their leaders, particularly the president (Monsma 1973: 35). Yet, at the same time, they believe that many politicians are corrupt and have obtained office through morally, ethically, and legally questionable means (ibid.: 28-29).

The resolution of this conflict will result in a maintenance, or even increase, of support for the criminal justice system in the post-Watergate era. Americans have always resolved their contradictory feelings about government by clinging to the belief that their basic institutions are sound and just, but that, occasionally, a "few rotten apples" abuse them. This same reasoning will be applied to Watergate. The people will see the checks and balances of the Constitution employed in such a way as to "throw the rascals out" of the executive branch and reinstate "honest men" in their place.[19]

Indeed, the demand for honesty in government occasioned by the outcry over Watergate will have far-reaching positive implications for the entire political system. Badly needed reforms in areas such as campaign financing and executive and legislative oversight of the CIA, FBI, and IRS can be expected to follow.[20] In the same way that Haynsworth and Carswell, in the wake of the Fortas Affair, found themselves facing a new and more demanding ethical standard during their abortive attempts to secure Senate confirmation as Supreme Court justices, other would-be office holders will be put to more rigorous moral tests.

This series of events, the third scenario concludes, can have no other consequence than the maintenance, or even increase, of support for the criminal justice system.

A PLEA FOR EMPIRICAL ANALYSIS

These three scenarios represent attempts to encapsulate views presently being propounded by many participants in the great national debate concerning corruption at the highest levels of government. As such, they are structured speculations at best—models from which hypotheses might be generated concerning Watergate's possible impact upon support for the criminal justice system.

These constructs are not presented as the only possible ones which might be distilled from the popular and professional literature.[21] Part, or perhaps all, of them might prove operational or valid. Hopefully, they may be of heuristic value as hypotheses available to criminologists to implement or discard as they attempt to reach empirically based conclusions concerning Watergate's implications for law enforcement, the courts, and corrections.

In this endeavor, students of the criminal justice system might well continue to make substantial recourse, on an interdisciplinary basis, to the most advanced methodologies for measuring support of societal institutions. Criminology's efforts to develop the public opinion poll into a powerful research tool have been impressive.[22] Perhaps they can bear even more fruit if criminologists comprehensively examine Watergate's impact upon support through critical analyses of their own and other social scientists' surveys.[23]

Watergate is similar to the assassinations of national leaders and urban riots of the late 1960s because it burst upon the scene with little warning. Like these other phenomena, its impact upon the critical variable of support for the criminal justice system has not been apparent. It may have profound implications for law enforcement, the courts, or correctional institutions, or its effects may be so insubstantial as to not rise above the trivial. At the least, the variety of contradictory interpretations encompassed in the three scenarios suggests that criminologists should pause before they give in to temptations to offer too-rapid assessments of Watergate's legacy.[24]

Politicians and journalists must provide immediate analyses of Watergate. Their constituencies and clienteles will not wait for sober second thoughts in these cataclysmic times. However, criminologists can move at a more cautious rate. A predominant portion of the American public may adopt the apocalyptic vision or the some-more-equal-than-others perspective, or both. Or it may embrace the conclusion that the system has been vindicated. Criminologists familiar with cognitive dissonance should not be surprised to find Americans accepting mutually contradictory scenarios at the same time.[25] Highly influential elites may agree with the public's assessment or reach very different conclusions. The chances are excellent that Watergate has very complex implications for support for the criminal justice system.[26] Such considerations caution against explanations not premised upon empirical data.

NOTES

1. The term, "criminology," is used in a general sense in this chapter, referring to any social science approach to the study of the criminal justice system.

2. "System" is defined here as an entity "composed of separate, distinguishable units that interact in order to perform certain functions. . . ." (Monsma 1973: 6).

3. This chapter defines "support" as approval of, and respect for, a political institution. It is reflected, for example, in the level of trust and confidence the public and the elite have in the institution.

4. By "public" is meant "the mass" or the group reflecting the views of the "average citizen." The "elite" might be described as a group in the society, composed primarily of members of the upper middle and upper classes, which possesses the major portion of that society's political power.

5. These scandals will be encompassed in the word, Watergate, for the purposes of this chapter.

6. Of course, there may be no dilemma at all for the individual who regards criminology as little more than one of the many battlefields for attackers and defenders of the present criminal justice system, as simply a medium for shoot-outs between ideologues of the left and right. This chapter is based on the assumption that the scientific method can be applied to many criminological inquiries; an attempt to strive for objective analysis in this field is neither hypocritical nor naive. For a persuasive defense of this approach in the context of the discipline of political science, see Isaak (1975: 47-61).

7. Kurt and Gladys Lang, among others, have attempted to chart the public's increasing concern with Watergate through a longitudinal analysis of public opinion polls (1975: 71-79).

8. A frequent tactic of the news magazines has been to draw upon a conglomeration of "experts" for predictions. See, for example, Time (1974b: 64-67 for a series of brief remarks by George Reedy, William Rusher, Richard Neustadt, Arthur Schlesinger, Jr., Emmet John Hughes, James MacGregor Burns, and Andrew Hacker, among others. See also "Watergate's Impact on Future as Political Scientists See It" (U.S. News and World Report, December 3, 1973)

for Watergate predictions based on a nationwide poll of political scientists.

The pooling of experts technique has also been employed in several books. See, for example, Bickel (1974) and Harward (1974).

9. See Rosenberg (1975) for an initial attempt to catalogue the mountain of literature on Watergate.

10. James Q. Wilson has charged that something like this happened when criminologists presented their opinions on how to combat crime to the President's Crime Commission. See Wilson (1975).

11. A similar view was recently expressed by a legal scholar-politician, former Attorney General Edward Levi:

> We are in a post-Watergate era. We are doing the usual thing of reliving the past where the lines of argument are set forth and they are easy to pick up. But the lessons of history are much more complicated than this assumes, and surely it is to the academic world one would hope to turn for the second and third thoughts on what we have learned, the corrective steps to be taken, and the problems which face us today. We know we are a country prone to cycles. Each branch of the government at times has abused its power, and all, unless memories are very short—which I am afraid they are—have done so in recent times. But the academic memory should be longer. For one thing you have time to think, a most precious asset which our country needs (1975b: 13).

12. For a classic study of mass and elite attitudes toward constitutionalism, see McClosky (1964).

13. Recent disclosures of the Pike and Church Committees have shown clearly that the fallout from Watergate is not diminishing. See, for example, Lardner (1976a, 1976b) and Washington Post 1976.

14. For an article predating the Nixon resignation which speculates insightfully on the impact of the Watergate machinations on support for the criminal justice system, see Oelsner (1974).

15. The Socialist Workers Party and the Young Socialist Alliance, prime targets of Nixon administration covert operations, have maintained that only the destruction of the present governmental system and the creation of a "socialist" one in its place can secure the "democratic rights" of the people:

As socialists, we believe there is more behind Watergate-
type attacks on democratic rights than the immorality of
the Nixon administration, sordid as that is. Such attacks
stem from the nature of capitalism—the role of a few
wealthy families who own the giant corporations and banks.
Such a tiny minority can only rule by secrecy, deception
and intimidation, and by gathering around it a loyal crew
of corrupt politicians and lying bureaucrats. We think
that to enjoy full democracy the American people will find
it necessary to sweep aside the Nixons, Rockefellers,
Hunts, Liddys, advertising men, and Cuban mercenaries—
and set up a government based directly on the working
people and the oppressed (Jenness and Pulley 1975: 8).

16. As Attorney General, William Saxbe suggested a post-
Watergate scenario not unlike the apocalyptic vision:

The setting of the proper example must begin with the
leaders of government. In recent years, the spectacles
we have seen are appalling, and I am not talking only
about Watergate now. The list of state and local officials
convicted of federal crimes—usually for violating the
public trust for an illegal buck—is scandalously long.
Disrespect for the law by those sworn to uphold it
can only encourage a tendency toward lawlessness in
others. . . .
The options are very limited as we face the future.
If we go on as we are, there is every possibility that
crime will inundate us.
The nation would then be faced with the prospect
of falling apart or devising a national police force in one
final effort to restore domestic order (Saxbe 1974: 16-17).

For an account of Attorney General Saxbe's alleged attempt to
"pull rank" on two police officers to prevent them from giving him a
traffic citation, see McCarthy (1974).
See, also, Pynn (1975: ix, 3) for the argument that Watergate
shook "the Constitutional structure of the rule of law in the United
States" and Harward (1974) for a collection of speeches on the "impact of Watergate" as a "crisis of confidence."

17. For an attempt to empirically test this proposition, see
Nagel (1970: 31-49).

18. Letters to the editor in the wake of the Nixon pardon frequently contained poignant versions of the some-more-equal-than-others
theme:

Having spent 45 years of my life as an educator in the
field of the social studies, I am distressed and sickened
by the unconditional pardon given to Richard M. Nixon.
Omitting my deep personal revulsion for the act, I am
more concerned for the teachers, both of social studies
and otherwise, who put forth such effort to instill in their
students that the laws of our country are equally for all.
If President Ford thinks the young will accept his excuse
that Mr. Nixon has "suffered enough," he lacks understanding of the students' ability to cut through sham. I
wonder how he in a classroom would meet the justifiable
cynicism of these young people (Davis 1974).

. . . Everything that I've been taught in school and held
sacred is for naught. The picture of the lady blindfolded
holding scales and sword, supposedly impartial and fair
to all, is a farce. Apparently some are more equal than
others.
     President Ford grants this pardon, saying that the
Nixon family has suffered enough. What about the families of the men and women who have had to and are still
paying their debt to society?
     Finally why does Nixon get a full pardon when
courageous men who refused to kill another human being
must come back on conditional amnesty? Nixon, like
the overlords of organized crime, has put his faith in the
American way of life and has won! (Blanton 1974).

For an attempt to objectively state the arguments on both sides
in the debate concerning the propriety of the Nixon pardon, see Hoyt
1974.

19. President Ford's declaration after the Nixon resignation
that "the Constitution works" is just one example, although perhaps
one of the most dramatic, of the many articulations of the system-
vindicated scenario which have appeared in the media. Anthony Lewis
has contended, for example, that Nixon's departure showed that the
"system functioned" and that the "old American promise of fealty to
law above men turned out to be true." For his defense of this position,
see Lewis (1977).
     Attorney General Levi has taken a similar tone, arguing that
the transformation in the White House which took place between 1974
and 1975 "is a strong reaffirmation of the vitality of our institutions"
(1975a: 1).

20. Congress appears to be moving decisively in the direction of significant reform of its oversight of the nation's intelligence agencies. See, for example, Pincus (1976) and Rich (1976).

Numerous social scientists have presented proposals for the reformation of American government in the post-Watergate era. For a report which makes a series of wide-ranging recommendations focusing primarily upon the executive branch, see Mosher et al. (1974).

21. Henry Steele Commager has argued eloquently, for example, that Watergate-style politics, with all its "knaveries, vulgarities, and dishonesties," more or less reflected American society, and even "the American character," and that, with Watergate, we were, in fact, getting the kind of government we wanted. See Commager (1975).

22. See, for example, Conklin (1971), Engstrom and Giles (1972), McDowell and Hogan (1975), Jacob (1971), Smith and Hawkins (1973), and Walker (1973), among many others.

Wesley Skogan (1975) has provided an insightful critique of one dimension of these studies. For a comprehensive exploration of the "nature, scope and sources of public opinion data" relevant to criminal justice research, see Hindelang (1976).

23. In this endeavor, they can contribute much through critiques of the literature. A Louis Harris column reported in early December, 1973, for example, that public confidence in the White House had sunk to such an all-time low, in the midst of the Watergate disclosures, that only 18% of the public expressed "a great deal" of confidence in the presidency (1973). Yet, three months later, with the Watergate affair increasing in its intensity, and with President Nixon continuing his desperate struggle to remain in office, Gallup reported that 69% of the public expressed "some confidence" in the presidency (Charlotte Observer 1974).

Perhaps the dramatic differences in these reports stem from the fact that Harris was communicating only responses indicating "a great deal" of confidence, while Gallup was focusing his attention upon replies reflecting "some" confidence.

It is possible, however, that some of the dissimilarity stemmed from the fact that Gallup asked his respondents to distinguish between the president and the office of the presidency, while Harris' question lent itself to a blurring of the distinction between the man and the institution: "How much confidence do you feel in the people who are running the White House—a great deal, only some, or hardly any confidence?"

In short, Harris mistakenly reported levels of public support for the leadership of the White House as if they were identical to those for the presidency itself.

24. For speculations by criminologists along the lines of the apocalyptic vision, see Gibbons and Hancock (1974).

25. For an intensive analysis of the role of cognitive dissonance in law and attitude change, see Muir (1968).

26. Some of the complexities and nuances of the relationship between Watergate and support for the political system are explored in Barger's excellent study of San Antonio elementary and secondary school children's pre- and post-Watergate attitudes. Of particular significance to students of the criminal justice system are two of this study's findings: (1) "The loss of affection, respect and esteem for the President of the United States" among the children has been 'so widespread and profound' in the wake of Watergate "that even if it is indeed focused on the individual the impact on the institution of the Presidency could be long-lasting and significantly" (Barger 1974: 11); (2) At least at the upper-grade levels, the "policeman's image of honesty apparently has suffered in tandem with the President's, although not as dramatically," suggesting "a spill-over effect from Watergate. . . ." (ibid.: 24).

A survey research study conducted among Appalachian elementary and secondary school children in Clay County, North Carolina suggests, however, that Watergate's impact upon their evaluations of political authority was minimal (Baggs 1975).

For an analysis of Watergate's implications for "specific and diffuse support" among the leading media of a major societal group, the business community, see Clark (1974).

REFERENCES

Baggs, A. 1975. Student evaluations of political authority: some preliminary observations on the applicability of the malevolent leader thesis to post-Watergate Southern Appalachia. Paper presented at the annual meeting of the North Carolina Political Science Association.

Barger, H. 1974. Images of the president and policeman among black, Mexican-American, and Anglo school children: considerations on Watergate. Paper presented at the annual meeting of the American Political Science Association.

Bickel, A. et al. 1974. Watergate, Politics, and the Legal Process. Washington, D.C.: American Enterprise Institute for Public Policy Research.

Blanton, M. 1974. Some are more equal than others. Charlotte Observer, Sept. 12.

Blumberg, A., ed. 1970. The Scales of Justice. New York: Transaction.

Brandeis, J. 1928. Dissenting opinion. Olmstead v. United States (277 U.S. 438, 485).

Charlotte Observer. 1974. Nixon hurts the presidency, survey says, Mar. 3.

Clark, J. 1974. Moral prerequisites of political support: business reactions to the Watergate scandal. Paper presented at the annual meeting of the American Political Science Association.

Commager, H. 1975. The shame of the republic. In Watergate and the American Political Process, ed. R. Pynn. New York: Praeger Publishers.

Conklin, J. 1971. Criminal environment and support for the law. Law and Society Review 6: 247-65.

Davis. M. 1974. A teacher's plight. Washington Post, Sept. 15.

Devine, D. 1972. The Political Culture of the United States. Boston: Little, Brown and Company.

Easton, D. 1965. A Framework for Political Analysis. Englewood Cliffs: Prentice-Hall.

Easton, D. and J. Dennis. 1969. Children in the Political System. New York: McGraw-Hill Book Co.

Engstrom, R. and M. Giles. 1972. Expectations and images: a note on diffuse support for legal institutions. Law and Society Review 6: 631-36.

Gardiner, J. and M. Mulkey, eds. 1975. Crime and Criminal Justice. Lexington, Mass.: Lexington Books.

Gibbons, D. and R. K. Hancock. 1974. Some criminological theory and forecasts for a society that is coming apart. Paper presented at the 1974 Annual Meeting of the American Society of Criminology.

Harris, L. 1973. Presidency rated below trashmen. Washington Post, Dec. 9.

Harrock, N. 1976. Nixon declares he sought to bar Allende election. New York Times, March 12.

Hartz, L. 1962. The Liberal Tradition in America. New York: Harcourt, Brace, Jovanovich.

Harward, D., ed. 1974. Crisis in Confidence—The Impact of Watergate. Boston: Little, Brown and Co.

Hindelang, M. 1976. Public opinoin regarding crime, criminal justice and related topics. Washington, D.C.: National Criminal Justice Reference Service, National Institute of Law Enforcement and Criminal Justice.

Hoyt, C. 1974. Pardon pros, cons. Charlotte Observer, Sept. 10.

Isaak, A. 1975. Scope and Methods of Political Science, Rev. Ed. Homewood, Illinois: The Dorsey Press.

Jacob, H. 1971. Black and white perceptions of justice in the city. Law and Society Review 6: 69-89.

Jenness, L. and A. Pulley. 1973. Watergate—The View From the Left. New York: Pathfinder Press.

Lang, K. and G. Lang. 1975. Televised hearings: the impact out there. In Watergate and the American Political Press, ed. R. Pynn. New York: Praeger Publishers.

Lardner, G. 1976a. FBI break-ins still go on, panel says. Washington Post, May 11.

———. 1976b. IRS power "abused," study says. Washington Post, May 12.

Levi, E. 1975a. Address before the American Bar Association Convention. Washington, D.C.: United States Department of Justice.

——. 1975b. Address before the Association of American Law Schools. Washington, D.C.: United States Department of Justice.

Lewis, A. 1974. The resignation proved impeachment works. New York Times, Aug. 11.

McCarthy, C. 1974. Government lawlessness. Washington Post, Jan. 29.

McClosky, H. 1964. Consensus and ideology in American politics. American Political Science Review 58: 361-82.

McDowell, G. and R. Hogan. 1975. Perceptions of the criminal justice system: the Memphis study. Memphis, Tenn.: Institute of Governmental Studies and Research, Memphis State University.

Monsma, S. 1973. American Politics—A Systems Approach, Second Ed. Hinsdale, Ill.: The Dryden Press.

Mosher, F. et al. 1974. Watergate—Implications for Responsible Government. New York: Basic Books, Inc.

Muir, W. 1968. Prayer in the Public Schools: Law and Attitude Change. Chicago: The University of Chicago Press.

Nagel, S. 1970. The tipped scales of American justice. In The Scales of Justice, ed. A. Blumberg. New York: Transaction Books.

New York Times, ed. 1973. The Watergate Hearings—Break-in and Cover-up. New York: Bantam Books, Inc.

Oelsner, L. 1974. That the laws be faithfully executed. New York Times, May 5.

Pincus, W. 1976. Oversight committee plans eyed. Washington Post, May 11.

Pynn, R. 1975. Watergate and the American Political Process. New York: Praeger Publishers.

Rich, S. 1976. Oversight unit is said to pose "grave risks." Washington Post, May 18.

Rosenberg, K. and J. K. Rosenberg, eds. 1975. Watergate: An Annotated Bibliography. Littleton, Colo.: Libraries Unlimited.

Saxbe, W. 1974. Address before the Major Cities Chief Administrators' Conference on Urban Crime. Washington, D.C.: United States Department of Justice.

Smith, P. and R. Hawkins. 1973. Victimization, types of citizen-police contacts, and attitudes toward the police. Law and Society Review 8: 135-52.

Skogan, W. 1975. Public policy and public evaluations of criminal justice system performance. In Crime and Criminal Justice, eds. Gardiner and Mulkey. Lexington, Mass.: Lexington Books.

Time, Inc. 1974a. Where America goes now. Time, Aug. 8: 64-67.

———. 1974b. More blunt talk in the oval office. Time, Aug. 19: 62.

Trebach, A. 1974. Remarks during panel on "governmental morality: implications of Watergate for criminology." Annual meeting of the American Society of Criminology.

U.S. News and World Report. 1973. Watergate's impact on the future as political scientists see it. Dec. 3: 78-82.

Walker, D. 1973. Paper presented at the annual meeting of the Southern Political Science Association.

Washington Post. 1976. Church eyes Dallas probe reopening. May 11: A16.

Wilson, J. 1975. Crime and criminologists. In Crime and Criminal Justice, eds. J. Gardiner and M. Mulkey. Lexington, Mass.: Lexington Books.

3

SOME PERSPECTIVES ON POLICE CORRUPTION

Mark Pogrebin and Burton Atkins

In the past decade social scientists have witnessed a rejuvenation of interest in the study of political corruption, fueled most recently by the Watergate scandals. This concern has not been limited to stellar individuals in high levels of government but has extended to all echelons of federal, state, and local politics. Paramount attention, at state and local levels, has been directed at various aspects of corruption in the criminal justice system and, particularly, corruption within police departments. Considerable publicity about police corruption in major cities such as Chicago, Indianapolis, Cleveland, Houston, and Denver has been generated by the news media within the past several years (Time 1974). Two of the nation's largest cities, New York and Philadelphia, were the focus of commission reports that found widespread corruption to the extent that illegal activities had become routine in the cities' police departments. Reports of organized theft rings being run through the police department of Newburg, New York, a medium-sized city along the Hudson River, suggests that corruption is not monopolized by the nation's cities but may, in fact, permeate many police departments across the country.

The existence of corruption among institutions sworn to uphold the law forces all of us to confront serious problems concerning whether the system of criminal justice is meeting its moral and political expectations. The issue of police corruption is particularly intriguing for social scientists since they can bring a varied perspective to bear upon that political, legal, and social aspect of "official deviancy." Indeed, given the pronounced effect of police corruption upon the legal system and the fundamental political and social problems raised, a variety of explanations for this dilemma have already been advanced by sociologists, criminologists, and political scientists. This chapter examines some of the explanations for police corruption which have emerged in this social science literature. While we do not intend to offer any new data, periodic reviews of literature do aid in allowing us to sort out conceptual problems associated with explaining and understanding phenomena like police corruption. For the purposes of this review we shall adopt Roebuck and Barker's definition of police corruption in which they include ". . . any type of proscribed behavior engaged in by a law enforcement officer who receives or expects to receive, by virtue of his official position, an actual or potential unauthorized material reward or gain (1974: 424). Although there are many other ways in which police misuse or misrepresent their official role, for example, not issuing traffic citations to acquaintances, we will be utilizing the term "corruption" only when it involves a monetary transaction for profit.

Before reviewing the literature on police corruption, it would be useful to set forth some of the premises that (1) define the boundaries between police and other public officials and (2) serve to isolate values and ethics associated with police work from those that may prevail in other sectors of the political system. The very use of the term "corruption" is perhaps pejorative in that it defines a type of behavior as beyond the boundaries of acceptability. Thus, there are aspects of police behavior that might be labeled as corrupt which do not necessarily violate any specific law or regulation. To that extent, the concept seems to imply that there are some abstract ethical standards that must be established and met. Since the line between malfeasance and misfeasance may be both fine and wavering, we need to realize that the concept of corruption may encompass ethical as well as legal standards established by the community. Additionally, theories and hypotheses concerning police corruption are, in reality, addressing only a subset of activities subsumed under the more general concept of political corruption. Still, our ability to grapple with the smaller units sometimes provides the necessary guideposts for dealing with the larger question.

POLICE VALUES IN A PLURALIST SYSTEM

If legal rules and sanctions are a reflection of societal norms that have evolved to the point of requiring formalization, then the interpretation and impact of such standards are, in many ways, dependent upon the value premises of those charged with carrying them out. One common interpretation of the American political system suggests that the standards set in public policy—whether specific dollar allocations for public programs or the normative presumptions concerning the program's existence—are a reflection of the values and ethics found among the political and economic elite controlling the system (Dye and Zeigler 1970). Thus, the social class that controls legislative, administrative, and even judicial institutions shapes the values that are the basis of our legal norms and public policies. While much of this interpretation is accurate, it fails to fully appreciate the practical impact of our pluralist system, particularly in the way in which values established by one sector may be easily refashioned to suit the needs of another.

For this reason, it seems that we have not thoroughly examined the role of the police in a pluralist society. While we may begin with the presumption that political and economic elites define our legal values, the fact remains that lower-echelon public officials like the police often function, in effect, to redefine many elements of the value system. Several processes inreract to create this flexibility. Consider, for example, how police recruitment affects the kinds of values brought into local law enforcement systems. For the most part, police recruits emerge from the working class. For individuals growing up in this milieu, police represent not only an abstract status symbol of authority but, in a more tangible way, a vehicle for entry into the system itself. Considerable research has shown that the values of working-class environs differ from those found in middle- and upper-class milieu. One concept that defines some aspects of these differences and which may be particularly relevant to understanding the attitudinal predispositions of police, is "working-class authoritarianism." Working-ciass authoritarianism refers to the matrix of social, economic, and political values that reflect, among other things, intolerance of deviant perspectives, reliance on authority, and rigid belief systems (Lipset 1963). While these characteristics are not peculiar to any one social strata, they do appear to be fairly commonplace in working-class settings. In other words, educational prerequisites and monetary compensation that are fairly low virtually lock police recruitment processes into tapping a certain type of ideology for police work. It may well be, then, that the values held by those charged with enforcing legal norms are at variance with the values of those who created them.

While this inherent value tension is not necessarily a unique phenomenon, it does take on some unusual characteristics as it affects police behavior. Our pluralist social system creates and perpetuates a pluralist value system. Each element of this larger, multifaceted arrangement which defines the American ideology nurtures itself by its anchor in a particular social class and occupational setting. These provide the necessary roots to the system. The potentially disparate views thus produced are moderated, however, by our penchant for group affiliation. It is this process of overlapping and multiple group memberships which moderate these value clashes. Curiously, several characteristics of their culture insulate police from this social-moderation mechanism. Like other professions, police develop occupational norms. Yet, unlike many other professions, police tend to internalize their norms to the extent that they feel, perhaps erroneously, that many segments of the community—particularly the middle and upper classes—view them with disdain. The dual values defining the policeman's "working personality"—danger and authority—further delineate and insulate the group (Skolnick 1966). In fact, it is commonplace for police and their families to limit their social contacts to other police. Whereas most other occupational and social groups allow for exchange and feedback processes for the purpose of testing and sharing value premises, police tend to perpetuate a fairly rigid normative system generated by their social class origins and perpetuated by their occupational hazards.

We point out these broad contours of the values inherent in the police culture only to emphasize the peculiarities of law-enforcement work which may allow corruption to flourish. This is not to suggest that working-class values themselves encourage corruption. Rather we are suggesting that in considering the theories of police corruption that follow, we should not lose sight of the somewhat unusual circumstances associated with this type of official corruption. Several of the explanations for police corruption emphasize the values engendered in the police subculture—cynicism and secrecy, for example—which may provide the psychological or emotional roots for corruption. It is useful to keep in mind through this review that the insulation of the police from many segments of society may act to foster values, and particularly actions based on those values, which society may view as corrupt.

INDIVIDUAL CAUSES OF CORRUPTION

In examining the major causes of criminal behavior among police, the Chicago Crime Commission placed much emphasis on the type of police officer on the force. The commission concluded that poor recruitment methods permitted many men to enter the department who were not suited for law-enforcement work. The commission recommended that all police candidates be subjected to a complete character investigation (Peterson 1960). This explanation implies that corrupt activities stem from the low moral caliber of certain police recruits. It suggests further that corruption could be avoided if recruiting methods were sufficiently rigorous that individuals prone toward corruption could be detected and kept off the force.

In a similar vein, Goldstein (1970) argues that a major cause of police corruption is the individual officer's misuse of authority in order to gain monetary compensation. This individualistic explanation of police corruption also places the responsibility of police misuse of official authority on the particular officer's character. According

to this school of thought, commonly known as the "rotten-apple" theory, the policeman seemingly chooses to involve himself in corrupt
activities. But like the analogous free-will explanation of criminal
behavior, this theory largely ignores the organizational social structure of police departments which may establish the norms and role
expectations that permit corruption to flourish.

Until recently the rotten-apple theory was usually advanced
by police officials as the most important explanation for police involvement in illegal activities. This theory, which obviously seeks
to protect the organization from blame, suggests that a few individual
policemen were swayed from the path of honest law enforcement and,
thus, the force itself is relieved of responsibility. Wilson (1970: 293)
suggests, however, that the rotten-apple theory is inadequate because
it does not explain the frequency of police misconduct in large cities.
In fact, to entertain this theory requires that one admit that police
recruitment practices have been a total failure, an admission unlikely
to be forthcoming from police departments. Indeed, Burnham (1972:
14-16) has argued that if one wants to explain police misconduct in
terms of applies, then perhaps the barrel itself needs to be examined.
He, like Wilson, suggests that police corruption should be viewed as
a failure of the criminal justice system and not as a flaw in the character of a few wayward policemen.

STRUCTURAL EXPLANATION OF POLICE CORRUPTION

Roebuck and Barker (1974: 425) present a structural explanation for police corruption. They claim that ". . . police corruption is
best understood not as the exclusive deviance of individual officers,
but as group behavior guided by contradictory sets of norms linked to
the organization to which the erring individuals belong, i.e., organizational deviance." In short, Roebuck and Barker are alluding to the
existence of a police subculture in which deviant means and practices
are often considered normal police behavior.

The subcultural theory of police deviancy is based on the proposition that organizational deviance is institutionalized and accepted to
some degree within almost all police departments. Stoddard (1968)
found that rookie patrolmen are socialized into the police subculture
and learn from the more experienced officers to become deviant in
many aspects of the job. He concludes that the police subculture is
self-perpetuating, and eventually all police are subject to its values.
Reiss (1971: 170) found that police officers are more prone to accept
illegal exchanges when such activities are accepted as an institutionalized and legitimized part of the police organization and subculture.
Moreover, when an officer's commitment to justice is not confirmed

by the legal system, or his moral commitment to the job is not sustained by his peers or the public, he tends to lessen his moral commitments and allow subcultural norms to predominate. The officer who has reduced his commitment to justice usually finds a sympathetic peer group within the organizational subculture resulting in the reinforcement of deviant values which often lend themselves to corrupt practices.

Secrecy, claims Westley (1970: 130), is the most vital component of the police subculture. The policeman who violates the code of secrecy could be deprived of his fellow officers' support in time of need. A breach of the unwritten code of secrecy is probably the worst internal offense an officer can commit. Reiss (1971: 213) expresses a similar view. He observes that testifying against a fellow patrolman is considered to be one of the most serious violations of police subcultural norms, leading, at times, to absolute exclusion from the informal network of communications and refusal on the part of other officers to work with that officer. In sum, secrecy is often perceived as having greater value within the hierarchy of police subcultural values than honesty and lawfulness. This seems to explain why corrupt activities become widespread in large city departments. The honest officer, by informing superiors in the organizational structure of peer corruption, may find his fellow officers perceiving him as untrustworthy or unreliable. Resorting to secrecy, concludes Manning (1974b), often frees police from constraints that deter participation in criminal activities.

CYNICISM AND LEGITIMIZATION OF GRAFT

The existence of certain norms and role expectations obviously affects a policeman's orientation towards the law-enforcement system; the evolution of a social infrastructure within police departments, according to the structural explanation, requires that the policeman adapt to expectations or be for all intents and purposes, excluded from the system. But some writers have advanced the view that the nature of the policeman's profession encourages corruption. According to Neiderhoffer (1967), members of the police rank-and-file often develop a cynical attitude toward their job which may result in a tendency to excuse graft. Those officers who internalize cynicism, observes Neiderhoffer, perceive police work as a business and, as a result of their attitude, place much value on attaining material goods, which often leads to graft. In contrast to the cynical rank-and-file officer who is more likely to participate in corrupt activities, the professionally oriented policeman perceives police work as a profession which requires high standards of conduct. Neiderhoffer implies that professionally oriented police are not likely to become involved in illegal exchanges with the public because of their commitment to the profession. In short, cynicism may provide the policeman with a justification to exchange police authority for graft.

Reiss (1971) notes that police are more prone to legitimize involvement in corrupt practices if there is an exchange of services with those who will benefit from police inaction:

> What may be most pertinent in the policeman's exchange with organized crime is the legitimacy that attaches to the exchange. To deviate on one's own is to be criminal, but where the offence is consensual, not only is there mutual implication in the offence, and therefore minimization of risk, but the offence is also easily legitimized. For an officer to share in a payment from illegal gambling is accepted, but for an officer to burglarize an establishment is to step beyond the bounds of what is legitimate. Deviation often is shared with fellow officers, providing open support for each (Reiss 1971: 171).

The President's Commission on Law Enforcement and the Administration of Justice (1967) suggests that the attitudes of police department administrators are carried directly to the personal and ethical standards of those lower in the organizational structure. The commission's viewpoint is that supervisors and executives exert great influence in establishing the department's attitude toward corrupt police behavior. If officers perceive that those in command condone dishonesty, then their perceptions of what is and is not proper police conduct may be based on their own concept of departmental norms. As a direct consequence, those involved in corrupt exchanges will legitimize their behavior.

Wilson (1970: 301) argues that corrupt activities are perceived by police to be justifiable given the weakening moral standard on the part of the public. Wilson observes that the citizenry is hypocritical when it comes to judging police integrity. Although the public will quickly denounce police who take graft, it is virtually expected in some areas that police will overlook certain offences for a small bribe. Thus, the officer is the object of conflicting standards because the community desires police officers who will not take bribes yet also wants to bribe them.

An interesting explanation for the legitimization of corrupt practices has been offered by Skolnick (1966). From his observation of a west-coast police department, Skolnick notes that the police distinguish among degrees of immorality involving certain victimless crimes. Bookmakers and numbers operators were viewed as businessmen by police, but narcotic users were seen as posing a serious danger to the community. By defining certain activities as more dangerous to the public than others, the police were able to perceive themselves as not being corrupt if they did not participate in illegal exchanges they felt were a threat to public safety. In short, it appears that police often justify their deviant activities by maintaining a concept of non-deviant self that utilizes the citizenry's involvement in idiosyncratic types of crime.

DETERRENCE AND ASSUREDNESS OF PUNISHMENT

The opportunity to engage in corrupt activities over a prolonged period of time may perhaps be related directly to the occupational structure of the profession. Police are often exempt from being policed; rarely does an officer report a peer to a higher authority. Obviously, the police subculture suppresses attempts to publicize illegal police activities. But another important explanation for this lack of reported deviant occupational behavior lies, in large part, with the fear that reporting the misconduct of a fellow officer may result in a counter-allegation concerning the reporting officer's conduct sometime during his career. The threat of retaliation is a very real fear of all officers simply because of the wide latitude of legitimate discretion utilized on the job.

Police administrators realistically admit that they are unable to eradicate all police corruption. Their real concern is maintaining a low degree of corruption in their departments (Neiderhoffer 1967). The predicament of police executives is awesome. They become almost powerless in controlling the deviance within their lines of command. The incapability to sanction corrupt subordinates is explained by Sayre and Kaufman (1960):

> The Police Commissioner must expend a great part of
> his energies in attempts at policing the police. His prob-
> lems are concentrated in police corruption. However
> aggressively the commissioner pursues the goal of police
> integrity by the use of special squads to investigate the
> force, by shake-ups and transfers of command, by swift
> suspensions and other forms of discipline, he accepts ul-
> timately that police corruption is endemic to his organi-
> zation, and that he is fortunate if he can prevent its
> reaching epidemic proportions. He lacks the resources
> to do more (: 289).

Police executives have further organizational problems in attempting to discipline subordinates for illegal behavior. Most urban departments come under the municipal civil service regulations which tend to restrict reform efforts of modern police commanders (President's Commission 1967: 210). In the past few years, local police organizations have proved very successful in coming to the defense of police who have been accused of corrupt activities, thus preventing punitive action toward those officers.

In short, very few police except reprecussions from their involvement in corrupt exchanges. They are not deterred by the law enforcement apparatus of which they are a part, nor do they fear departmental sanctions for their illegal behavior. The likelihood of punishment, either by the district attorney or another outside investigative body, is usually lacking; therefore, corrupt activities on the part of police endure. Internal control appears to prove insufficient and external control is successfully intimidated by local police benevolent associations.

VICTIMLESS CRIMES, PUBLIC CONSENSUS, AND POLITICAL AUTHORITY

Manning (1974b) presents the viewpoint that "any well-organized consensual, secretive organization can resist the efforts of an unorganized public. . . . As long as there remains a lack of consensus on the enforcement of our moralistic laws, police corruption and selective law enforcement will continue" (: 195). A similar point of view is shared by Chambliss and Seidman (1971) who note that those persons who provide illegal services to the community are usually in a financial position to pay off the police in exchange for tolerance of their unlawful enterprises. Although the entire enterprise is surreptitious, a trade-off is performed in which certain community services are tolerated by the police in exchange for compensation which permits the service to exist. Because of the ambiguity concerning the activity, the graft is justified by the benefits alleged to flow to the community:

> The law enforcement system is placed in the middle of two conflicting demands. On the one hand, it is their job to enforce the law, albeit with discretion; on the other hand, there is considerable disagreement as to whether or not certain particular activities should be declared criminal. Faced with such a dilemma, the police are likely to do what any well-managed organization would do under similar circumstances: follow the line of least resistance. They resolve the problem by establishing procedures which minimize organizational strains and provide

the greatest of rewards for the organization and the individuals involved. Typically what this means is that law enforcers adopt a tolerance policy toward the vices and selectively enforce those laws when it is to their advantage to do so (Chambliss and Seidman 1971: 490).

Victimless crimes were found to be a type of enforcement activity in which the police often received monetary compensation for participating in illegal exchanges. The Knapp Commission's (1974) findings in New York City clearly illustrated the extent of police corruption's relationship to victimless crimes. The commission found that plainclothes detectives divided payoff money which they received as a result of their unlawful involvement in gambling, narcotics, extortion, prostitution, construction payoffs, payoffs from unlicensed bars, and sabbath-law violations.

A real concern of police in the enforcement of moral laws (victimless crimes) is the extent to which organized crime corrupts police. Some claim that corruption is the major obstacle to the control of organized crime (Ruth 1967). The pressures felt by the police from political leaders, businessmen, and the public lead to inaction by all but the most courageous police commanders. It is doubtful, argues Hills (1969) that organized crime could be so successful in this country without the cooperation of some of our police and political machinery. Moreover, it may well be that, since the responsibility for the maintenance of social order in the United States is so decentralized, the police may often take enforcement cues from local political officials who themselves have a tolerant view of organized crime. According to Manning,

> Many factors pattern this enforcement but they all reflect the political organization of society. The distribution of power and authority, rather than the striving for justice, or equal treatment under the law, can have a direct bearing on enforcement (Manning 1974a: 103).

Gardiner also argues that decentralized local government encourages corruption by dispersing authority and control. Gardiner claims that ". . . the best thing for the existence of illegal activities is a political system which is so decentralized that no political force is powerful enough to challenge any individual officials who have been corrupted" (1970: 8). Along similar lines Goldstein sees a strong relationship between the extent of police corruption and the moral climate of the community. That is, where one finds government and business affairs operating with a high degree of integrity and honesty, one will usually find a police department that also operates with a high level of integrity (1975: 14). Goldstein concludes that to expect police to adhere to honesty and profess a high degree of integrity in a community where governmental officials are corrupt is unrealistic. However, he suggests that even the most astute and honest government official is still political, and thus opportunities will always be available for corrupt practices to affect decisions relating to law enforcement (1975: 24). On the basis of Goldstein's findings, it may be surmised that the amount of police corruption in a community may be directly related to the amount of corruption tolerated by local governmental officials. Moreover, it would follow from both Gardiner's and Goldstein's analyses that police corruption would probably be but one element within a corrupt political system. Obviously, to the extent that one seeks to explain police corruption by reference to the political system in which the police department operates, the attempt to sort out possible relationships becomes enormously complex. In light of this it is useful to underscore several questions posed by Gardiner and Olson (1974: 130), answers to which might yield valuable data concerning the linkage between police departments and their respective political systems: (1) What factors affect the likelihood that a particular type of government activity will involve corruption? (2) How do corrupt relationships become established? (3) What are the relationships between the involved parties? (4) What are the consequences of corruption both for the parties involved and for others? and (5) What changes might reduce the likelihood that corruption will occur in the future?

EFFECTS OF POLICE CORRUPTION

Much of this research, of course, presumes that police corruption has detrimental effects upon law-enforcement activities in general. Corruption, claims Wilson, tends to demoralize the individual officer who does not share in the rewards of corruption, fosters disrespect for criminal law, provides incentives to participate in corrupt exchanges, and encourages the individual officer to perceive the community as cynical and hypocritical (1963: 189). But the effects of police corruption go beyond the departments themselves. Police corruption, claims the National Council on Crime and Delinquency, erodes public confidence in law enforcement as well as contributing to disrespect for the law itself. Thus, one extremely important result of corrupt police activities may be the public's unwillingness to report crimes. "Increased trust in the police improves the reporting of information and raises the level of citizen cooperation" (National Council on Crime and Delinquency 1974: 19). A recent survey published by the Law Enforcement Assistance Administration (1974) indicates that the actual incidence of crime is indeed much higher than reported. This is not to say that distrust of the police on the part of the public is the only cause for the high percentage of unreported crimes. However, wide-scale police corruption does seem to cause a loss of public confidence in law enforcement which could account in part for the lack of public willingness to report crimes to the police.

CONCLUSIONS

How might these various conclusions be placed in perspective? In the first place, this review has tended to consider police corruption as a unique phenomenon. While there are certain identifiable aspects of police corruption that we sought to identify at the outset, one cannot ignore the linkages between the police and the rest of society. It may well be that those officials charged with enforcing the law are doing so within an ethical framework imposed on them by others. Obviously, it would be virtually impossible for a totally moral police department to operate in a political and economic system which allows corruption to exist and, in fact, may even tacitly condone it. As Patrick Murphy has written:

> Legislators, politicians, businessmen, even the general public have all contributed to the problem. The business ethic, anything for a price, establishes a climate in which corruption is rationalized as just something everybody is doing. The political ethic, anything to stay in office, fosters a cynical atmosphere in which corruption can thrive (1973: 37).

Murphy seems to suggest that political corruption of various types is part and parcel of the American ethic. Others have gone even further in their condemnation of the societal standards that perpetuate corruption. One observer has noted that the order of causality may in fact flow in the opposite direction—that it is not society that provides the ethical flavor but rather that the ideal of American virtue (the police officer) are models of corruption and violence for the rest of society (Bayley 1969). If this is so, it would seem to be the role society has given police officers that, in effect, places them above the law. No other individual can so blatantly ignore basic values as part of their official duty. Police may invade privacy, destroy property, routinely ignore traffic regulations, detain citizens on mere suspicion of wrong-doing, and if need be, kill (Neiderhoffer 1967). Obviously, the need for law enforcement is satisfied with considerable cost.

The causes and consequences of police corruption probed in this review suggest that considerable research is needed for adequate explanations of official misconduct to be offered. The relationship between governmental processes and police corruption needs further investigation. The research discussed in this chapter has shown that courts, prosecutors, elected officials, and administrative appointees all affect the degree of corruption that exists in local police departments. It is necessary to investigate the extent and type of interrelationships that local governmental agencies and elected officials have with each other in communities that have a corruption problem. Also, the conditions which cause the public to have a high degree of tolerance for corrupt activities, in the police organization and in other units of local government as well need further study. Further research is thus needed in public perceptions of police, especially in communities alleged to have corrupt police departments. This, in turn, suggests that research designs should be formulated that compare not only political structures among cities with and without police corruption, but provide comparative analysis of the public perception of police. Certainly, it is necessary to better understand the conditions which appear to permit corruption to flourish. By studying the interrelationships between police, government, and the public, we may acquire the knowledge of structural variables which will provide an explanation for corruption. That knowledge can be applied to prevent police and other units of government from unlawful abuses of authority.

REFERENCES

Bayley, D. 1969. The Police and Political Development in India. Princeton: Princeton University Press.

Burnham, D. 1972. The study of official corruption. In Quest for Justice. Washington, D.C.: American Bar Association Commission on a National Institute of Justice.

Chambliss, W. and R. Seidman. 1971. Law, Order and Power. Reading: Addison-Wesley.

Dye, T. R. and L. H. Zeigler. 1970. The Irony of Democracy. Belmont, Calif.: Wadsworth Publishing Co.

Gardiner, J. 1970. The Politics of Corruption: Organized Crime in an American City. New York: Russell Sage.

Gardiner, J. and L. Olson. 1974. Theft of a City. Bloomington: University of Indiana Press.

Goldstein, H. 1970. Police discretion: the ideal vs. the real. In The Ambivalent Force, eds. A. Blumberg and A. Neiderhoffer. Waltham: Ginn and Co.

————. 1975. Police Corruption: A Perspective on Its Nature and Control. Washington, D.C.: Police Foundation.

Hills, S. 1969. Combatting organized crime in America. Federal Probation 33 (March): 23-28.

Knapp, E. 1974. The Knapp Commission Report on Police Corruption. New York: George Braziller.

Law Enforcement Assistance Administration. 1974. Newsletter, March.

Lipset, S. M. 1962. Political Man. Garden City, N.Y.: Doubleday.

Manning, P. 1974a. The policeman as hero. In The Crime Establishment, ed. I. Silver. Englewood Cliffs: Prentice-Hall.

————. 1974b. The police mandate, strategies, and appearances. In Criminal Justice in America, ed. R. Quinney. Boston: Little, Brown.

Murphy, P. 1973. Police corruption. The Police Chief 40 (Dec.).

National Council on Crime and Delinquency. 1974. Official corruption: a position statement. 20 (January): 15-19.

Neiderhoffer, A. 1967. Behind the Shield. Garden City: Anchor Books.

Peterson, V. 1960. The Chicago police scandals. Atlantic, October: 58-64.

President's Commission on Law Enforcement and the Administration of Justice. 1967. Task Force Report: The Police. Washington, D.C.: Government Printing Office.

Reiss, Jr., A. 1971. The Police and the Public. New Haven: Yale University Press.

Roebuck, J. and T. Barker. 1974. A typology of police corruption. Social Problems 21: 423-27.

Ruth, H., Jr. 1967. Why organized crime thrives. Annals of the American Academy of Political and Social Science. November: 113-22.

Sayre, W. and H. Kaufman. 1960. Governing New York City. New York: Russell Sage Foundation.

Skolnick, J. 1966. Justice Without Trial. New York: John Wiley and Sons.

Stoddard, E. 1968. The informal code of police deviancy: group approach to blue coat crime. Journal of Criminal Law, Criminology and Police Science 59: 201-13.

Time, Inc. 1974. Time, May 6.

Westley, W. 1970. Secrecy and the police. In The Ambivalent Force, eds. A. Blumberg and A. Niederhoffer. Waltham: Ginn and Co.

Wilson, J. 1970. The police and their problems: a theory. In The Ambivalent Force, eds. A. Blumberg and A. Niederhoffer. Waltham: Ginn and Co.

4

THE IMMORALITY OF PLEA BARGAINING

Marshall J. Hartman and Marianna Koval

The process of plea bargaining is absolutely and fundamentally immoral, and yet it is probably the key mechanism by which the criminal justice system in this country operates today. It is a process whereby Americans accused of criminal offenses barter away constitutional rights—trial by jury, privilege against self-incrimination, confrontation of witnesses, and proof of guilt beyond a reasonable doubt—in exchange for a lighter sentence. The result of this system is that those who do exercise their constitutional rights may receive a more severe sentence.

The justifications for this process, which has become so widely sanctioned, are three: first, plea bargaining is more economical—without it, this country could never afford all the courtrooms, judges, and court personnel needed for trials; secondly, the process is advantageous to defendants; and finally, that the public is served by it. Each of these justifications will be discussed in turn.

Operationally, the system works as follows: The defendant, through his attorney, finds out from the prosecutor what charges will be dismissed or reduced or what lesser sentence will be recommended if a guilty plea is entered. Then the defendant's counsel, after learning the prosecutor's "deal," relays the information back to the defendant for a counter-offer. At some point in the proceedings, they may check with the court, to make sure the court will agree to the bargain and, finally, after a series of offers and counter-offers, a deal is struck and the defendant pleads guilty. Until very recently, these negotiations were not made part of the official court record, but that policy has now ended in most jurisdictions.

THE BUREAUCRATIC PERSPECTIVE

The advantages of plea bargaining are apparent from the statistics. "Roughly 90 percent of all defendants who were indicted entered a plea of guilty prior to trial" (President's Commission 1967). This figure is directly attributable to the technique of plea bargaining, where the defendant is told, in no uncertain terms, that if he does not plead guilty, he will suffer the consequences.

The report of the American Bar Association on Minimum Standards for Criminal Justice, Standards Relating to Pleas of Guilty points up the weapons of the prosecutor in this game, listing his arsenal of prosecutorial options:

> First, the charge may be reduced to a lesser or related offense. Second, the prosecutor may promise to nolle prosequi other charges. Third, the prosecutor may agree to recommend or not to oppose the imposition of a particular sentence (American Bar Assn. 1968; Sec. 3.1).

In practice, the purpose of plea bargaining is reduction of sentence, and reduction of charge or the releasing of charges are only means to that end. Perhaps a more appropriate term for the process would be "sentence bargaining."

An example of reduction of charge would be the reduction of a murder charge to one of manslaughter based upon an agreement to plead guilty. In most jurisdictions, a conviction for murder carries a mandatory minimum sentence. In Illinois, for example, it is fourteen years. Similarly, in most jurisdictions, manslaughter, a lesser included offense within the murder family, carries no minimum sentence. Therefore, faced with the fear of the mandatory minimum or, in any event, a much heavier sentence, the defendant will plead guilty to get the benefit of the bargain for a reduced sentence.

Or, a prosecutor may agree to dismiss some charges if multiple charges are involved. For instance, a defendant may be charged with five burglaries. A plea of guilty to one may bring dismissal of the other four. Such a dismissal will usually bring with it a lower sentence than the defendant would have received had he been convicted of five burglaries.

Finally, the defendant may plead as charged, if the prosecutor will agree to "go easy" and recommend a lighter sentence that he would have had the defendant gone to trial. Therefore, the process of plea negotiation—whether charges are reduced or dropped, or there is a plea to the original charge for a reduced sentence—results in a less severe sentence if the defendant pleads guilty; by doing so, the defendant trades away the right to require the prosecution to prove actual guilt at trial.

The anomaly of this process is that we sentence defendants who we know are guilty to less severe sentences than those defendants about whose guilt we may be uncertain. Those defendants who plead guilty admit to the crime in open court and full view of the public. There can be no question about their guilt. On the other hand, with defendants who are convicted after a trial, there still may be some doubt as to their guilt. To give the admitted criminal a lighter sentence is not only anomalous, it is patently unjust.

The present plea-bargaining system inhibits the rights of those people who have a realistic change of being acquitted at trial. Some innocent defendants are persuaded that it is advantageous to plead guilty, despite their innocence. Therefore, it becomes a moral injustice to give persons who plead guilty a lesser sentence than those who assert their innocence and their right to trial.

THE CONSTITUTIONAL BASIS OF THE RIGHT
TO JURY TRIAL

Prior to the 1960s, virtually none of the rights contained in the first ten amendments of the constitution were applied to Americans in state courts. Although they were always deemed available to defendants accused of federal offenses, these rights were denied to those accused of equally serious state offenses, as well as all defendants in misdemeanor cases.

The major thrust of the Warren Court during the 1960s was to apply the Bill of Rights to the states and, for the first time, to provide for every American all the liberties guaranteed by the Constitution, regardless of the court's jurisdiction. Through a doctrine of selective incorporation, led by Mr. Justice Black, the Bill of Rights received this wider application, while the other justices on the Warren court felt that there was no historical precedent which mandated their application in one fell swoop. Yet the majority did accept the proposition that they would extend the appropriate key amendments to the states, one at a time, on a case-by-case basis whenever they determined that a specific provision was fundamental to the American scheme of justice.

The Sixth Amendment right to jury trial, pivotal in establishing the unconstitutionality of plea bargaining, was guaranteed in every state criminal justice system in the country with the landmark decision in Duncan v. Louisiana. A nineteen-year-old youth was charged with simple battery, an offense punishable by a maximum of two years imprisonment. Under Louisiana law he was not entitled to a jury trial, and was found guilty by the trial judge. In reversing the decision, Justice White held that the Sixth Amendment right to a jury trial was applicable to the states through the Fourteenth Amendment:

Because we believe that trial by jury in criminal cases is fundamental to the American scheme of justice, we hold

that the Fourteenth Amendment guarantees a right of jury
trial in all criminal cases which—where they are to be
tried in federal court—would come within the Sixth Amendment's guarantee. Since we consider the appeal before us
to be such a case, we hold that the constitution was violated when the appellant's demand for jury trial was refused.

It is an axion in American jurisprudence that no person can be
penalized for exercising a constitutional right, yet the primary role
of the plea bargaining system is to assure that the right to a jury trial
is seldom utilized. It follows, therefore, whenever a person is sentenced more severely for the exercise of his constitutional right to
trial, the constitutionality of that sentence becomes questionable.
The syllogism proceeds as follows: (1) plea bargaining rests on the
assumption that a person who foregoes the right to trial will receive
a lesser sentence; (2) it is unconstitutional to demand (the inverse of
1) a more severe sentence for an accused because the constitutional
right to jury trial has been exercised; therefore, (3) plea bargaining
is unconstitutional.

The economic efficiency of plea bargaining is the strongest argument in favor of maintaining the system. In the federal system
alone, it has been estimated that the number of trials would double if
the percentage of guilty pleas decreased by just 10 percent. The
Federal government would need to multiply the number of judges,
prosecutors, juries, and other court personnel many times to adequately handle this increased case load. Some proponents of the current system claim that without plea bargaining, the system would
break down. Yet one can have no sympathy for this view. American
resources are such that they may be allocated whenever the need
arises and it is merely a question of priorities. The criminal justice
system demands such priorities; it is the hallmark of the American
democratic system and we pride ourselves on it as we export our
system to other parts of the world.

Allowing bureaucratic values of efficiency to override
constitutional guarantees is contrary to the essential purpose of the Bill of Rights. These fundamental protections
of the individual are conditions imposed on all state actions; they would be nullified if the state could sacrifice
them simply to facilitate more economical implementation
of its goals (HLP: 1406).

Such arguments based upon cost and efficiency have been raised
before only to yield to constitutional considerations. In <u>Bruton</u> v.
<u>United States</u>, it was held that the co-defendants cannot be tried

together if one has confessed but refuses to take the stand, and thus cannot be cross-examined. In discussing the resulting burden on the courts, the court recognized that "joint trials do conserve state delays in bringing those accused of crime to trial." But, to "secure greater speed, economy, and convenience in the administration of the law at the price of fundamental principles of constitutional liberty," was to pay too high a price. State fiscal integrity cannot be protected at the expense of crucial individual rights in the criminal process.

Although the guilty-plea process is efficient—which explains its present prominence and perhaps guarantees its continued use—it is only relatively so. The guilty-plea process is inefficient in that it generates extensive appellate litigation which results in frequent remands to the trial courts for evidentiary and other kinds of hearings.

Another point that helps to dispel the myth of economic efficiency in the plea-bargaining process is that it often occurs simultaneously with the processing of the case through the formal steps of the proceedings. When a bargain is arrived at, the case is simply pulled out from wherever it happens to be. The resulting need to pull cases out of the process—sometimes on the morning of the trial—makes efficient scheduling of cases difficult or impossible. Thus, plea bargaining makes it difficult to use judicial and prosecutorial time effectively. When a trial is cancelled at the last minute because a defendant has agreed to plead guilty, it is often impossible for the judge and the lawyers to reschedule other trials. The result is wasted time (National Advisory Commission 1973: 43).

The argument that plea bargaining saves the court time and expense does not justify penalizing defendants because they exercise their constitutional rights. There may be policy reasons why a person who pleads guilty ought to receive a benefit from the system. However, the Constitution must take precedence over expediency.

THE DEFENDANT'S BENEFITS

Another reason for the preservation of plea bargaining is the claim that defendants seek plea negotiations because it benefits them and, therefore, it ought to be sanctioned as part of the criminal justice process. Yet, in fact, defendants really do not prosper at all from plea negotiations.

It may be conceded that the first defendant who practiced plea bargaining in a jurisdiction might get a break. Thereafter, however, the sentencing system adjusts and defendants who plea bargain and plead guilty get the sentence they ought to get, but defendants who demand trial and are convicted get longer sentences.

This assertion is based on experience as well as study.[*] In one of the major urban juvenile courts of our land, prior to the Gault decision, requiring counsel in the juvenile court, all cases were tried prior to disposition. The procedure of the juvenile court prior to that decision was that first, there would be a hearing to determine whether or not the child was guilty of the alleged offense. If the defendant was found delinquent, the case was continued for a period of three weeks during which time a social investigation was made of the child's background. Then a dispositional hearing was held to determine the best plan for the child based upon his background, the nature of the crime, and other relevant factors.

Unfortunately, after Gault, when criminal-court practitioners began to come into the juvenile courts, they brought with them not only the concept of due process and fundamental fairness inherent in our adult criminal system, but also the plea bargaining process. As a result, very few trials have been held in the juvenile courts since Gault. Instead of determining, after an evidentiary hearing, what the best plan would be for a child, plea bargaining takes place prior to that hearing. The result is that some children, who should go to reformatories for their own and the state's best interests, are now released because they plead guilty. Under the old system, some children who went to trial would very likely have been released on probation; the advent of plea bargaining has produced a new ethic and a new view towards those children who sought trial.

States' attorneys were as unhappy about having trials in the juvenile court as they were in the criminal court. With the advent of plea bargaining in juvenile cases, those youths who demand trial are less likely to be considered for probation than if they had admitted

---

[*]Most judges do admit that they consider favorably the fact that a defendant pleads guilty when deciding what sentence to impose. Empirical studies also prove that judges sentence defendants who plead guilty more leniently than those who are convicted (by a jury). The Influence of the Defendants Plea on Judicial Determination Sentence, 66 Yale Law Journal 204, 206-209 (1956). Defendants convicted after trial receive a longer sentence than those who plead guilty. One study shows a 10% to 95% variance in punishment pursuant to guilty pleas. Ferguson, The Role of the Judge in Plea Bargaining, 15 Crim. L.Q. 25, 50-1 (1972). Whatever the precise degree of the sentence discount, the consensus is that it is substantial. Official Inducements to Plead Guilty: Suggested Morals for a Marketplace, 32 U. Chicago L. Rev. 167 (1964).

their guilt initially. As a matter of fact, another argument offered for maintaining the plea bargaining system is that defendants who actually admit their guilt to the court are on the road to rehabilitation and thus ought to receive less severe sentences.

Again, two facts must be pointed out. First, the privilege against self-incrimination contained in the Fifth Amendment militates against forcing defendants to admit their guilt. This is a long and hallowed tradition stemming from the Magna Carta in 1215 and it is a basic precept of Anglo-American jurisprudence. This privilege is vital to our criminal process. Therefore, if one penalizes defendants for exercising their constitutional privilege against self-incrimination, one is penalizing them for utilizing a basic constitutional right— and that is unconstitutional. Second, one might argue that a person deserves a lighter sentence for pleading guilty because of a contrite heart. However, in most jurisdictions the time difference between pleading guilty and opting for a trial is often a matter of years.

The threat of sentence differentiation is a common form of judicial coercion which makes plea bargaining the only feasible choice for the defendant. A vivid example of this occurred a few years ago in an urban jurisdiction. A defendant was charged with robbery and after plea negotiation was offered one to ten years in the penitentiary if he would plead guilty. He refused and asserted his innocence. After two days of trial, the defendant told his counsel that he was convinced by the State's case that the jury was going to find him guilty. Therefore, he wanted to plead guilty and take the original sentence offer. The lawyer notified the judge and the prosecutors of his client's intention. But the prosecutor decided that because the defendant had taken up the State's time and the court's time, the recommendation would be that he receive three to ten years in the penitentiary. The judge acquiesced to the statement of the prosecuting attorney. Defense counsel returned to his client and informed him of this development. The defendant expressed indignation and anger that because he had taken two days of the State's time, he would have to spend an additional two years in prison and refused to take the plea, and opted to take his chances with a jury trial. He did that and at the close of the case the jury found him guilty. The court promptly sentenced him to a term of seven to fifteen years in prison.

This substantial difference cannot be attributed merely to the lack of a contrite heart, but is part of a premeditated plan to induce defendants to forego their constitutional rights in the interest of saving court time. Under this scheme, defendants are eligible for lenient sentences only if they cooperate with the system.

Succinctly put, "sentences reflect the amount of trouble caused to all in authority by the obviously guilty defendant" (Newman 1966: 216). A trial is trouble. While few, if any, judges admit that they penalize the defendant for exercising his right to trial by invoking heavier sentences, they concede that the defendant who pleads guilty receives a more lenient sentence. In Dewey v. United States, the court took judicial notice of the fact that trial courts generally impose a lighter sentence on pleas of guilty than in cases where the accused pleaded not guilty but was found guilty by a jury.

THE PUBLIC PERSPECTIVE

The final justification for plea bargaining is that the public is served. Assuming that the defendant is not served and the Constitution is not served, then, at least, the public is served because of the principle of sure justice, that is, instead of letting some guilty defendants escape, via a jury trial, they all plead guilty and the State has sure, swift convictions. In reality, the public benefits least of all from the plea-bargaining process.

First of all, the public does not play an active role when a jury trial is circumvented by the plea-bargaining process. The formal, public condemnation or vindication of an accused which follows a trial benefits society by enhancing the legitimacy of the criminal justice system. Trials increase the participation of the community in the criminal justice system and make the guilt determination process more visible. Trials are also valuable for the public and the accused as lessons in legal procedure, dignity, fairness, and justice. Second, if it is agreed that under this system some innocent people will plead guilty rather than risk the uncertainties of a criminal trial, then it is reasonable to assume that some of the people will find themselves in our prison system undergoing rehabilitation for crimes they never committed.

Several factors contribute to the temptation of plea bargaining; the judge has a busy calendar, the prosecuting attorney has numerous cases before him, and the public defender or defense lawyers are usually overworked and underpaid. However, the public is not served because some defendants use the plea-bargaining system to achieve lighter sentences while at the other end of the spectrum, defendants who ought to be serving less time are penalized for exercising their constitutional rights. Plea bargaining results in inconsistencies that reduce the deterrent impact of the law.

Moreover, probation officers' reports and presentence investigations are given short shrift in the plea-bargaining process. The real factors that count in determining how heavy a sentence an individual will get after a plea bargain include the strength of the state's case and the weaknesses of the defendant's case.

The plea-bargaining process places a premium on experience as a defendant, so that it can benefit older, more experienced defendants. Often, young defendants, or those with little past experience with the law, have neither the knowledge nor the means to manipulate the system as effectively as career criminals.

No one profits from a system in which a hard-core criminal gets a lighter sentence because of a plea bargain. Everyone should get the sentence he or she deserves based on pre-established sentencing guidelines, prior background and needs, and not based upon whether he or she plea bargains.

THE DEFENDANT'S PERSPECTIVE

There is one other aspect that is often forgotten: the impression that the plea-bargaining process makes upon the nearly eight million defendants who are arrested annually. They are told by an assistant public defender or private defense lawyer that they ought to plead guilty because if they don't the judge will give them more time. How many of them are institutionally coerced into pleading guilty to save themselves from a more severe sentence? How many of them receive an impression of the government, represented through its criminal justice system, which says that the presumption of innocence is a mockery, a sham, and a farce? And how many return from court convinced that there is simply no room in the American criminal justice system to allow them their day in court?

The plea-bargaining process has created a criminal justice system in which one is presumed guilty if arrested and will surely be convicted if indicted. If people cannot redress their grievances under the law, they will take their arguments to the streets. If we expect justice in the courts instead of violence in the streets, our courts must reflect our constitutional heritage and not engage in "bargain basement" techniques and "cut rate" sentences only for those who play the game.

The New York State Special Commission on Attica concluded:

What makes inmates must cynical about their preprison experience is the plea-bargaining system. . . .

Even though an inmate may receive the benefit of a shorter sentence, the plea-bargaining system is characterized by deception and hypocrisy which divorce the inmate from the reality of his crime. . . . The Hughes Committee (the Joint Legislative Committee on Crime) made a study of prisoner attitudes towards plea bargaining . . . and found that almost

90 percent of the inmates surveyed had been solicited to
enter a plea bargain. Most were bitter, believing that
they did not receive effective legal representation or that
the judge did not keep the state's promise of a sentence
which had induced them to enter guilty pleas.

As the Hughes Committee observed, the large segment
of the prison population who believe they have been 'victimized' by the courts or bar 'are not likely to accept the
efforts of another institution of society, the correctional
system, in redirecting their attitudes.' The Hughes Committee warned that no program of rehabilitation can be
effective on a 'prisoner who is convinced in his own mind
that he is in prison because he is the victim of a mindless,
undirected, and corrupt system of justice' (1972: 30-31).

It would be far better, as Justice Black stated, to put the state
to its test and let those cases that are winnowed out by the jury process go free and those defendants that are convicted receive their just
desserts. Otherwise, plea bargaining corrupts the entire system of
corrections and criminal justice in this country.

THE CONSTITUTIONAL BASIS OF PLEA BARGAINING

Plea bargaining is now officially permissible, in Federal courts
at least, if it is conducted in accordance with the guidelines laid down
in Rule 11 of the Federal Rules of Criminal Procedure. Nevertheless,
the constitutional status of plea bargaining remains uncertain. The
Supreme Court has contented itself with broad statements which en-
dorse the general practices of plea bargaining. As yet, it has not
dissected the bargaining process into its discrete components and
evaluated their respective legitimacy under prevailing interpretations
of the due process and equal-protection guarantees.
The Supreme Court allowed a guilty plea even though the defendant told the judge in open court that he was innocent of the charge,
but was pleading guilty to avoid the death penalty in North Carolina
v. Alford, saying:

While most pleas of guilty consist of both a waiver of trial and an express admission of guilt, the latter element
is not a constitutional requisite to the imposition of a
prison sentence even if [the defendant] is unwilling or unable to admit his participation in the acts constituting the
crime. . . .

and held that where "a defendant intelligently concludes that his interests require entry of a guilty plea and the record before the judge contains strong evidence of actual guilt" a plea may be accepted even if accompanied by protestations of innocence.

This is the same court which has stated that "the disposition of charges after plea discussion is not only an essential part of the process but a highly desirable part for many reasons." The case was Santobello v. New York:

> It is now virtually certain that a prosecutor's subsequent failure to keep a promise made during the plea bargaining process is grounds for plea withdrawal. In Santobello a second prosecutor's inadvertent failure to keep a promise given by the original prosecutor that no sentence recommendation would be made was grounds for plea withdrawal, even though the trial judge claimed that the recommendation had no effect on the sentence rendered.

SUMMARY AND RECOMMENDATIONS

The trial is the cornerstone of the American jurisprudence system, and American jurisprudence is the cornerstone of American society. From all aspects, plea bargaining is a blot upon the criminal justice system. It is unacceptable from the defendant's point of view. It is unacceptable from the public's point of view. It is even unacceptable from the system's point of view, because what we do to defendants in the police station and the courtroom has an impact of what they do while on probation and parole and in the prisons.

> The practice of plea bargaining forfeits the benefits of formal, public ajudication; it eliminates the protections for individuals provided by the adversary system and substitutes administrative for judicial determinations of guilt; it removes the check on law enforcement authorities afforded by exclusionary rules; and it distorts sentencing decisions by introducing noncorrectional criteria. This nullification of constitutional values should not continue without careful examination (Comment 1970: 1398).

The National Advisory Committee on Criminal Justice Standards and Goals has recommended that plea bargaining be abolished "no later than 1978."

The fundamental questions are, How to accomplish that goal? Can we prevent defendants from pleading guilty if they so choose? Can we prevent prosectors from telling defendants what lenient sentences

they will receive if they will only plead guilty? Can we discourage
defendants from seeking reductions of charges to avoid mandatory
minimums?

The answer to all of these is obviously no. How, then, is plea
bargaining to be abolished? There is no simple answer. However,
it would be remiss to fail to present at least one possible recommendation for the abolition of plea bargaining:

> The elimination of plea bargaining will obviously place
> the existing criminal justice system under severe stress,
> and no court is fully capable of restructuring the system
> in response to the change. But legislatures also have an
> obligation to seek out other means of mitigating the con-
> flict between administrative efficiency and fundamental
> rights, means which will withstand constitutional scrutiny.
> Thus, society might allocate more resources to the crim-
> inal process. It might choose to penalize many fewer
> forms of individual behavior. By appropriate reductions
> of penalties, the right to jury trial might be bypassed for
> many offenders. Indeed, a system that depended less on
> incarceration and more on parole and similar programs
> might prove effective as well as less expensive (Comment
> 1970: 1411).

One solution to the problem permits pleas of guilty. Many
people would prefer to plead guilty to avoid the rigors of trial, or to
avoid embarrassment of friends and family. Still another group,
who had relied on their cleverness in not being caught, would plead
guilty upon apprehension. And there are those who simply want to
admit guilt and throw themselves on the mercy of the court without
attempting to gain any advantage by manipulating the system. These
guilty pleas would be unaffected by the proposed solution. It is directed at eliminating a specific form of abuse—the guilty plea induced
and spawned by fear of a heavier sentence, or even fear of death.

The solution is not complex and was examined in U.S. v.
Stockwell, in which the trial judge informed the defendant that if he
pleaded guilty, he would receive a three-year sentence. However,
if he chose to stand trial and was subsequently convicted, he would
receive from five to seven years. The defendant was, in fact, convicted after a trial and the judge rendered a sentence consistent with
his warning and well within the statutory range allowed by law. Nevertheless, the Circuit Court reversed the sentence explaining that

> Courts must not use the sentencing power as a carrot and
> stick to clear congested calendars and they must not create
> the appearance of such a practice.

Accordingly, once it appears in the record that the court has taken a hand in plea bargaining, that a tentative sentence has been discussed, and that a harsher sentence has followed a breakdown of negotiations, the record must show that no improper weight was given to the failure to plead guilty. In such a case, the record must affirmatively show that the court rendered sentence solely upon the facts of the defendant's case and personal history, and not as punishment for refusal to plead guilty.

In People v. Darrah, Justice Schaefer of the Illinois Supreme Court took this same idea further stating that we should consider adopting a rule prohibiting any differentiation between a sentence imposed after a plea of guilty and one imposed after a trial. This would allow defendants to explore what they might receive from the court upon conviction, and prosecutors to inform defendants that they might expect probation. But it would operate so that what a defendant was informed he would receive prior to trial, he would receive after trial, barring some new fact brought forth at the trial. It is not known whether enforcement of this rule by itself would abolish plea bargaining, but it would certainly go a long way toward correcting what is today the major abuse in our criminal justice system.

REFERENCES

American Bar Association. 1968. Project on minimum standards for criminal justice, standards relating to pleas of guilty, approved draft.

Bond, J. E. 1975. Plea Bargaining and Guilty Pleas. New York: Clark Boardman, Co.

Bruton v. United States. 1968. 391 U.S. 123.

Comment. 1956. The influence of the defendant's plea on judicial determination of sentence. 66 Yale Law Journal 204.

Comment. 1964. Official inducements to plead guilty: suggested morals for a marketplace. 32 University of Chicago Law Review 167.

Comment. 1970. The unconstitutionality of plea bargaining. 83 Harvard Law Review 1387.

Dewey v. United States. 1959. 288 F. 2d 124, 128 (8th Cir.)

Duncan v. Louisiana. 1968. 391 U.S. 45.

Ferguson, L. A. 1972. The role of the judge in plea bargaining. Ferguson 15 Criminal Law Quarterly 25.

Gault. 1967. 384 U.S. 997, 86 D. Ct., 1922, 16 L. Ed. 2d 1013.

Griffiths, J. 1970. Ideology in the criminal process or a third model of the criminal process. 79 Yale Law Journal 358.

National Advisory Commission on Criminal Justice Standards and Goals. 1973. Report on Courts. Washington, D.C.: Government Printing Office.

New York State Special Commission on Attica. 1972. Attica, New York: Bantam.

Newman, D. J. 1966. Conviction: The Determination of Guilt or Innocence Without Trial. Boston: Little, Brown.

North Carolina v. Alford. 1970. 400 U.S. 25, 91 S. Ct., 160 27 L. Ed. 2d 162.

People v. Darrah. 1965. 210 N.E. 2d 478 (Ill.)

President's Commission on Law Enforcement and Administration of Justice. 1967. Task Force Report: The Courts 9. Washington, D.C.: Government Printing Office.

Santobello v. New York. 1971. 404 U.S. 257, 925 S. Ct., 495, 30 L. Ed. 427.

United States v. Stockwell. 1973. 472 F. 2d 1186 (9th Cir.).

5

TOWARD A CONTROL THEORY OF UPPERWORLD CRIME AND INDISCRETION: EXPLAINING WATERGATE

John Hagan

"Crime, Freud told us, is the price we pay for freedom" (1958). What Freud didn't tell us is that the freedom to commit crimes varies by vocation and social class. We optimistically call this freedom "discretion," hoping, presumably, for a self-fulfilling prophecy in which the use of this freedom will be as our euphemism suggests: discreet. Call it what we will, however, the upperworld vocations within government and business carry with them an enlargement of freedoms involving public and financial trust. Violations of these trusts can be considered crimes against the public interest. They are, in short, criminal indiscretions. Our interest is in explaining upperworld crime, using the American experience with Watergate as a catalyst for theoretical thought.

THEORIES OF UPPERWORLD CRIME

The term "upperworld crime" was first used nearly forty years ago in an early textbook discussion by Albert Morris (1935). Parallel concepts emerged from Edwin Sutherland's (1949) study of white collar crime, Richard Quinney's (1963) research on "occupational crime" among retail pharmacists, and Donald Cressey's discussions on embezzlement (1953) and related "respectable crimes" (1965). Yet, little consistent attention has been given to the development of a theory of upperworld crime. Further, it will be argued that the few theoretical efforts available are inadequate.

For the purposes of discussion, we will designate the existing sociological explanation of upperworld crime as "strain theories." Basically, these theoretical accounts assert that the differential response to some kind of strain or tension mediates upperworld crime.

An early form of this argument was proposed by Vilhelm Aubert. The source of strain in this account is the conflict between societal values and operating norms. Aubert argues that "The laws against white-collar crime are usually not in obvious and apparent harmony with the mores," and that, therefore, ". . . ambivalence may arise in the attitude towards white-collar crimes. . . ." (1952: 178). It is this ambivalence that is the presumed motivant of upperworld crime.

A similar hypothesis underwrites a study of the wholesale meat industry by Frank Hartung (1950). The proposition here is that society contains, in addition to those values shared in common, specific value systems organized around the work-conditions of specialized occupational groups. Hartung argues, with the meat industry as an example, that this value conflict is commonly resolved in favor of the immediate requirements of work.

A difficulty with both of these discussions is the disparity assumed between the general public's evaluations of upperworld crimes and those of occupationally involved individuals. Independent studies by Donald Newman (1952), Ruth Cavan (1964), and Peter Rossi et al. (1974), spanning three decades of public opinion, reveal a uniform evaluation of upperworld crimes as less serious than other criminal offenses. Thus, the public condemnation of upperworld illegalities assumed in Aubert's and Hartung's explanations is not present. The importance of this finding will become increasingly apparent as our discussion continues.

A final version of the strain argument is found in Donald Cressey's (1953: 1965) theory of embezzlement. The essence of Cressey's theory lies in the actor's verbalized neutralization (or, rationalization) of the offensive act. Thus, Cressey argues that

> . . . verbalization is the crux of the problem. I am convinced that the words that the potential embezzler uses in his conversation with himself are actually the most important elements in the process which gets him into trouble, or keeps him out of trouble. If he sees a possibility for embezzlement, it is because he has defined the relationship between . . . [an] unshareable problem and an illegal solution in language that lets him look on trust violation as something other than trust violation. If he cannot do this, he does not become an embezzler (1965: 14).

In this same article, Cressey suggests that his theory of embezzlement has the potential for wider application, fitting other respectable crimes as well.

However, a major difficulty with this theory is that it assumes feelings of guilt-induced strain that may not be commonly experienced. In short, the strain that would require neutralization through verbalization may not be forthcoming. For example, the evidence mentioned earlier indicates that the general public does not condemn upperworld offenses and suggests a common absence of values in need of neutralization. It can further be hypothesized that those who contemplate upperworld crimes would be least likely to feel the constraint of values that might proscribe these acts. In short, the assumed source of the need to verbalize, rationalize, or neturalize is not apparent. This does not deny the possible maintaining and facilitating functions of these verbalizations; rather, it is their causal priority and prominence that is questioned.

To this point, our discussion has dealt in abstract theoretical terms. Our attention turns next to an example—the American experience with Watergate. This episode will be explored in terms of the theories discussed, and in view of a theory to be proposed.

WATERGATE

The American experience called "Watergate" is a chronology of events that spans from June 17, 1972, to August 8, 1974. The outline of these events will be familiar to most readers, beginning with the unsuccessful break-in of the Democratic National Committee Headquarters in Washington's Watergate complex, and ending with Richard Nixon's resignation as President of the United States. Perhaps most important to this sequence was Mr. Nixon's admission, three days before his resignation, that six days after the initial break-in, he had discussed with his top aides the political implications and necessities of a "cover-up." This admission solidified final support for the House Judiciary Committee recommendation that Mr. Nixon be impeached for obstruction of justice.

The most comprehensive view of executive activity during the course of these events is provided in the Presidential Transcripts, the abridged, 1200-page record of selected White House conversations. These transcripts provide an invaluable resource for recounting the motives expressed in the course of òne set of upperworld crimes. Of course, a problem in utilizing these materials is that they are assumed to be incomplete. However, since the motives implied in the strain theories of upperworld crime involve sympathetic representations of purpose, we will assume that material relevant to these theories are unlikely to be deleted from the transcripts. We will argue also that in spite of the self-serving potential of the transcripts, they actually provide support for an explanation of Watergate that is considerably less flattering than the strain approach.

A careful reading of the transcripts (1974) reveals few references to, or considerations of, societal values. Occasional mention is made of the Nixon administration's "commitment" to "law and order," however, the references are in passing (: 362, for example), and never a matter of extended consideration. Instead, the discussions recorded are predominantly tactical in content, dealing with the perceived costs, risks, and benefits of day-to-day strategy. During these discussions, rationalized motives are expressed. However, it is the manner in which these rationalizations are considered that is essential in explaining Watergate.

At least five rationalizations for the cover-up are proposed during the course of Mr. Nixon's conversations. They include (1) protection of national security: ". . . the whole thing was national security" (: 125); (2) protection of the presidency: ". . . it isn't the man, it's the office" (: 267); (3) support of the defendants: ". . . this was not an obstruction of justice, we were simply trying to help these defendants" (: 339); (4) loyalty: "Well, the point is, whatever we say about Harry Truman, etc., while it hurt him a lot of people admired the old bastard for standing by people" (: 359); and (5) the country's future: "If there's one thing you have got to do, you have got to maintain the Presidency out of this. I have got things to do for this country. . . ." (: 673).

The most important of these rationalizations, judging from the attention it received from the participants, was the assertion that administration agents were simply trying to help defendants by offering them cash payments. Although the president protested that he opposed these payments and was unaware of their delivery, the support rationalization became important as a broader defense for his subordinates. The president phrased the problem clearly: "Dean's the case in question. And I do not consider him guilty. Now that's all there is to that. Because if he—if that's the case, then half the staff is guilty" (: 339).

Discussions relating to the support rationalization reveal that its importance was clearly as a justification, rather than as a cause for the payments being made. For example, in the March 21, 1973 conversation in which the decision was made to pay Howard Hunt "hush money," the discussion is entirely tactical. Neither considerations of societal values nor rationalized motives impede a conversation directed explicitly at "keeping the cap on" the unfolding story of Watergate. In a well-known passage from the transcripts, the pragmatic decision is made.

PRESIDENT: That's why for your immediate things you have no choice but to come up with the 120,000, or whatever it is. Right?
DEAN: That's right.
PRESIDENT: Would you agree that that's the prime thing, that you damn well better get that done?

DEAN: Obviously he ought to be given some signal any-
way.
PRESIDENT: (Expletive deleted), get it (: 133).

Nowhere in this discussion is support of Hunt's family or legal
expenses considered. Several weeks later, on April 14, the support
rationalization appears for the first time, with little effort to deny
its justificatory character:

PRESIDENT: Support. Well, I heard something about
that at a much later time.
HALDEMAN: Yeah.
PRESIDENT: And, frankly, not knowing much about ob-
struction of justice, I thought it was perfectly proper.
EHRLICHMAN: Well, it's like—
PRESIDENT: Would it be perfectly proper?
EHRLICHMAN: The defense of the—
PRESIDENT: Berrigans?
EHRLICHMAN: The Chicago Seven.
PRESIDENT: The Chicago Seven?
HALDEMAN: They have a defense fund for everybody.
PRESIDENT: . . . So it's common practice (: 242).

Later in the same conversation, the ad hoc character of the
rationalization becomes even more obvious.

HALDEMAN: What Dean did, he did with all conscience
in terms . . . (of) the higher good.
PRESIDENT: Dean, you've got to have a talk with Dean.
I feel that I should not talk to him.
EHRLICHMAN: I have talked to him.
PRESIDENT: I mean about motive.
EHRLICHMAN: I have talked to him.
PRESIDENT: What's he say about motive. He says it
was hush-up?
EHRLICHMAN: . . . He says he knew, he had to know that
people were trying to bring that result about (: 272).

In the end, even the President, in a discussion with Assistant
Attorney General Henry Peterson, is forced to acknowledge the false
character of the expressed motivation:

PETERSON: The strange thing about this one, Mr. President, is that they could have done it openly.
PRESIDENT: Why, of course!

PETERSON: If they had just come out in the Washington
Post (they) could say, "Well these people were—"
PRESIDENT: They helped the Scotsboro people, they
helped the Berrigans, you remember the Alger Hiss defense fund?
PETERSON: And we're going to help these—They were
going this—Once you do it in a clandestine fashion, it
takes on elements—
PRESIDENT: Elements of a cover-up (: 679).

Similar discussions surround the remaining rationalizations.
In each case, the verbalization is introduced in a justificatory context.
The concerns are tactical: the avoidance of legal prosecution, political embarrassment, and moral blame. These concerns relate to consequences, not causes, of upperworld crime.

TOWARD A CONTROL THEORY OF UPPERWORLD CRIME

A "Watergate" is dramatic, but not definitive, evidence for or
against any particular theory. Nonetheless, such a case study can
serve a catalytic function, in that it sensitizes us to the deficiencies
of theories and suggests new directions for consideration. Having
demonstrated some of the deficiencies of the strain theories of upperworld crime, our attention is thus focused on alternative formulations.
Our argument is that a control theory of upperworld crime is
the most appropriate of these formulations.[1] With Hobbes, the control theorist asks a basic question: "Why do men obey the rules of
society?" The nature of this question reveals the bias of control theory: deviance is taken for granted, leaving conformity as the phenomenon to be explained. The problem at hand, then, is to explain
why all upperworld citizens are not criminals, or, stated more accurately, why some of us are less criminal than others.
Answers to the control theorist's questions come from within
and without. The first response focuses on the "inner person." With
Durkheim, it is assumed that social conformity is based on moral
constraint. Thus, for some individuals, considerations of morality
are important, while for others they are not. Unfortunately, this
first line of defense becomes problematic in a society whose conception of upperworld morality is ill-defined. Research indicating the
uncertainty of these conceptions was reviewed earlier in our discussion.
By default, then, the second level of the control theorist's considerations, external or situational controls, increases in importance.
Holding moral ties constant, it is the perception of risks, costs, and
benefits that is assumed to guide upperworld behavior. It is argued

that, in lieu of a public morality that harshly condemns upperworld crime, the occurrence of such behaviors will depend largely on the perceived risks and rewards associated with violating public and financial trusts. Further, as the perception of risk decreases, and agreement with this perception proliferates, social pressure may be added to individual profit as an inducement to involvement in upperworld crime. These propositions, if accurate, suggest that upperworld crime may be both commonplace and contagious.

It can be argued that the case of Watergate is a supportive illustration of control theory. The actors involved proved unconstrained by either moral ties or by a set of operating principles that were themselves unclear. In short, the problem was one of discretion without direction. Repeatedly, the rights and obligations of the executive branch (for example, the limits of "executive privilege," the meaning of "national security," and the scope of "high crimes and misdemeanors") were debated in terms of a vague Constitution and undecided public opinion. Similarly, the situational controls operative at the time of the initial Watergate offenses were inadequate. White House aides were able to manipulate funds and personnel for criminal and political purposes, with little expectation of detection. The product, in sum, was undirected indiscretion. Furthermore, once they were caught, punishment became problematic in an atmosphere confused by discussions of pardons. The uncertainties surrounding these events emphasize, then, the porous nature of the controls operative in one upperworld setting.

If there is a message in the experience of Watergate for the policy-minded and for a control theory of upperworld crime, it is that checks and balances of power are crucial. Upperworld vocations, particularly politics and business, often carry with them a freedom to deviate which is unparalleled in the underworld. Our mistake has been believing that upperworld discretion could provide an antidote to upperworld deviance. Neither time, experience, nor control theory recommends such a belief. As Freud would remind us, unchecked freedom is a criminogenic condition.

NOTE

1. For a discussion of the control theories of deviance, see Hirschi (1969: Chapter 2), Nettler (1974: Chapter 9), and Hagan (1977: Chapter 3).

REFERENCES

Aubert, V. 1952. White-collar crime and social structure. American Journal of Sociology 58 (November): 263-71.

Cavan, R. S. 1964. Underworld, conventional, and ideological crime. Journal of Criminal Law, Criminology, and Police Science 55 (June): 35-240.

Cressey, D. R. 1953. Other People's Money. Glencoe, Illinois: Free Press.

———. 1965. The respectable criminal: why some of our best friends are crooks. Transaction 2 (March-April): 12-15.

Freud, S. 1958. Civilization and its Discontents. Garden City, New York: Doubleday & Company.

Hagan, J. 1977. The Disreputable Pleasures. Toronto: McGraw-Hill Ryerson Ltd.

Hartung, F. E. 1950. White-collar offenses in the wholesale meat industry in Detroit. American Journal of Sociology 56 (July): 25-34.

Hirschi, T. 1969. Causes of Delinquency. Berkeley: University of California Press.

Morris, A. 1935. Criminology. New York: Longmans, Green, and Company.

Nettler, G. 1974. Explaining Crime. New York: McGraw-Hill Book Co.

Newman, D. J. 1952. Public attitudes toward a form of white-collar crime. Social Problems 4 (January): 228-32.

Quinney, R. 1963. Occupational structure and criminal behavior: prescription violations by retail pharmacists. Social Problems 11 (Fall): 179-85.

Rossi, P., E. Waite, C. Bose, and R. Burk. 1974. The seriousness of crimes: normative structure and individual differences. American Sociological Review 39(2): 224-37.

Sutherland, Edwin. 1949. White Collar Crime. New York: Holt, Rinehart and Winston.

Transcripts. 1974. The Presidential Transcripts. New York: Dell.

6

THE PREVAILING MORAL ORDER: INCENTIVES FOR A NEW PERSPECTIVE ON CRIME

Nancy J. Beran

In the sociological community at large, the 1960s produced an assault on value-free and apolitical claims. The structure-functionalist orientation, so firmly entrenched in the discipline, was increasingly criticized for its tacit commitment to established social orders. The role of values in the sociological enterprise was widely appraised and reappraised at a variety of levels. In theoretical and research pursuits, in the classroom and in the field, sociologists were enjoined by others, and each other, to critically examine what it was they took for granted. While some seemed to simply stand back shocked or embarrassed, the challenge to practice what we preach to Introductory Sociology students was undertaken with glee by some and with resentment by others. As discussion and debate intensified, conflict theory finally began to come of age in American sociology. The alienation theme culminated in entreaties, if not demands, to focus attention on structural variables, especially power (Coser 1956, Gouldner 1970, Reynolds and Reynolds 1970). The sociologists advocating critical structural analyses of social systems were often labeled radicals, an ironic underscoring of the status-quo commitment of mainstream sociology. In a recent discussion of the fact that sociology rarely addresses "big issues," Horowitz observed:

> One might argue that the very comfort of sociologists, their bureaucratic structures and their organizational definitions, conspire to disguise and to dampen their inclination to pursue fundamental inquiry. Serious inquiry involves high risks and high risks are exactly what people of comfort and sociologists living in comfort would prefer to avoid (Horowitz 1975: 73).

These developments in the sociological community have been reflected in the area of deviance studies. Indeed, some of the most widely discussed arguments have come from students of deviance, for example, Becker and their critics, such as Gouldner. In a 1968 article that has had significant impact upon the field Gouldner recalled his attack in 1961 on value-free doctrines in social science and then proceeded to express and elaborate his subsequent ". . . fear that the myth of a value-free social science is about to be supplanted by still another myth, and that the once glib acceptance of the value-free doctrine is about to be superceded by a new but no less glib rejection of it" (Gouldner 1968: 103). Gouldner further reports that his concerns regarding this issue culminated upon reading Becker's paper (1967) entitled "Whose Side Are We On?". In the latter, Becker articulates the position that sociologists must in fact take sides, but that the demands of the science can be satisfied by making clear which vantage point has, in fact, been chosen.

Gouldner's reaction to this argument is detailed and complex but clearly indicative of the position that the resolution of the value issue is not simple:

> Of course, it is a good thing for sociologists to know what they are doing; and it is a good thing for them to know and to say whose wide they are on. But a bland confession of partisanship merely betrays smugness and naivete. It is smug because it assumes that the values that we have are good enough; it is naive because it assumes that we know the values we have (Gouldner 1968: 112).

Gouldner argues further that Becker and other students of deviance (many from the labeling perspective) do indeed take a side—the side of the underdog, against the middledog, with funding from the overdog. In a "sociology of and for the new welfare state," the underdog is seen as a victim of mid-level zookeepers or caretakers of deviance:

> If this is a liberal conception of deviance that wins sympathy and tolerance for the deviant, it has the paradoxical consequence of inviting us to view the deviant as a passive nonentity who is responsible neither for his suffering nor its alleviation—who is more 'sinned against than sinning' (1968: 106).

The liberal focus, Gouldner continues, is on "man-on-his-back" as opposed to "man-fighting-back"; a concern with political deviance is excluded, as is a critique of the social institutions that engender deviance. The latter is more characteristic of radical sociologists who also take the viewpoint of the underdog, Gouldner says, but apply it to the study of overdogs.

The criticism that students of deviance do not try to relate phenomena to "larger social, historical, political, and economic contexts" has also been advanced by Liazos (1972: 104):

> Reading these authors, one would not know that the most destructive use of violence in the last decade has been the war in Vietnam. . . . Moreover, the robbery of the corporate world—through tax breaks, fixed prices, low wages, pollution of the environment, shoddy goods, etc.— is passed over in our fascination with 'dramatic and predatory' actions (: 107).

In a similar vein, Thio has argued that students of deviance avoid analysis of the established power structure and neglect the deviance of the powerful:

> The sociologists of deviance may be said to tacitly support the power elite because both their research and analysis imply that the powerful are not only morally superior but should not be held responsible for causing deviance within their society (1973: 1).

While the labeling school has been most frequently singled out for this sort of criticism, it should be noted that this orientation has addressed the question of social power to a much greater extent than most other perspectives on deviance. Sagarin has identified five central themes to the labeling perspective, and one of these he states as follows:

> It is not especially useful to look at the nature of the act or the characteristics of the individual in order to understand the phenomenon of deviance; rather, one must examine the nature of the condemning society and the process by which some people gain the power and ascendancy to successfully place the label of deviant on others (Sagarin 1975: 128).

However much labeling students focus on middledog power, as opposed to overdog power, they surely accord the variable a greater role than do psychoanalytic, psychological, biological, and most sociocultural theories of deviance. Indeed, the widespread popularity that the labeling orientation gained during the 1960s testifies to some perceived need to broaden perspectives beyond the prior, almost exclusive, focus on the deviant individual. In the final analysis, the situation is best summarized by Taylor et al.:

Whilst the social-reaction perspective deals with the
power of public pressure and differential rule-enforce-
ment in the creation of deviancy, it does not deal with
the larger processes which form the governing framework
for the smaller processes and transactions.
When we single out these theorists as being guilty
of this omission, it is not because it is (sic) any more
guilty than any other variety of sociological theorizing in
criminology but because it held out the promise of a fully
sociological account, and failed to deliver (1973: 169-70).

Moreover, issues in the specific area of deviance have recently emerged in the even more delimited field of criminology, in addition to the larger sociological community. Essentially, the "old"
criminology has come under assault by the "new," "radical" criminologists who advocate the adoption of a conflict-theoretical and action orientation. As Reasons suggests:

Events of the last decade have increasingly thrust on the
criminologist questions for which his professional training has largely failed to prepare him. War crime, political crime, corporate crime, government crime, environmental crime, and white-collar crime have raised
issues concerning the adequacy of criminological theories
and the focus of criminological research (1975: 336).[1]

Noting that "the prevailing ideology which dominates research
and theory in criminology is liberalism," Platt indicts this orientation
for a variety of faults, including its assumption of a state definition
of crime (1974: 1). Liberal reformism, which is based on "the belief
that it is possible to create a well-regulated, stable and humanitari-
an system of criminal justice under the present economic and political
arrangements" is criticized for supporting "the extension of welfare
state capitalism and gradualist programs of amelioration, while rejecting radical and violent forms of social and political change"
(1974: 3). Platt further elaborates dissatisfaction with liberalism in
criminology for its "emphasis on behaviorism, pragmatism, and social engineering," "underlying cynicism and a lack of passion," "lack
of a historical and dialectical perspective," "nihilism," "wishy-washy
relativism," and "elitism and paternalism" (ibid.). In a similar vein,
Krisberg notes that the "old" criminology has been charged with
prostituting itself to law enforcement and criminal justice agencies:

Criminological theory has fostered and disseminated the
hegemonic concepts of the ruling class, and empirical

criminological studies have often supplied the technology
of social control that has been employed in both domestic
and foreign spheres (1975: 16).

Reasons suggests that, while criminologists have traditionally
been submerged in a consensus perspective of society, recent developments are impacting upon this position and "some criminologists have
begun to investigate critically the origin, enforcement, and administration of laws within the context of interests, power, and conflict" (1975:
343). There are a variety of indicators that some criminologists are
indeed broadening their perspectives in analyzing crime and the criminal justice system. One is the considerable amount of attention that
has been accorded victimless or willing-victim crime since the mid-
1960s especially with regard to decriminalization (see Schur 1965).
Another is renewed interest in white-collar crime. Recent years
have also witnessed the emergence of work in the area of political
crime—both crimes against the state and crimes of the state and its
leaders. Most suggestive, however, is the development of "radical
criminology" (Platt 1974: 1-10), "new criminology" (Taylor et al.
1973), and various other conflict perspectives toward crime (Turk
1969, Quinney 1970). In discussing the emergence of the new criminology, Taylor et al. suggest:

It is not just that the traditional focus of applied criminology on the socially deprived working-class adolescent
is being thrown into doubt by the criminalization of vast
numbers of middle-class youth (for 'offences' of a hedonistic or specifically oppositional nature).[2] Neither is it
only that the crisis of our institutions has deepened to the
point where the 'master institutions' of the state, and of
the political economy, are unable to disguise their own
inability to adhere to their own rules and regulations.[3]
It is largely that the total interconnectedness of these
problems and others is being revealed (1973: 278).

The thrust of these new orientations is reflected in the comments of Krisberg who states that "the promise of the New Criminology
is to link the study of crime with the larger pursuit of social justice
and thus to aid in struggles to achieve human liberation from various
forms of social oppression" (1975: 2):

The New Criminology directs us to ask basic questions
about the quality of justice in our society; it asks us to
evaluate the democracy of our political institutions, the
fairness of our economic institutions, and the humanity

of our social relationships. The nature of crime in our
society and the quality of justice rendered by our legal
institutions reveal fundamental facts about the overall
fairness of our social structure. Investigating the relationship between crime and the maintenance of social
privilege is thus central to the New Criminology (: 4-5).

Reasons notes that, by focusing on the political nature of criminal definitions and their application and enforcement, the power-
conflict perspective asserts that crime is a product of current power
differentials and conflicting world views:

Crime is a definition of behavior made by officials of the
state and not inherent in an act. Those behaviors which
are offensive to the powers that be will be made crimes.
Rather than focusing on the common crimes of the common criminals, emphasis is placed on the lawless behavi-
or of the state and those in positions of power (1975:
348-49).

An example of the structural orientation in these new approaches
in criminology is Gordon's analysis of capitalism, class, and crime
in America (1973: 163-86). Gordon's argument runs as follows:
Most crimes in this country represent rational responses to the com-
petitiveness and inequality of life in capitalist societies. Many apparent differences in crimes—in degree of violence, for example—
can be explained by the structure of class institutions in this country
and the duality of the public system of the enforcement and administration of justice. That duality, in turn, can be explained by a dynamic
view of the class-biased role of public institutions and the vested interests which evolve out of the state's activities. For many reasons,
finally, it is unlikely that we can change the patterns of crime and
punishment, for the kinds of changes needed would substantially
threaten the stability of the capitalist system (Gordon 1973: 184).

Taylor et al. maintain that the whole thrust of the conflict theorists of deviance "is that society is riven with antagonisms of a kind
that even middle-range anomie theory is inadequate to depict" (1973:
255). These analysts (themselves new criminologists) suggest that
the conflict perspective will make substantial contributions to the field
of criminology, especially in conjunction with labeling theory (: 266-67).
Reasons maintains that the "kinds-of-people" paradigm, the "kinds-
of-environments" paradigm, and the "power-conflict" paradigm are
vying to be "the paradigm," and that "the future portends not a lessen-
ing, but an intensification, of this competition and the future politi-
cizing of crime and the criminologist" (1975: 349).

The developments that have been discussed above in the sociological community at large, the area of deviance studies more specifically, and the field of criminology even more specifically, are clearly
related to the sociopolitical climate of the times. Taylor et al. note
that challenges against structure-functionalism "have been most effective during periods of political uncertainty, or, in other words,
during periods when men are less than secure about the stability,
permanence, or legitimacy of existing social arrangements" (1973:
237). In discussing the development of radical criminology, Platt
suggests that

> The roots of this radicalism are to be found in political
> struggles—the civil rights movement, the antiwar move-
> ment, the student movement, Third World liberation
> struggles inside as well as outside the United States, and
> anti-imperialist movements—and in the writings of par-
> ticipants in these struggles—George Jackson (1970, 1972),
> Angela Davis (1971), Eldridge Cleaver (1968), Tom Hay-
> den (1970), Sam Melville (1971), Bobby Seale (1969),
> Huey Newton (1973), Malcolm X (1964), and Ruchell
> Magee, to name a few (1974: 2).

Dissatisfaction among students of criminology has also sprung
from increasing problems in the daily operation of the criminal justice "nonsystem." That is, the efficacy, as well as the legitimacy,
of criminal justice policies and practices has become highly questionable, from arrest through final disposition. A dramatic, recent
study of the effectiveness of correctional treatment essentially concluded that "nothing works"—at least nothing which has been attempted
to date (Lipton et al. 1975).

In this context, and given the assault on both the feasibility
and desirability of value-free approaches, it should perhaps not be
surprising that some of the academic treatises dealing with these issues are proposing potential solutions and definitive action, including
macroscopic social reconstruction. Horowitz has recently stated that

> the practice of sociology is the extension of human life
> through the use of reasoning and planning. . . . All soci-
> eties are subject to revolution, to reconstruction, to
> grandeur, and to decay. In this sense, sociological ana-
> lysis can never simply be a matter of information about
> social stratification and differentiations. It must also be
> a question of what sort of sociology we choose to live with,
> how we choose a society, and finally, whether a choice
> even exists in the arena of social systems (1975: 78).

Taylor et al. take the position that: "There is a crisis not just in social theory and social thought (Gouldner 1971) (sic) but in the society itself. The new criminology must therefore be a normative theory: it must hold out the possibilities of a resolution to the fundamental questions, and a social resolution" (1973: 280). They go on to suggest that

> . . . the causes of crime must be intimately bound up with
> the form assumed by the social arrangements of the time.
> Crime is ever and always that behaviour seen to be prob-
> lematic within the framework of those social arrangements:
> for crime to be abolished, then, those social arrangements
> themselves must also be subject to fundamental social
> chage (: 282).

After claiming that ". . . the growth of our new approach to understanding crime requires us to participate in struggles for social justice" (1975: 168), Krisberg later adds, ". . . the basic principles of a social structure should be respect for the dignity of human life and the equal value of each individual. Practically, this means combatting structures of institutional privilege and affirming the ideal of human liberation and self-determination" (: 171). In a similar vein, in concluding his radical economic analysis of crime discussed earlier, Gordon says:

> If we managed somehow to eliminate ghetto crime . . . the
> competitiveness, inequalities, and racism of our institu-
> tions would tend to reproduce it. And if, by chance, the
> pattern of ghetto crime was not reproduced, the capitalists
> might simply have to invent some other way of neutralizing
> the potential opposition of so many black men, against
> which they might once again be forced to rebel with 'crim-
> inal acts.' It is in that sense of fundamental causality
> that we must somehow change the entire structure of in-
> stitutions in this country in order to eliminate the causes
> of crime (1973: 184).

In all, these arguments suggest that, as sociologists, students of deviance, and criminologists, we have much to gain from the modification, if not outright abandonment, of established orientations toward our subject matter. Remembering Kaplan's discussion of the principle of the drunkard's search (1964), we should acknowledge that the bulk of our activities to date has contributed little to finding the key to the crime problem. This fact should in itself be sufficient reason to explore new approaches, and the arguments presented above provide additional and persuasive incentive to do so. By demonstrating that neither we nor the phenomena we study are apolitical or value-free, these discussions encourage us to recognize the role of power and conflict in human relations. The adoption of a more macroscopic perspective holds promise for dealing with long-neglected structural, systemic variables. As Liazos has written:

> . . . we must see that covert institutional violence is much more destructive than overt individual violence. We must recognize that people's lives are violated by the very normal and everyday workings of institutions. We do not see such events and situations as violent because they are not dramatic and predatory; they do not make for fascinating reading on the lives of perverts; but they kill, maim, and destroy many more lives than do violent individuals (1972: 111-12).

From a similar perspective, one could ask: Where are the structural incentives for people to behave "morally"? Daily realities seem more conducive to erosion of faith in the system, to cynicism toward hopes of finding meaning in it, and to a bizarre combination of apathy and aggression. How else can people react to Watergate, to the oil industry, to the cost of living, and to so many other suspected systemic hypocricies? The graffiti in a recent daily newspaper read, "The world is a rat race and the rats are winning." The alienation theme of much of radical sociology is no accident, for disenchantment with contemporary lifestyles and the values they imply became painfully evident during the 1960s. And in this decade we are witnessing the spreading of this disenchantment from youth and the working class to the middle-aged and middle class. Widespread liberation movements clearly imply widespread feelings of entrapment.

One of the few things that proves to be more difficult than wrestling intellectually and emotionally with these issues is getting funding to study them. Given the investment of the monied overdogs in the protection of their interests, funding policies and practices continue to support mainly lower-range and, at best, occasional middle-range analyses of crime and the criminal justice system. A more philosophical problem revolves around definitions of and relationships between the concepts of crime and morality. Attempts to define "the criminal" confront serious dilemmas, not the least of which is substantial variation in time and space. Efforts to identify universal components of definitions find the mala prohibita category grossly outweighing the mala en se. The same sorts of problems confront any effort to define morality. Even the taking of a human life is at some times and some places by some people sanctioned under such circumstances as war killing, capital punishment, euthenasia, and abortion.

While it is discouraging that all known definitions of crime and morality are relative, it is encouraging that specific persons at specific times and places seem both capable of and wont to substantive decision making regarding the morality of behavior within their immediate lifespace. And indeed, those directly involved act on these decisions, feeling no need for recourse to a criminal justice system. While offensive behaviors apparently have always been with us, their definition and management by "outside experts" evolved alongside industrialization, urbanization, and other macroscopic social developments in recent history.

From this perspective, both the radical criminologist and the radical criminal, both the radical sociologist and the radical citizen may represent healthy reactions to the politically and economically entrenched moral order that nurtured the excesses of industrialization and urbanization. The "social consciousness" movement they have aroused contains, in addition to the arguments presented above, some themes that clarify critical issues and suggest some potential avenues toward resolution. One is the notion of relativism which assaults the simplistic morality of "good guys and bad guys." In balance, the theme of existentialism suggests renewed emphasis on responsibility in the conduct of living, both toward oneself and toward others. Closely related to this is the theme of "oneness" characteristic of the Eastern religious orientations which coordinate with the widespread theme of environmentalism and its focus on the unity of all life forms. Similar in nature is the theme of communalism. These themes seem to reflect a negative reaction to the fragmentation of modern social-psychological life and to the neutralizing effect such fragmentation has on our values.

Strongly reminiscent of Benedict's notion of synergy, Taylor et al. have suggested that "we have to address ourselves to the kind of structural reorganization which would render individual, societal and industrial interests identical" (1973: 260). And furthermore,

a truly post-capitalist society . . . is a society in which authority as such as divorced from the domination of men by men. It is also a society in which the power to 'criminalize'—if not abolished—is made subject to a genuine, rather than simply powerful, consensus (: 252).

NOTES

1. Reasons footnotes these comments with the suggestion that while a few criminologists such as Sutherland and Alfred Morris have

addressed some of these issues in the past, the major thrust of criminological training and practice has largely neglected them.

2. See Cohen (1971) and Taylor (1971).

3. See Kennedy (1970) and Pearce (1973).

REFERENCES

Becker, H. 1967. Whose side are we on? Social Problems 14: 239-47.

Cohen, S. 1971. Protest, unrest and delinquency: convergences in labels or behavior? Paper presented to the International Symposium on Youth Unrest, Tel-Aviv.

Coser, L. 1956. The Functions of Social Conflict. New York: Free Press.

Gordon, D. 1973. Capitalism, class, and crime in America. Crime and Delinquency 19: 163-86.

Gouldner, A. 1968. The sociologist as partisan: sociology and the welfare state. American Sociologist 3: 103-16.

———. 1970. The Coming Crisis of Western Sociology. New York: Basic Books.

Horowitz, I. 1975. Science and revolution in contemporary sociology: remarks to an international gathering. American Sociologist 10: 73-78.

Kaplan, A. 1964. The Conduct of Inquiry. San Francisco: Chandler.

Kennedy, M. 1970. Beyond incrimination: some neglected facets in the theory of punishment. Catalyst 5 (Summer): 1-37.

Krisberg, B. 1975. Crime and Privilege: Toward a New Criminology. Englewood Cliffs, N.J.: Prentice-Hall.

Liazos, A. 1972. The poverty of the sociology of deviance: nuts, sluts, and preverts. Social Problems 20: 103-20.

Lipton, Martinson, and Wilks. 1975. The Effectiveness of Correctional Treatment. New York: Praeger.

Pearce, F. 1973. Crime, corporations and the American social order. In Politics and Deviance, eds. L. Taylor and I. Taylor. Harmondsworth: Penguin.

Platt, T. 1974. Prospects for a radical criminology in the United States. Crime and Social Justice 1: 1-10.

Quinney, R. 1970. The Social Reality of Crime. Boston: Little, Brown and Co.

Reasons, C. 1975. Social thought and social structure: competing paradigms in criminology. Criminology 13: 332-65.

Reynolds, L. and J. Reynolds. 1970. The Sociology of Sociology. New York: David McKay.

Sagarin, E. 1975. Deviants and Deviance. New York: Praeger.

Schur, E. 1965. Crimes Without Victims. Englewood Cliffs, N.J.: Prentice-Hall.

Taylor, I. 1971. The new criminology in an age of doubt. New Edinburgh Review 15 (November): 14-17.

Taylor, I., P. Walton, and J. Young. 1973. The New Criminology: For a Social Theory of Deviance. Boston: Routledge and Kegal Paul.'

Thio, A. 1973. Class bias in the sociology of deviance. American Sociologist 8: 1-12.

Turk, A. 1969. Criminality and the Legal Order. Chicago: Rand McNally.

PART
II

INSIGHTS INTO CRIMINALIZATION

7

PUNISHMENT IN A JUST SOCIETY

Scott H. Decker

INTRODUCTION

It seems problematic that any theory of justice would fail to account for a thorough system of laws and coercive devices to assure compliance with those laws. But John Rawls' Theory of Justice, a complete work in many other senses, is guilty of such a charge. Though he does note the need to account for such a system, he fails to consider two important questions: (1) Can punishment be justified under his conception of justice? and (2) If it can be justified, what form must it take to be consistent with the two principles of justice which he offers? This chapter will take up the issue of coercive penal sanctions, as well as the philosophical dilemma stated by Rawls: "whether those who do affirm their sense of justice are treating these persons unjustly by requiring them to comply with just institutions" (1972: 575). The first section of this chapter presents a summary of Rawls' conception of justice. The next section considers whether punishment can be justified within this conception, as well as the grounds for such justification. The third part presents the four traditional models of punishment. Finally, the traditional models are evaluated from a Rawlsian position, and an ideal theory of punishment consistent with his two principles of justice is presented.

The starting point for Rawls is what he terms "the original position." From this position, rational persons who wished to further their interests would accept what he calls the two principles of justice. The first principle is that "each person is to have an equal right to

*The author is indebted to Dr. Alan Mabe and Dr. Charles Wellford for their critical comments on earlier versions of this paper.

the most extensive total system of basic liberties compatible with a system of liberty for all" (1972: 303). The second principle speaks to social and economic inequalities; these inequalities "are to be arranged so that they are both: (1) to the greater benefit of the least advantaged, consistent with the just saving principle, and (2) attached to offices and positions open to all under conditions of fair equality and opportunity" (ibid.).

Attached to these most basic principles of justice are priority rules, a means of determining answers to more complicated questions. The first priority rule ranks the two principles in lexical order. Lexical order is a phrase derived from the term "lexicographical." In moral philosophy this term has been used to rank needs or moral qualities in an order such that those at the top of the list must be satisfied before those ranked beneath it can be fulfilled. In this case liberty can only be restricted for the sake of greater or more secure liberty. Thus the criterion of the first principle must be met before the second principle may be fulfilled. The second priority rule deals with unequal distribution of social and economic goods. It states that they are to be distributed equally unless an unequal distribution of these goods would lead to the greater advantage of the least-favored group. From the original position, general, rather than specific, principles should be developed. They must be universals, able to settle the major disputes in society. These principles are to be constructed behind "the veil of ignorance," that is, one has no knowledge of how a decision will affect one's own life. All particular information is withheld from those in the original position; they know only the general level of their own society and some basic facts of human society generally. A unanimous choice of a particular concept of justice is then possible. Given these constraints on the choices of persons who desire to devise a conception of justice, Rawls posits that the two principles will be the outcome.

CONDITIONS FOR PUNISHMENT

Though he doesn't develop a comprehensive statement on punishment, Rawls himself states the need to develop a system to insure adherence and punish offenders. One must advance a further reason for considering a crime-control system in the context of Rawls' book. Such a coercive, punitive institution would represent a grave challenge to the primary value of the just society, liberty. It is a prima facie contradiction to elevate liberty as the prior good above all others, and to have a formal, official means of denying liberty to some within a society.

It must now be considered whether a system of punishment is consistent with justice. All entered into the social union under the same conditions, and were subject to the same considerations. All initially affirmed their sense of justice in entering the social union. To require all to reaffirm the principles, professed in the original position, could not be termed unjust. The reasons for this are fairly straightforward, since the union was freely entered into by all. Further, the principles were chosen as the best possible outcome by all, consistent with their status as free and equal moral beings. No accidental social circumstances or natural contingencies would play a part in determining either the principles or the social structure from the standpoint of the original position. In this sense one could not feel to be the victim of improper or unjust actions, for one would need only be reminded that those forces to which all are subject were those of one's own choice, based on the constraints of the original position. To allow every member of the social union the ability to shed the self-chosen liberties and constraints whenever it was perceived to be in one's interest to do so would yield anarchy and its attendant vices—instability, disorder, and lack of cooperation among citizens. In fact, it could be maintained that all members would agree that it was to their own greatest personal advantage that the principles and their attendant institutions be affirmed at all times. To require others to comply with just institutions is to require them to comply with their own nature and their own choices, a position which in no way could be termed unjust.

The focus must turn to the need for coercive penal sanctions in a society guided by these two principles of justice. Under the ideal conception, Rawls assumes that full compliance with the two principles will occur. Therefore, the need for penal sanctions or any coercive measures would not exist. It will be argued here that a partial compliance theory is a much more plausible and realistic approach to the issue, based on several statements Rawls makes, as well as our historical knowledge of the inevitability of some form of deviance in every society.[1] Even under full compliance, a limited theory of penal sanctions would be necessary under his conception of the rule of law. The desire for maintaining the law stems from the necessity for order and stability in society. These ends are achieved and affirmed when the law is enforced and maintained within society. An effective penal system lends security to all. Faced with the choice between liberty, as defined in the original position, coupled with a system of punishment for law violators and that of a society where law breakers are not dealt with as threats to the order and stability of society, it is rational to opt for the former. This is because stability and order in society allow persons the greatest opportunity to fulfill their life plans, and achieve their potential.[2]

These are the major points upon which Rawls bases the need for a system of punishment. Punishment is defined here as "any form of coercion resulting in any form of deprivation" (Turk 1972: 19). This may appear to be an overly broad and sloppy definition of the term, but a more limiting definition would ignore the content and ordering of the two principles of justice. Under the two principles, deprivation must be regarded as stemming from coercion, rather than from personal ability or social conditions as might occur in modern-day society. Furthermore, any coercion which leads to deprivation under the two principles may be viewed as the formal action of the social union.

Now the groundwork assumptions have been laid. It has been demonstrated that punishment under the two principles would not necessarily be unjust, that it may, in fact, be the most just way to deal with those who transgress in a society guided by the two principles. The need for a coercive penal machinery has been grounded in the desirability of a stable social order. Finally, the partial-compliance theory has been shown to be a more plausible working assumption than full compliance.

One must now move to a consideration of the end which punishment is to serve. It will be recalled that stability was cited as the major goal of coercion. Rawls argues that the stability of a particular social union is greatly enhanced when persons in that union can put trust and confidence in one another (1972: 346). The existence of an effective system of punishment will provide security in relations among people. In this way injustices can be minimized. For Rawls, a legal system should be "an order of public rules addressed to rational persons in order to regulate their cooperation and give appropriate weight to liberty" (1972: 241). Under such a system, punishment would accomplish the following specific objectives beyond the general one of stability: (1) uphold the criminal law, (2) uphold basic natural duties, (3) forbid us to injure others in life or limb, and (4) forbid us to deprive others of their liberty or property. The operation of such a system must be clearly and precisely defined especially regarding what behavior will be penalized and what limits on the power to punish there will be. Establishing such a system will be tolerable only if it is congruent with the two principles. The guidelines for such an institution must be consistent with choices made in the original position. Unless this is the case, the institution would seek to extend its limits into areas not initially agreed to by all and, therefore, could not lay binding claim upon members of the social order. Quite simply, the strongest claims upon individuals can be made by principles chosen in the original position. Finally, punishment is acknowledged for the sake of liberty, the foremost of the two principles and the basis upon which a just society must be built.

Attention will now be turned to a consideration of the specific conditions which must be met prior to meting out punishment. The first and most important claim is a reiteration of the guilding principles for punishment. It is essential that the laws exist for the sake of liberty. Their purpose must not be to restrict or inhibit, but in a sense to free or liberate individuals from the constraints and obstacles which prevent them from realizing their rational life plans. All must know the law and have been given a fair opportunity to comply with it, if the law is to be considered just. In this context, Rawls notes, "This principle is simply a consequence of regarding a legal system as an order of public rules addressed to rational persons in order to regulate their cooperation, and of giving the appropriate wight to liberty" (1972: 241). Such a system must demonstrate that the accused did, in fact, commit the alleged act and bore responsibility for its commission. It must be shown that, at the time the accused was thought to have committed the act, none of the following conditions were present: unintentionality, duress, or the accused's being below the age of responsibility, or suffering from mental disease. [3]

The considerations for invoking punishment are the following: the primacy of liberty, the necessity for order, the greater injustice done by not invoking the punishment, knowledge of the law, and a fair process for determining the existence of guilt. We may assert that Rawls' penal institutions exist to protect the liberty of all in society. It must be determined whether considerations of order will be balanced against those of liberty, for it is quite clear that in some instances the two may be contradictory. A system which seeks to preserve order and stability could restrict liberty merely on the grounds that actions of a person or group of persons was threatening and thus in need of corrective attention. But this cannot be the method of punishment for "justice as fairness." The first reason for this is Rawls' condition that a man must have intentionally committed a criminal act. And secondly, criminal acts reaffirm the liberty principle, rather than the desire for order.

At this time a more thorough discussion of the term "order" must be undertaken. Rawls has asserted often that order is necessary for a just society. It is a condition which free and equal moral beings would desire. Justice as fairness serves all by aiding in the fulfillment of their rational life plans, and providing the best possible set of circumstances for members of the union to achieve their ends, consistent with that same desire in each other. It may be viewed as a cooperative stability, maintained so that all may do as much as they please, congruent with the desire of others to do so within a framework of a predominantly just society. A stable society provides all with the best chance to live up to their hopes and aspirations. It is clear that a society regulated by the two principles could tolerate certain unstable elements. This is so because of the priority of liberty. The critical determination is the point at which the disorder of some becomes so great a threat to the liberty of others that it must be curtailed. Clearly, the fulfillment of rational life plans provides the best basis for such a restriction. When disorder stemming from the acts of others becomes great enough to require individuals to seriously alter the means of attaining their goals, such that they give up or are led to give up the pursuit of their rational life plans, then the liberty of some must be curtailed. A certain amount of disorder will always accompany society, especially under partial-compliance theory. It may be argued that a certain amount of disorder would be desirable in a just society, since that would be evidence of the priority of liberty, and give confidence to creative agents whose acts of disorder may lead to greater benefits for all.[4] But, in times of great social upheaval and instability, there would be extensive use of penal sanctions. In the absence of such conditions only those acts that presented grave threats to the fulfillment of rational life plans would be dealt with by such sanctions.

Some mention must be made of the penal machinery as it fits into a total system of meting out punishment. Such a system may include many other institutions, such as police, courts, parole, and probation, each of which must be in accord with the two principles. If one of the aforementioned institutions were unjust, the entire system must be declared unjust. As Rawls has argued, the principles regulate the whole structure of society, as well as its component parts (1972: 276). It is instructive, at this point, to refer to Turk's definition of punishment offered earlier: "any form of coercion resulting in any form of deprivation." Such an inclusive definition of punishment may be inaccurate for any system of justice other than that guided by the two principles. The necessity for such a definition with justice as fairness lies primarily in the philosophical priority of liberty.

THE FOUR TRADITIONAL MODELS OF PUNISHMENT

Punishment has traditionally followed one of four models: deterrence, reformation, retribution, or treatment. Each of the four will be presented and evaluated as possibilities for a social union founded on and guided by the two principles of justice.

The deterrence model originated with the classical school of criminology. The founders of this position are Caesere Beccaria, Jeremy Bentham, and Sir Phillip Romilly (Phillipson 1923). Writing late in the eighteenth century, they sought to make the law a clear and well-defined body of regulations. Behavior was explained by hedonistic assumptions about motivation. Thus, deterrence sought to provide a punishment in order to outweigh the "pleasure" obtained by committing a criminal act. Bentham worked out an extensive calculus, showing the amount of pleasure gained by performing certain criminal acts and the requisite punishment to act as effective deterrence in the future. In order to be effective, the punishment must be certain, swift, uniform, and proportionate to the act committed. Deterrent punishments are both forward and backward looking; forward looking in attempting to deter both the offender and the general public from committing criminal acts in the future (general deterrence) and backward looking in attempting to punish the offender for his actions (special deterrence). Thus, protection and prevention are the primary ends of such a model of punishment.

The reformation model stems from the Pennsylvania penitentiary system in the United States. Based on Quaker beliefs, it seeks to provide the means for the prisoner to see the "error of his ways" and subsequently alter behavior in light of such reflection. It operates through isolating the individual in a socially neutral situation and exposing him to the values which society desires him to take on. The reformation model rests on a free-will scheme, wherein the prisoners are capable of comparing their lives to a life regarded as better, thus stimulating a desire for change. Once the desire for change has been brought about, prisoners will seek to alter their own lives. This model is essentially forward looking, hoping to change the behavior for the future while dealing only minimally with past actions.

Reciprocity is the norm in retributive schemes of punishment. The state seeks to make the prisoner suffer to the extent that he inflicted harm upon others. This was the earliest form of punishment. It originated in tribal customs and can be found in the Bible. Today, it is resurfacing in a somewhat different form known as victimology. This model presupposes responsibility and is a highly relativistic means of determining and applying punishments. It is strictly backward looking, seeking solely to compensate the victim, or more often to "even the score" between society and the offender.

The final form of punishment to be discussed is that of treatment. It is proposed that this is not really a form of punishment at all. But in light of the definition of punishment used here, it can be regarded as such. In this context one should note the work of the American Friends Service Committee (1971). Throughout, a convincing argument is made for the view that treatment is another form of punishment. Further, the operational definition of punishment used here clearly renders treatment punitive. Under this model, criminality is thought to be the result of sickness, a pathological element in an individual. To deal effectively with it, one treats the offender as being ill, a socially sick person. Treatment is based upon a scientific model, in which individual change is brought about through the use of forces beyond the offender's control. Behavior is viewed deterministically in this model, and responsibility for crimes takes on a different meaning than it does in the other models of punishment. Responsibility is of value only in being able to say that a specific person did, in fact, commit a specific criminal act. Responsibility thus becomes a relationship of act to offender, rather than motive to act.

RAWLS AND THE TRADITIONAL MODELS

The deterrent model is most congruent with justice as fairness. The tradition of which it is a part closely parallels Rawls' account of the rule of law. Throughout his account of this topic, the priority of liberty is stressed. Laws are to provide stability to a social order as a "system of public rules addressed to rational persons" (1972: 236). Rawls' conception of the rule of law embodies four central features. First, acts which are proscribed in the law must be things which persons are both capable of doing and capable of avoiding. The second requirement of the rule of law is that similar cases must be treated similarly. Third, there can be no violation without a specific law that prohibits such acts. Finally, a just set of institutions must exist for the determination of guilt and assignment of penalties. The notions of special and general deterrence would accomplish the ends which punishment must meet under the two principles of justice, reaffirming the trust of citizens in one another and in their social union. The existence of a penal system so structured would generate the confidence necessary for the social union to operate properly. Its members would have confidence that the penal machinery would function effectively, thus minimizing the chance that rational life plans would have to be altered due to the existence of socially disruptive forces. A viable form of general deterrence would assure all members of society that proscriptions for illegal behavior exist and are effective. It would further serve to discourage those who consider committing criminal acts, by reducing the plausibility of, and benefits thought to derive from, crime. The aims of prevention and protection are consistent with the available means of choice in the original position, as are the desire for certainty, celerity, proportionate severity, and uniformity. In punishing the individual by means of separation (special deterrence), society would be protected. Further criminal acts may be deterred in that a rational persons would regard their liberty as their most valuable possession and the fulfillment of their rational life plans as their greatest good.

One possible source of injustice under a deterrent system of punishments must also be noted. For deterrence to be effective, theory states, severe penalties must be handed out for crimes whose perpetrators are hard to catch. But justice as fairness would not tolerate such uneven penalties. First, under Rawls' scheme, many of the laws whose violators are hard to catch—for example, victimless crimes—would not be considered criminal, since the violators present no great disorder to society. Second, in justice as fairness, the need to make examples of those who were unable to successfully complete a crime would be minimized because of the increased accuracy required in detection and adjudication. Third, those on the verge of committing acts for which a member of society was recently caught and punished would have to reconsider the value of the act and the threat presented to their liberty by the changes of being caught. Also of importance would be the consideration of whether potential imprisonment would represent greater progress toward the fulfillment of their rational life plan than would remaining free. It is only rational to assume persons would decide against committing criminal acts more often in Rawls' just society.

The notion of reformation is not altogether inconsistent with the guidelines for punishment in justice as fairness. Both notions are based upon free will and the ability of men to make rational choices. Faced with two alternatives in a neutral situation, a person should choose the alternative which is best for him, most consistent with his welfare. The conditions specified for reformation are very similar to those of the original position: free will, rationality, limited alternatives, a socially neutral situation. The reformation model also resembles Rawls' concept of moral education. The values to which a prisoner would be exposed are those to which he or she has already agreed—the principles of justice. In justice as fairness, the notion of special deterrence could take the form of reformation. Thus, every prisoner could be placed in the original position again (a socially neutral situation), upon entering prison. Guided by rationality and his or her notion of the good, the prisoner would thus choose the two principles of justice and a rational life plan consistent with those principles. Such a choice would represent the best possible solution to the alternative presented under the specified conditions, as well as a repudiation of past conduct. In this sense, prisoners would be affirming their own good as well as that of the rest of society. This would serve to generate confidence in the stability of society and effectively minimize or eliminate claims that punishment was unjust. Thus, individuals would be choosing punishment for themselves, as well as the specific form which it would take if they were to be placed in the original position again, and asked to judge the actions of one who had transgressed in a manner similar to their own, provided the veil of ignorance prevented them from knowing the course of action which they had taken.

It can be shown without much difficulty that retribution and treatment are notions which would be largely antithetical to justice as fairness. Retribution is, in principle, institutionalized revenge and, as such, has a psychological motivation. Rawls has declared that the principles and the institutions of a just social union are not to be guided by psychological premises (1972: 121, 137). Opposition to retribution due to the priority of liberty could also be demonstrated. Retribution would not serve to enhance or further liberties in any way. It would serve the second principle while ignoring the first. In no way would it affirm the liberty of the victim or society as a whole, but would address primarily the value and sanctity of wealth and property. A strictly backwards-looking punishment model such as retribution, with its emphasis upon repayment of debt, would not characterize a society that emphasized liberty above all other values. While it may be argued that retribution does affirm the good of liberty by punishing those who have blocked the liberty of others, it cannot be held that it in any way serves to better the chances for full expression of liberty in the future. On those counts it fails as a plausible description of punishment for a society guided by the two principles of justice.

The treatment model as a form of punishment would be held inconsistent with the general precepts around which a penal system is to be structured in Rawls' just society. Unlike retribution, treatment attempts to be preventive and seeks to halt future crimes. But it does so in a way that does not enhance the liberty, freedom, or rationality of all men. By locating the origins of criminality in the pathological status of the offender, treatment models deny individuals the opportunity to make choices freely. Behavior is seen as a set of determined responses. The rationality of decisions becomes rather suspect under such a conception. Rational decisions can be made but they are not the result of the actors doing. Rather, rationality under such a conception would be an externally imposed category, wholly inconsistent with the two principles of justice and their ordering. In seeking to preserve the general liberties of society, treatment can tolerate great abuses to special (individual) liberties. These threats to liberty usually come through the use of differential treatment, open-ended sentences, involuntary treatment practices, and the imposition of the values of another cultural group upon the prisoner. It could be argued that such a model presupposes a theory of behavior that is the antithesis of that around which those, guided by the two principles, would structure their lives and make their decisions.

CONCLUSION

A system of punishments under the two principles of justice must be guided by the priority of liberty over the distributive principle.

All that exists in society must exist primarily for the sake of enhancing the liberty of all. The only tolerable penal system under such guidelines would be one that made it possible for all in the social union, including the offenders, to have more extensive freedom. The method of punishment must also be one that free and equal moral beings would rationally choose, under the conditions of the maximizing rule. It must enhance their prospects for successfully fulfilling their rational life plans. Finally, all of this must be chosen from the standpoint of the original position, wherein the veil of ignorance limits available knowledge. Because of the inherent threats to liberty and the great potential for abuse that exists in a system of punishments, its formation should be guided at all stages by the maximizing rule (1972: 152-57). The maximizing rule can be used as a basis for decision making. It encourages individuals to structure decision making processes in such a way that they would suffer the least if their enemies were in positions of making decisions. It is a way of getting the least bad of several bad outcomes. Under this stipulation no one knows the changes of one's criminalization prior to entering the social union, thus fulfilling the first postulate of the rule. And in conjunction with the second postulate—that each cares little to gain above the minimum—all must desire a penal system to be so structures as to deter behavior which would net great benefits by risk taking. Thus, neither the need nor the motive to engage in theft and other crimes to sustain life would be present. By following the third precept of the maximizing rule, there would be more carefully structured safeguards to prevent the imprisonment of innocent persons, and the penal system itself would be developed as consistently as possible with the two principles of justice specified in the original position. The general guideline of the rule, that alternatives be structured such that one would be subject to penalties chosen by an enemy, would further insure a penal system that would foster the liberties of all, not just of those who are not incarcerated. In this way, no one could claim to have been subjected to laws not consented to, judicial practices not agreed to, or punishment that one had not specified. Thus, all persons under justice as fairness creates the laws which judge them, the procedures by which that law is applied, and any subsequent punishment which may adhere to a determination of guilt. We have demonstrated that only two of the four traditional punishment models would be consistent with Rawls' two principles of justice. Punishment is just when it is based upon deterrence and reformation, and not upon retribution and treatment.

NOTES

1. This stance is premised upon both philosophical and sociological grounds. It is most visible in the work of Durkheim (1965:

65-66). The natural propensity of man towards quarrel and its attendant result, anarchy, is the basis upon which Hobbes (1970: 99-100) builds his case for a strong sovereign. Finally, Hirschi (1971) notes that deviance theorists have approached the problem in a backwards fashion. He argues that, in the face of so much deviance, what is needed are explanations of conformity.

2. On this point Rawls' statements are similar to the contract tradition of Hobbes (1970) and Locke (1965). In this regard (the need for a system of laws and punishment), he does not show much divergence from his predecessors in the contract tradition. It is precisely at this point, though, that the similarities end, and the differences begin to take on important dimensions.

3. Though Rawls does not state this explicitly, his discussion of nullen crimen sine lege (: 238-39), mens rea (: 241-43), and references to H. L. A. Hart (1961, 1968) make it abundantly clear that this is his intention. It is interesting that his entire discussion of the rule of law (: 235-41) bears a remarkable similarity to several of the important precepts of classical criminology. Despite this similarity, nowhere, throughout this discussion, can one find a reference to Beccaria, Bentham, or Romilly, the three figures central to this perspective.

4. This argument parallels Rawls' position on the positive functions of civil disobedience. He argues that, ultimately, civil disobedience should compel some to recognize the injustice which others are enduring. This recognition should lead to the enhancement of liberty for all.

REFERENCES

American Friends Service Committee. 1972. Struggle for Justice. New York: Hill and Wang.

Durkheim, E. 1965. The Rules of Sociological Method. New York: The Free Press.

Hart, H. L. A. 1961. The Concept of Law. Oxford: Clarendon Press.

———. 1968. Punishment and Responsibility. New York: Oxford University Press.

Hirschi, T. 1969. Causes of Delinquency. Berkeley: University of California Press.

Hobbes, T. 1970. The Leviathan. Indianapolis: Bobbs-Merrill.

Locke, J. 1965. Two Treatises of Government. Cambridge: Cambridge University Press.

Phillipson, C. 1923. Three Criminal Law Reformers: Beccaria, Bentham, Romilly. New York: E. P. Dutton.

Rawls, J. 1972. A Theory of Justice. Cambridge: Harvard University Press.

Turk, A. T. 1969. Criminality and Legal Order. Chicago: Rand McNally.

8

THE PROTESTANT ETHIC AND DECRIMINALIZATION

Vergil L. Williams and John C. Watkins, Jr.

> Criminal conviction represents the degrading public
> revelation of what Anglo-American society has long con-
> demned as a moral defect, and the existence of criminal
> sanctions may serve to reinforce this cultural taboo. . . .
> (Powell v. Texas).

The argument presented in this article is that much of the failure of the criminal justice system to reduce certain forms of criminality can be attributed to obsolete criminal law. The contention is
that detrimental laws and policies are the result of centuries of constructing laws which serve only to institutionalize a value system
derived from a secularized puritan moral code. The original rigidi-
ties of the code and the subsequent changes in the mores of society
have rendered much of the legal structure inappropriate and dysfunc-
tional. Criminal law should be purged of its theological content and
restructured around behavioral science concepts.

MORALITY AND THE LAW

The tendency to mix theology and criminal law may be viewed
from two perspectives: (1) the viewpoint of the theologians, and, (2)
the viewpoint of the law makers. Theologians are in the business of
promoting a particular interpretation of a body of holy writings; in
the United States, the predominant reference point of religious scholars is the Holy Bible. Even so, the interpretations are substantially
different as evidenced by the existence of the Jewish community and
the major divisions of the Christian community into Protestantism
and Catholocism. To further complicate the philosophical framework
of theology, the branches of Christianity are literally divided into
hundreds of sects.

Despite the disagreement among theologians, there is substantial historical evidence that they are able to unify their efforts sufficiently to bring about political pressure on law makers in an attempt to mold criminal law to suit their objectives of achieving a moral populace. The history of birth-control legislation, for example, illustrates this point (Wilcox 1969: 335-43). Early legislation restricting the dissemination of birth control information and technology was fostered by Protestants. Information on birth control and the sale of prophylactics were grouped with pictures and books considered to be obscene and suppressible by federal law. When Protestants began to lose interest in using legislation to slow the sale of birth-control devices and the free flow of birth-control information, the Catholics began to use their powerful lobby to achieve the same ends. The combined efforts of Protestant and Catholic groups delayed the progress of birth-control education for decades.

There is an element of irony in the efforts of theologians to influence the content of criminal law. One occasionally hears a theologian express the thought that humanity has passed thousands of laws attempting to enforce the Ten Commandments. That thought contains the implicit assumption that the ultimate goals of the theologians and the ultimate goals of the law makers are the same, and, consequently, it is perfectly natural for the law makers to cooperate with the theologians by providing criminal sanctions for immoral acts. It is almost incumbent upon the law makers to do so. A second implicit assumption in the statement provides the irony. The statement is somewhat facetious in that it openly recognizes that it is impossible to achieve the desired morality with mortal law. The religious scholar who expresses that thought is presenting a concise history of the failure of criminal law built upon a theological base.

Making the implicit assumption explicit allows a closer examination of the relationship between theology and criminal law. It is basically true that the ultimate goals of the law makers and the theologians are the same. Both seek an orderly society wherein men are considerate of one another and reasonably free of fear in order to develop their higher faculties—whether these faculties are considered to be intellectual or spiritual. However, there is a considerable difference in the primary methodology employed by the two groups. The theologians rely, for the most part, on achieving an orderly society by the building of internal restraints. They seek voluntary compliance with a moral code. Religious history provides a number of examples of over-zealous churchmen who attempted to achieve morality by applying force. Nonetheless, most theologists acknowledge that persuasion is preferable to coercion. Conversely, the prevalent tool of the law maker is coercion. The existence of the criminal law is, itself, coercive in that it instills an element of fear or dread in the generally law-abiding citizen who might violate the law. In that sense the criminal law sets up an internal restraint. However, external restraint is the main principle involved. The offender is punished because he has violated the criminal law. This coercion acts to incapacitate him and to provide an example suitable for deterring others who might commit the same act (see Bentham 1789).

We must assume that both theologians and law makers are important to the achievement of ordered liberty, and that both groups are somewhat successful in their efforts. Surely social conditions would be less stable without their intervention. By the same logic, one can argue that both groups are failing to some extent. Crime, as defined by the criminal law, does exist. Immorality, as defined by the theologians, does exist. Neither group—acting singly or in concert—has achieved the ultimate goal. Within the framework of our philosophy of government, coercion is to be deplored and used as a last resort. If the theologians were completely successful in their efforts to achieve an orderly society via persuasion, there would be no need for coercive criminal law. But, in recognizing that there is a need for criminal law, there seems to be no compelling reason for the law makers to look to the theologians for leadership. After all, they have failed in their efforts to achieve an orderly society and the law maker is faced with the task of providing a different vehicle for achieving that goal. The law maker, however, finds it almost impossible to approach his task objectively. In order to understand this lack of objectivity, one must look at the mixture of theology and criminal law from the perspective of the law maker.

SECULARIZING MORAL CODES

The law makers include both legislators who are in a position to create statutory law and appellate judges who have the power to create new principles of case law. Let us make a leap of epistemological faith and assume that all such law makers are capable and dedicated people who approach their task of law making with the utmost sincerity. Can they do their jobs objectively? We would argue that they do not and that they cannot unless they make a great effort to change their orientation. Objectivity, if it can be achieved at all, it requires extreme effort to break away from one's past experiences and present emotions. It requires a willingness to selectively utilize the work of authorities in the social sciences. It requires the will and effort to learn a new methodology.

Learning a new methodology is difficult for both legislators and judges. Most of them receive formal training in the law which gradually conditions them to accept the law's traditional methodology found in the doctrine of <u>stare decisis</u>. Reliance upon precedent helps to prevent chaos in the legal framework because change can come about only slowly. It assures consistency, predictability, and constancy (Belli 1968). Unfortunately, chaos can also develop if the law is so inflexible that it cannot change as rapidly as social conditions.

A total reliance on precedent effectively eliminates any possibility of achieving the objectivity necessary to break with reliance on the theologists for leadership in the formulation of criminal law. Law makers are subject to two types of pressure from the theologians. One type of pressure is the relatively obvious political pressure already discussed. With determination, law makers can resist that type of pressure if they deem it wise to do so. However, there is a second type of pressure that is too subtle to detect without prolonged and concentrated effort. Legislators are individuals who are products of their culture and environment. Theologians have helped to shape their thinking patterns throughout their lives, both directly and indirectly. Chances are good that many legislators themselves belong to a flock presided over by a theologian and have definitive moral codes which they will voluntarily promote during their law-making activities.

Let us assume that a particular law maker is an atheist. Does that mean that he or she can be more objective? The answer must be "not necessarily." Theological doctrines have become secularized over long periods of time and their origin is not apparent. The process began when a major portion of a population embraced a particular theological doctrine. Religious doctrines define many acts as being taboo. After several generations have passed, the theology may be modified rather extensively, but a value system remains in the form of groundless taboos (superstitions). The source of the taboo may not be readily apparent after the original theology has been modified, but new generations (including a few atheists) have by now embraced the value system. At this point, secularization of a moral code has occurred.

An illustration of this can be found in the classification of certain crimes as <u>mala in se</u> and <u>mala prohibita</u>. The notion that some acts are wrong in and of themselves (<u>mala in se</u>) can only derive from theological constructs. In our experience, groups of college students (which include agnostics and atheists) have relatively long lists of acts that they classify as <u>mala in se</u>. This attitude indicates to us that they have rather fixed ideas regarding the "morality" of a given act even when the logic of prohibiting the act is not easily discerned. For example, an atheist may define an act of homosexuality between consenting adults in private as being "wrong." The source of such feelings, we would argue, is frequently the secularized moral code of some previous era. Individuals are prone to define acts as moral or immoral even without professing a religious affiliation.

It is probably fortunate that such moral codes persist. However, we fear that they often stand in the way of rational approaches to law making. For instance, virtually every individual professes to know what is right and what is wrong concerning sexual behavior. In almost every case, such attitudes stem from reference to teachings from theology or from a secularized theological position as opposed to conclusions drawn from scientific research. Judging from the large number of criminal laws purporting to regulate sexual behavior in the United States, one gains the feeling that sex is something to be tolerated only under rigorously prescribed conditions. If one studies sexual behavior only by referring to the criminal law, it would not be stretching a point too much to note that, in many cases, any sex act is criminal unless it is performed by a lawfully married couple using the face-to-face missionary position in the privacy and darkness of their bedroom. The implicit assumption in the criminal law is that sex is wrong and not to be enjoyed, although it may be used under certain conditions to foster procreation. How did such odd notions creep into our criminal jurisprudence? Actual human behavior would not seem to form a logical basis for this potentially burdensome body of laws. We suggest that certain segments of criminal law, nonetheless, reflect a secularized value system which originated in our early historical encounter with Puritanism. The Puritan theology has been modified extensively, but the resulting value system lingers even today. The doctrine of stare decisis helps to perpetuate its obsolete behavioral expectations in the criminal law.

THE PROTESTANT ETHIC

Before illustrating some areas of criminal law where attention is needed, we will delineate some of the elements of the Protestant ethic that have been secularized and incorporated in toto into the character structure of middle-class Americans. We bow to the recognized authority on this topic by summarizing some elements of Max Weber's The Protestant Ethic and the Spirit of Capitalism.[1] Key elements of this essay are briefly noted in the following paragraphs.

Accumulation is a key element. An individual has a duty to increase his wealth and to continually prove that he is chosen, successful, and valuable. A second value is quantification. Success must be illustrated in quantifiable terms. Labor has a central place in the value system. Work in an acceptable occupation is a duty and the only acceptable way of life. It has the characteristics of an ultimate end. Individualism is a vital element. The individual must strive for success in isolation. <u>Competition</u> is the main driving force to prove one's value through success. Successful members of the middle class consider themselves to be an elite group much like the elite of Puritanism. Success must be accomplished by competition to set apart the "blessed" from the "rejected." <u>Rational conduct</u> is necessary. This implies that success is to be pursued in a conscious and systematic way. One must have a life plan, be purposive and systematic. Other types of behavior—emotional, spontaneous, or impulsive—are morally wrong. <u>Asceticism</u> occupies a central role in the value system. Enjoyment stemming from the senses and from sexual activity must be repressed. Luxurious consumption is suspect (see Weisskopf 1955: 12-13).

We contend that the secularized value system described by Weber is still a viable part of our character structure and a detriment to objectivity in constructing a workable criminal jurisprudence. In order to effectively deal with our cultural heritage, we must discipline ourselves to rely on a forward-looking methodology.

CRIME AND SIN—IMPLICATIONS FOR POLICY SHIFTS

With the issuance in 1967 of the report by the President's Commission on Law Enforcement and Administration of Justice, a resurgence of public sentiment swept the nation urging those in positions of influence to "do something" about crime. New programs were suggested, new recommendations made, and a new source of federal funds created to assist criminal justice agencies in the performance of their tasks. Oddly enough, however, one can search the pages of this report in vain for any suggestion about the innovative restructuring of our penal laws in the pursuit of a more rational penal policy. As Jack Douglas noted, "Instead of asking itself what should be legally defined as 'crimes' in our society today, the commission in its report takes it for granted that those activities should be crimes that are now legally defined as crimes" (1971: xiii).

It is this acquiescence, this "taking for granted" attitude on the part of policy makers in this field that we find disturbing. It would seem, quite possibly, that many of those in a consulting role to the President's Crime Commission unconsciously took the same stance toward crime in general as did the Dutch criminologist Hermannus Bianchi (1956: 6) when he wrote that "Crime is a sinful, ethically blameworthy, defiant and erroneous act, eventually prohibited by penal law, at any rate deserving to be followed by conscious counteraction on the part of the society."

It cannot be gainsaid that there are some forms of criminality that would still lend themselves to Bianchi's characterization. In point of fact, violent crimes against persons and property, and a host of less dramatic acquisitive offenses, would persistently commend themselves to almost universal disappropriation. But, equally important is the fact that there are also a host of activities branded "criminal" by the law that should not be so designated.

Norval Morris and Gordon Hawkins (1970) suggest that "Politicians rely heavily on the criminal law and like to invoke criminal sanctions in connection with most social problems, if only to indicate their moral fervor and political virtue." Of course, the "moral fervor" of some law makers is intensified in direct proportion to their own personal identification with the tenets of the Protestant ethic or some derivative. In criminal law, this concept can be dangerous—dangerous because such a stance often confuses crime with sin and concomitantly introduces a degree of moral absolutism that stifles rational debate. The problem becomes particularly acute in the area of the so-called "victimless crimes."

It is small wonder that vagrancy, drunkenness, gambling, certain forms of delinquency, and selected types of sexual activity have been branded criminal by legislators and jurists down through the years. These divergent forms of social interaction have been labeled as such precisely because there has been an almost perfect meeting of the minds between the law maker and his theological counterpart in this otherwise murky area. It is our contention that the Protestant ethic is, at best, a doctrinaire rationale for the continued criminalization of discrete forms of antisocial conduct on the outermost fringes of the criminal law. Today, few social scientists would argue that offenses, such as vagrancy or certain acts of delinquency, represent a type of "moral defect" in the psycho-social or religious makeup of the average defendant. Yet, courts and legislative assemblies continually give lip service to such worn out bromides when debating these issues. Such phrases may soothe our collective conscience, but they lack any genuine utility in the formulation of a new penal policy toward victimless crimes.

If we move along a continuum from vagrancy and delinquency to such things as drunkenness, gambling, and proscrived sexual activities, we are immediately thrust headlong into a vortex of unending controversy. On the one hand are those who fear a complete moral breakdown if these offenses are removed from the statute books. Arrayed on the opposite side (although fewer in number) are advocates of what we shall characterize as "hard core" decriminalization—a decriminalization that would ultimately refashion American penal law policy along lines that might prove to be counterproductive. This either/or approach to the problem simply will not achieve its intended purpose. A rational penal policy would attempt to ascertain what antisocial phenomena are clearly within the reaches of the criminal justice system's sanctioning policies and what phenomena are clearly outside the system's competency. It would take a hard look at what consequences the continued criminalization of these offenses will have within a nationwide framework aimed at both crime prevention and control.

Policy makers should be aware of at least three basic defects in the criminal justice system that have a bearing on decision making. The first, already noted, is overcriminalization. The second is a critical lack of coordination among local, state, and federal criminal justice agencies. Third, and perhaps most crucial, is the lack of an adequate data base in criminal justice upon which decisions can be made. Many more problem areas could be cited, but these three are the ones that, it appears, should be corrected first if we are to move toward a more workable and responsive body of criminal law.

Obviously, some of the issues discussed in the earlier portion of this chapter do not pertain to the second and third defects mentioned above. But when discussion focuses on overcriminalization, the Protestant ethic colors and channels debate into unrewarding responses to serious policy questions. Responsible proponents of decriminalization are often literally reconceptualized in the role of the Devil's advocate. When this occurs, the die has been cast, emotion overcomes rationality, and meaningful penal reforms again are shelved. As a result, we are faced with an overburdened substantive law of crimes that grows more ponderous and ethically biased with each succeeding legislative session.

Few serious promoters of responsible decriminalization are given an attentive legislative ear because of the overwhelming penchant to discover a "moral defect" in the commission of certain criminal activities that smack more of sin than of crime. It is this blind association with crime qua sin that has, in large measure, rendered some portions of criminal law sterile instruments of social control. A policy shift is called for. This shift should be in the general direction of recognition that the law of crimes cannot fulfill its manifold responsibilities as it is presently conceived and administered. It should be in the direction of recognizing that criminal law does not impact on many of the social and psychological causes of crime, especially in the specific area under discussion. Finally, it should be in the direction of avoiding, whenever possible, any direct association with particular theological premises in deciding whether certain discrete forms of behavior should come within the sanctioning power of the state.

THE ROLE OF SOCIAL SCIENCE IN DECRIMINALIZATION

With a review of a substantial amount of criticism of the traditional methodology of criminal jurisprudence, it is possible to suggest a solution. Law makers cannot attain the objectivity that we recommend without some assistance. It is tempting to recommend that criminal jurisprudence develop a research arm. Instead, we recommend that criminal jurisprudence develop a research-dissemination arm as a more economically expedient alternative. This recommendation is based on the premise that sufficient research is already underway, but research findings are not in a form that is accessible to law makers. A new research arm would be expensive and would probably duplicate work already being done.

It is proposed that a criminal policy research-dissemination arm be developed along the following lines. It does not matter greatly whether the arm, which might be designated as the Council of Behavioral Science Legal Advisors, be under the aegis of government or a private organization. It is crucial, however, that the council be funded adequately to be able to attract an array of prominent scholars from several branches of the behavioral sciences. The council membership should be made up of at least one outstanding scholar from each of the following areas: (1) criminology, (2) theoretical sociology, (3) social psychology, (4) clinical psychology, and (5) economics. The scholars, each representing a particular discipline, should have a small staff of apprentice scholars from their respective field who represent an array of specialties within that field. The council should also have a noted legal scholar as part of its membership and sufficient editorial talent to produce a monthly publication of high quality.

The obvious function of this council would be the dissemination of research information that would be directly helpful to law makers. In accomplishing this goal, the members would perform a number of necessary tasks. The reason for recommending that a prominent scholar from each of several disciplines be appointed is that such a scholar would be expected to be aware of the social science research occurring in a given field. In addition to this awareness of significant research, the scholar would be able to make some judgments concerning the quality and possible validity of the research in light of the knowledge about other research in the discipline. Furthermore, he or she could assess the significance of new research findings in the various fields and gauge its applicability to criminal law with the help of the staff legal scholar. Finally, by removing excessive specialized jargon, findings could be interpreted and conclusions condensed so that they could be published in a form that could be comprehended by legislators and other policy makers.

Dissemination to law makers would be the most crucial step in this process. A monthly publication that would reach the vast majority of persons who influence legal policy in the United States is suggested. The council could not hope to have sufficient impact unless it could achieve widespread dissemination of its material.

It might be preferable to provide government financing to achieve this end as opposed to the alternative of making the Council a self-supporting operation.

In summary, this recommendation is a way out of the morality morass into which legal policy makers have fallen. Although we might assume that we are moving forward in the decriminalization sector, the evidence to date suggests a contrary interpretation. This proposal would address itself squarely to that issue.

NOTE

1. An excellent summary of Weber's essay, including a more detailed explanation of the process through which a moral code becomes secularized, can be found in W. Weisskopf (1955: 12-13).

REFERENCES

Belli, M. 1968. The Law Revolution. Los Angeles: Sherbourne Press.

Bentham, J. 1789. An Introduction to the Principles of Morals and Legislation. London: Athlone Press.

Bianchi, H. 1956. Position and Subject-Matter of Criminology. Amsterdam: North Holland Publishing Company.

Douglas, J., ed. 1971. Crime and Justice in American Society. Indianapolis: Bobbs-Merrill Company.

Morris, N. and G. Hawkins. 1970. The Honest Politician's Guide to Crime Control. Chicago: University of Chicago Press.

Weisskopf, W. 1955. The Psychology of Economics. Chicago: University of Chicago Press.

Wilcos, C. 1969. Toward Social Reform. Homewood, Illinois: Richard B. Irwin Publishing Company.

9

IS IT POSSIBLE TO AVOID THE
LEGISLATION OF MORALITY

Jeffrey H. Reiman

The question posed in the title of this chapter is of central importance to criminal justice. Indeed, it is a question relevant to a wide variety of pressing criminal justice issues. There are, for instance, those who oppose antidiscrimination laws on the ground that "you can't legislate morality." There are others who call for the decriminalization of so-called "morals" offenses, like prostitution or homosexual behavior, because "you shouldn't legislate morality." Both of these positions presuppose that it is possible to avoid the legislation of morality. It will be argued that the legislation of morality cannot be avoided, and that those who think it can are guilty of serious conceptual confusion. This is not to undermine the view of those who urge the decriminalization of "morals" offenses, but rather to demonstrate that that view has a more cogent foundation than the incoherent call for an end to the legislation of morality. This foundation lies in a more sophisticated understanding of the relationship of law to moral values. Indeed, my overriding purpose in examining and disposing of the various justifications for ending the legislation of morality is to sketch out the nature of the relationship between law and moral values. I believe this to be the precondition for intelligently resolving any dispute about morality and criminal justice.

There is one way to avoid the legislation of morality. This may seem paradoxical in the light of the above; however, a little discussion will dispel this appearance. The way to avoid the legislation of morality, is to avoid all legislation. Whatever the practical limitations of anarchism, no one has proven that anarchism is logically impossible. Anarchy is just that—a social order without an "archon," a law-giving authority. If it is possible to live without making rules that the community is prepared to back up with force (laws), then it is surely possible to live without legislating morality. But even this needs qualification.

If an anarchic social order were established self-consciously, then it could be said to have at least one law: the rule that any attempt

to establish public law-making authority will be resisted with force
by the community. And since this "law" clearly expresses a moral
preference (the moral preference for anarchism), it could be argued
that even anarchism requires the legislation of morality. But this
is only true of self-consciously established anarchy. If a social order simply and spontaneously developed without law makers and without even giving a thought to law makers, then it could be said to literally have no laws and no legislation. And thus, it could avoid the legislation of morality.

This unlikely possibility appears to be the only exception to
the principle that it is impossible to avoid the legislation of morality.
That is, since falling into anarchy is hardly a live possibility for us,
we cannot avoid legislation and, therefore, cannot avoid the legislation of morality. To put the proposition in unqualified form: given a
criminal justice system, we cannot avoid the legislation of morality.
The idea that we can have a criminal justice system which does not
embody moral preferences in the law is an incoherent one. It remains to be seen what effect this will have on the movement to decriminalize "morals" offenses. First, however, it will be helpful
to examine some other possible interpretations of the notion that you
cannot legislate morality.

I have already referred to those who oppose desegregation or
antidiscrimination laws with this assertion. Assuming that this is
sincerely meant, and not just a smokescreen thrown up to block social change, it has three possible meanings:

1. It is not possible to shape moral attitudes and behavior by
laws;
2. Moral actions are only moral if they are done freely, and
since law is coercive, it is not possible to bring about moral action
by law;
3. In a free country, it is wrong to force people (even legally)
into specific moral attitudes and behavior.

Each of these claims is of a very different nature. The first
is an empirical claim; it makes a prediction that is either borne out
by the facts or not. The second is a conceptual claim; it argues that
law and morality are two concepts that cannot occupy the same ground,
since the first is necessarily coercive and the second is necessarily
noncoercive. The third is a moral claim; it urges that it is wrong to
force a moral preference on people, if we assume that freedom is a
moral good. What these claims have in common is that they are all
false.

The first claim is most clearly false with regard to moral behavior. Unless we assume that people are simply impervious to the

threat of punishment, it is clearly possible to change people's behavior by enacting and using a legal sanction. Few can think that desegregation laws have not changed behavior in the South over the last decade, or that laws are not presently changing behavior towards women. As for moral attitudes, they are undoubtedly harder to reach by law, particularly in a nation committed to punishing people only for their actions and not their thoughts. Nevertheless, attitudes do not exist in a vacuum. They are maintained and passed on in a context of institutions and social practices. When institutions and practices change, attitudes gradually change as well. How long can a racist attitude based on myths about black inferiority survive in a social order in which blacks come to hold positions of political, economic, or academic prominence?

If the defenders of this first claim mean that you can't change moral attitudes on behavior overnight, they are certainly right. One cannot pass a law saying that, as of its effective date, all racists must shed their racism. But then a law against murder doesn't eliminate murder overnight either. This is more than can be asked of any law. If, however, a law can change behavior and, more gradually, attitudes over a period of time, this is enough to deny the first claim.[1]

Another version of this first claim might take Prohibition as its model and argue that this proves that one cannot change widely practiced moral behaviors by law. If Prohibition proves anything, it proves that extreme changes require extreme methods, and that in a democracy extreme methods require widespread and firm support. The most we can say about the lesson of Prohibition is that the effectiveness of a law will depend upon the willingness and ability of the government to enforce it thoroughly, and that the government will be less willing and able to enforce it if the public is divided in its attitudes towards the law. Since Prohibition was widely supported in rural areas and widely resisted in urban areas—even though it became part of the Constitution (through a procedure, incidentally, which favored the rural interests)—there was neither the support nor the cooperation necessary to enable the government to stop the flow of alcohol.[2] But this doesn't prove that law cannot change moral behavior or attitudes. It simply spells out a practical problem which must be met for any law to be effective.

The second claim asserts that law and morality are conceptually antithetical since the former is coercive and the latter must be voluntary. This simply rests on an understandable mistake about the nature of morality. There are some moral acts which must be uncoerced to be what they are. There can be no such thing as forced benevolence, anymore than there can be forced faith. A person who donates to the poor at gunpoint is not thereby charitable, just as a person who recites a catechism as an alternative to burning at the stake is not a believer. Furthermore, so far as an individual is concerned, we are prone to say that one is morally praiseworthy only insofar as he or she freely chooses to take a moral course of action. A person who doesn't steal only out of fear of being punished is hardly entitled to be praised for honesty.

Clearly, with all these qualifications admitted, there are acts which are morally preferable regardless of whether the actor is free or coerced. Even if people who refrain from stealing out of fear of punishment don't deserve moral praise, there is no doubt that the world is better off because they have refrained, regardless of the reason. If I have a right to free speech, you may refrain from gagging me either because you respect my right to say what I please or because you are afraid of being arrested. But regardless of why you refrain, a moral value—the right to free speech—is sustained. In fact, it might be said that the law pertains precisely to those situations in which a moral value is at stake which cannot depend on persons' freely given support to exist. The law cannot force a moral virtue like charity on us, but it can support a moral value like life, by coercively preventing the taking of life.

What this suggests is that, contrary to the second claim, there are at least some realms of morality quite compatible with legal coercion.[3] These are the realms in which a moral value like life or liberty is gained simply by preventing others' encroachments, even if they are prevented by the threat of punishment.

This should be enough to dispose of the third version of the claim as well. If there are moral values like liberty which can be protected by legal coercion, it hardly makes sense to hold that it is incompatible with the values of freedom to use law to force people into specific moral attitudes and behavior. In fact, it suggests the reverse: that in a free society, certain moral behaviors must be enshrined in law and backed up with the threat of sanction.[4] In what follows, it will be further argued that any legal system must enforce moral preferences. For the time being, it should be noted that the view that antidiscrimination laws and the like should not be passed because "you can't legislate morality" has been rebutted. Let us move on to analyze the notion that we shouldn't legislate morality, urged by the defenders of decriminalization of morals offenses.

In response to this, we should note a simple but often overlooked point: It is not possible to divide the criminal law into a part that enforces morality and a part that is morally neutral. Every criminal law, with the exception of technical laws—such as those which establish a legal deadline for income tax submission, and so on (we can disregard these since a criminal justice system constructed out of only such laws is unimaginable)—embodies some moral judgment in law. Every criminal law takes a stand in a real or potential moral dispute. It is not possible, therefore, to defend the decriminalization of so-called morals offenses, like prostitution or homosexuality, on the principle that one should not enforce morality. To refuse to legislate morality is to refuse to legislate.

Every law posits at least one and probably several moral values. So, obviously, a law such as that which prohibits and provides sanctions for premeditated murder legislates at least the following moral judgments:

1. That it is preferable to preserve human life;
2. That it is acceptable for the state to harm individuals who take human lives;
3. That individuals who take human lives after rational deliberation are more deserving of punishment than those who take lives on impulse, or for that matter, accidentally, ignorantly, or out of insanity.

This list could probably be extended further. It takes little reflection to see that in each case the criminal law establishes as binding some moral principle which is not necessarily shared by all human beings. To reply that laws like those against murder are necessary for society to exist at all is, first, probably either empirically false or impossible to prove, and second, doesn't avoid the moral judgment. Such a reply simply places the moral value elsewhere—on the existence of society. More importantly, however, this overlooks the fact that societies don't simply have laws against murder; they have laws that define murder. That is, out of the various ways in which people kill each other—in duels, in war, by accident, out of passion, by negligence or by neglect, and so on—each society selects some ways and defines them as murder—that is, as prohibited and punishable. Surely here, just as in the decision as to what forms of removing property from a person are theft, a moral judgment is embodied in the law. The inescapable conclusion is that all criminal law is the legislation of morality.

If this is the case, what becomes of the movement to decriminalize prostitution or homosexual behavior, and of the assumption that laws against such practices are no more than the writing of prevailing moral beliefs into law? If the law inescapably expresses moral belief no less when legislating against murder or theft as when legislating against homosexuality or prostitution, is there no basis for the decriminalization of morals offenses? Must the individual who is struggling to remove such offenses from the statute books merely accept the argument that the law unavoidably expresses moral beliefs which not everyone shares and, therefore, laws prohibiting morals offenses have as rightful a place on the books as those pertaining to violence and fraud?

The proponent of decriminalization can indeed answer this argument successfully and, furthermore, can answer it in moral terms. But it should be clear that it cannot be answered by oversimplified attacks on the legislation of morality, or on the basis of a view of the criminal law that sees some laws as morally neutral and others as expressing moral beliefs. One must answer it on the basis of a more sophisticated understanding of the relationship of law and moral values. On the basis of such an understanding, it is possible to show that laws which penalize homosexual practices and the like have no place in Anglo-American law. Such an understanding and such an argument will be offered in the hope of shedding some light on the philosophical grounds for decriminalization. Before taking this up, we should consider a popular, but ultimately misguided, attempt to supply an alternative argument for the decriminalization of at least some morals offenses. This is the argument that activities like prostitution and homosexual behavior are transactions entered into by freely consenting individuals and are therefore "victimless crimes."

Clearly, an act which victimizes no one has no place in the criminal law, for this is to miss the point for which acts are labeled crimes. It seems self-evident that acts are labeled and treated as crimes in order to protect society from those acts. An act which victimizes no one is an act for which protection is unnecessary. The idea of a victimless crime is, strictly speaking, an incoherent one like the idea of a square circle. To admit that an act has no victim and think it should still be a crime is to talk through one's hat; it would be just as sensible to outlaw Tuesday. Furthermore, it is obvious that crimes like assault have very visible victims who are ready to complain and press charges against their assailants, and this distinguishes them from those victimless crimes such as prostitution or homosexuality between consenting adults. But this distinguishing fact does not constitute an argument that crimes of the latter sort are victimless, and thus have no rightful place in the criminal law.

The basis for this assertion should be made clear to avoid confusion. Prostitution and homosexual relations are victimless and have no place in the criminal law. But this is not proven by the fact that they are consensual acts. That a criminal act has no victim can mean two things which are quite different but easily confused. It may mean (1) that there is no individual who feels directly harmed by the act and who is therefore willing and able to complain and present evidence against the perpetrator of the act. On the other hand, it may mean (2) that there is no one harmed in any way by the criminal act.

It is evident that any act of which (2) is true ought not to be a crime. It is also plausible to hold that, if an act is a consensual transaction freely entered into, then (1) is true. That is, for activities like prostitution or homosexual relations, there is no individual who feels directly harmed and is willing and able to complain and present evidence against the perpetrator. The meaning of this is not as obvious as first meets the eye. There are, of course, individuals who feel harmed by the existence of prostitution and/or homosexual relations, and who are more than ready to complain. What distinguishes them is that, unlike victims of assault or robbery or rape, they cannot point to the specific act of prostitution or homosexuality by which they are harmed. Since the criminal law is aimed at individual harmful acts rather than "conditions," this means the would-be complainant is not in a position to complain in the terms that the criminal justice system is set up to hear. With this understood, it seems fair to say that for consensual morals offenses (1) is true. Those who argue for decriminalization of consensual morals offenses because they are "victimless crimes" do so on the assumption that the truth of (1) implies the truth of (2). But the truth of (2) is quite independent of the truth of (1), and it is precisely the truth of (2) which proponents of maintaining the criminal status of consensual acts would refuse to concede.

In other words, if I believe, for example, that prostitution ought to be a crime, I am ready to concede the truth of (1) but not of (2), and this is a perfectly consistent position. I acknowledge not only the fact that there is no individual who feels harmed and who is willing and able to complain and testify; I acknowledge as well that this fact causes unique practical problems for law enforcers. But I still do not acknowledge that prostitution harms no one. Rather, I hold that it harms the prostitute, the patron, the surrounding society and so forth, in indirect, yet sufficiently important, ways to justify using the legal apparatus to discourage its occurrence. In fact, my position would not be that prostitution ought to be a crime even though it is victimless. My position would be that prostitution is not a victimless crime at all, but rather a crime whose victims are not ready or able to complain and are therefore all the more in need of the state's protection.

If the proponent of decriminalization can prove that morals offenses are victimless in the sense of (2), then there exists a conclusive argument for decriminalization. However, this is not at all an easy thing to prove; it is clearly not proven by establishing the truth of (1), since it is perfectly possible for an act to harm people who either don't feel harmed (the prostitute or the patron may be psychologically harmed in ways that dull their very sensitivity to the harm they endure[5] or who feel harmed but not by an specific incidence of the act

(the community may well be harmed by the overall impact of many
acts of prostitution though no one act can be identified as the offending
one, just as lawns are damaged because many people walk across
them even though no single act of walking on the grass does any damage).[6] Hence, if valid moral grounds for decriminalization consistent
with the ideals of our criminal law exist, they must be sought elsewhere. As suggested above, this problem leads us in search of a
proper understanding of the relationship of law and morality in the
Anglo-American tradition.

The Anglo-American legal tradition is not morally neutral. It
is hoped that by now the reader is convinced that no legal system
could be morally neutral. What distinguishes the Anglo-American
tradition is its attempt to base the law on a minimal moral foundation
to which all rational individuals can be presumed to agree, regardless
of their other moral-belief differences. The promotion of two values
appears to be at the core of our legal tradition: the prevention of suffering and the protection of liberty. Unlike Greek and medieval legal
systems which often sought to build into the law a picture of human
virtue which might not be generally shared by all, the strength of our
law lies in its attempt to skim the values in the law down to those
which it may presume all individuals share. That is, regardless of
how individuals differ as to what constitutes moral excellence or virtue, we can assume that they want to avoid suffering and to have the
liberty to act out their conception of excellence or virtue. This isn't
to say that every last human being would agree on this, but rather to
point out why our law seems at its core not to rest on narrow sec-
tarian moral preferences.

There is a unique advantage to be gained from basing a legal
system on what might be called "lowest common denominator" values.
The advantage is in what is generally called "legitimacy." Legitimacy
is the quality we ascribe to a political-legal order when we believe it
has a right to make and enforce its rules and that we have a general
moral obligation to obey those rules—"general" since it is no incon-
sistency to disobey a particular law on moral grounds while still
acknowledging the legitimacy of the larger legal order. Even in the
requirement that disobedience be justified on moral grounds, we
acknowledge our moral obligation to obey the law ceterus parebus.[7]
On the whole, a legal order will be legitimate to all those who find it
serves to promote the values they cherish. It is for this reason that
basing a legal order on a particular picture of human excellence, or
on a particular religious confession, inevitably leads to the alienation
of nonbelievers. If they comply with the law, they do so out of fear
of punishment not out of recognition of its legitimacy, and a legal order is only likely to be effective if it is widely perceived as legitimate.
To keep the law down to protecting values which presumably all share

because they are human beings, not because they belong to some particular religion or profess some particular creed, is to base the law on a foundation most likely to be widely viewed as legitimate. [8]

It is this very virtue which leads to the confusion of believing that the law can be purged of morality. Basing the law on "lowest common denominator" moral values is to base them on values so widely shared that commitment to them is taken for granted. The desire for liberty and the avoidance of suffering are so closely connected to what we are, as human beings capable of shaping our destinies and vulnerable to pain and frustration, that we easily forget that commitment to these values is a moral commitment. Forgetting this, it becomes possible to believe that the law is distinguishable into laws which express moral preferences (laws against prostitution) and laws which do not (laws against murder).

The real distinction is between laws resting on "lowest common denominator" moral preferences and those resting on more narrowly held moral beliefs. What is ordinarily styled as the legislation of morality, is the "legislation of narrowly held moral beliefs." The drive to purge the law of the legislation of morality, is in truth the drive to purge the law of all moral preferences which are not widely viewed as legitimate. And this drive is crucial precisely because, to the extent that the law expresses narrow moral beliefs, it is in danger of violating the broad moral beliefs on which it rests and from which it derives its legitimacy. To understand this is to grasp the soundest argument for the decriminalization of the so-called "morals" offenses.

The very values a legitimate legal order protects are those most directly threatened by law itself: liberty and the prevention of suffering. First of all, any law as a prohibition is necessarily a limitation of liberty. Secondly, any law, as a threat of punishment, is necessarily a specification of conditions under which suffering (including the deprivation of liberty) will be imposed. The virtue of laws based on these lowest common denominator values is that they promote more liberty and prevent more suffering than they threaten. In other words, even a law against murder limits liberty (the liberty to rid your world of an unwanted person for good) and threatens suffering (the suffering of punishment for violating the law). It seems obvious, however, that there is more liberty and less suffering in a society which limits the liberty to take a life and threatens punishment for it than one which does not. Hence, such a law can clearly be justified as promoting liberty and freedom from suffering.

Compare this with a law such as that prohibiting homosexual relations between consenting adults. [9] As a law it is already a limitation on liberty (on everyone's liberty, whether one chooses to exercise it or not) and a threat of suffering. What does it gain for a society to balance this cost against basic values? Since we are talking about a consensual act one need not be a party to it if one does not wish to be. Thus, no one's liberty is enhanced by laws which forbid homosexual relations, and no one's suffering is materially lessened. It might be argued that the existence of homosexuality itself limits some people's liberty to stroll comfortably in certain areas of town, and imposes suffering on some people, that is, the suffering of knowing that the "natural order" as they conceive it is being violated. Quite simply, these deprivations are the sort which must be disregarded in a society committed to liberty. If the suffering and the deprivation of liberty to move about which stem simply from the bare knowledge that something personally offensive is going on were to count against an act then there could be no liberty do to anything which others didn't like—that is, no liberty at all.[10] None of this argues against laws which protect people from having certain practices imposed on them even in the form of offensive public displays. It does argue that to make a consensual act a crime simply because it is offensive to some people is to limit liberty and impose suffering with no countervailing gain of similar worth.

It seems that the strongest case against keeping the so-called "morals" offenses on the books is to be found here. If a given act imposes no harm that limits liberty or causes suffering other than that which results from the bare knowledge that it is going on, then to make it a crime is to violate the very moral values that make the legal order worthy of widespread allegiance. Such laws are not to be eliminated because the legislation of morality should be eliminated. They are to be eliminated precisely because a legitimate legal order is one which legislates the most universally held moral preferences.

NOTES

1. For an interesting study of the impact of law on moral attitudes towards drugs, see Duster (1970).

2. For a look at the impact of Prohibition Era politics on law enforcement, see Richardson (1974: 86-93).

3. On the difference between legal rules and moral rules, see Baier (1965: 67-109) and Hart (1961: 163-76). Lon Fuller makes the distinction between the morality of aspiration and the morality of duty, the former excompassing acts like charity and heroism which must be freely undertaken to be of value, the latter encompassing acts like forbearing from violence and theft, which are still valuable if realized through legal coercion (1969: 5-9).

4. On the relationship between coercive legal institutions and individual moral autonomy, see Wolff (1970) and my reply to him (Reiman 1972).

5. Some have held that the prostitute in particular is victimized by prostitution, see Women Endorsing Decriminalization (1973).

6. For a good discussion of the thorny problems raised by the notion of "victimless crimes," see Schur and Bedau (1974). For some of the philosophical problems involved in defining the concept "victim," see Reiman (1974a).

7. On the issues of legitimacy, legal and moral obligation, and civil disobedience, see Rawls (1968) and Reiman (1972).

8. This is no doubt one source of the appeal of social contract theories of justice and political obligation (see Rawls 1971), and social contract theories of the source of criminal justice authority (see Reiman 1974b). For a critical view of social contract theories, see Macpherson (1962).

9. For a discussion of the moral issues posed by laws against homosexuality, see Leiser (1973: 33-68).

10. A similar conclusion is reached by Hart (1963: 46).

REFERENCES

Baier, K. 1965. The Moral Point of View. New York: Random House.

Duster, T. 1970. The Legislation of Morality: Law, Drugs, and Moral Judgments. New York: Free Press.

Fuller, L. 1969. The Morality of Law. New Haven: Yale University Press.

Hart, H. L. A. 1961. The Concept of Law. London: Oxford University Press.

———. 1963. Law, Liberty, and Morality. New York: Random House.

Leiser, B. 1973. Liberty, Justice, and Morals: Contemporary Value Conflicts. New York: Macmillan.

Macpherson, C. B. 1962. The Political Theory of Possessive Individualism: Hobbes and Locke. New York: Oxford University Press.

Rawls, J. 1971. A Theory of Justice. New York: Harper & Row.

———. 1975. The justification of civil disobedience. In Today's Moral Problems, ed. R. Wasserstrom. New York: Macmillan.

Reiman, J. 1972. In Defense of Political Philosophy. New York: Harper & Row.

———. 1974a. Victims, harm, and justice. In Victimology: A New Focus, Volume I: Theoretical Issues in Victimology, eds. I. Drapkin and E. Viano. Lexington, Mass.: Lexington Books.

———. 1974b. Police autonomy vs. police authority: a philosophical perspective. In The Police Community: Dimensions of an Occupational Subculture, eds. J. Goldsmith and S. Goldsmith. Pacific Palisades, Calif.: Palisades Publishers.

Richardson, J. F. 1974. Urban Police in the United States. Port Washington, New York: Kennikat Press.

Schur, E. and H. A. Bedau. 1974. Victimless Crimes: Two Sides of a Controversy. Englewood Cliffs, New Jersey: Prentice-Hall.

Wolff, R. P. 1970. In Defense of Anarchism. New York: Harper & Row.

Women Endorsing Decriminalization. 1973. Prostitution a non-victim crime? Issues in Criminology 8 (Fall): 137-62.

10

PRE- AND POST-WATERGATE MORALITY: A CASE OF LEGAL AND NORMATIVE AMBIGUITY

Jerome Himelhoch

On October 15, 1973, in a press conference three days after his resignation, former Vice-President Agnew resorted to an unusual form of self-exculpation. He asserted that the case against him "boils down to the accusation that I permitted my fund-raising activities and my contract-dispensing activities to overlap in an unethical and unlawful manner. Perhaps judged by the new, post-Watergate political morality, I did. But the prosecution's assertion that I was the initiator and gray eminence in an unprecedented and complex scheme of extortion is not realistic" (New York Times: 1973; emphasis added). This time the great phrase-monger coined a term which, this chapter will argue, elucidated an important sociological truth: a significant constriction, after Watergate, of the range of tolerable behavior for the members of the political and economic elite. Since the Agnew speech, there have been many words and some federal and state legislative deeds which reflect the new ethical perspective. For example, as one Washington correspondent commented on Edward M. Kennedy's withdrawal from the 1976 battle for the presidency:

> [the decision] reflected also the realities of post-Watergate political morality. . . [many Democratic leaders] believed that the Watergate scandal put a new premium on the political and personal morality and integrity of candidates for public office. . . . Politicians agree that the Chappaquiddick issue has become much more damaging to Kennedy since the Watergate scandals (St. Louis Post-Dispatch: 1974).

This research was supported by the Center for Metropolitan and Community Studies, University of Missouri, St. Louis.

I wish to thank Charles P. Koor and Harry H. Bash for their comments on this paper.

This is not to suggest that we have already built a new Jeru-
salem on the Potomac, but to hypothesize that a whole area of presidential behavior has been legally and normatively redefined. The
exposure by the media, the observations of presidential critics, the
Ervin Committee hearings, the firing of Archibald Cox, the grand
jury indictments, the House Judiciary Committee's Articles of Impeachment, Nixon's increasingly obvious evasion, equivocation, and
refusal to supply evidence, and finally, the publication of the presidential tapes have produced these redefinitions. In Marxist terms,
the whole generation of "false consciousness" which supported the
warfare state, the imperial presidency, and the American empire
has been partially—but only partially and perhaps only temporarily—
dissipated.

In this chapter, a portion of an integrative psychosocial model
of deviance causation will be applied to these shifts on conventionality
and legality.[1] According to the model, everyone acts in a psychosocial field which may be represented by a circle divided into a number of sectors. These sectors vary in terms of degree of conventionality from unconventional ("unethical" or "deviant") through normatively ambiguous to conventional ("ethical" or "conformist").
While the placement of specific acts in one of these categories will
vary from one subculture to another, there is evidence to suggest
that at a given point in time the overwhelming majority of Americans
will have developed a normative consensus concerning certain acts—
for example, murder, aggravated assault, and child molestation.
Concerning certain other acts, like abortion, defiance of court-ordered
busing, marijuana smoking, and bugging the premises of radical or
militant groups, there is normative dissensus. Some regard such
acts as ethical, other as unethical, and many others are uncertain.
For the last group, the acts would be normatively ambiguous. During
periods of sharp value conflict between large, legitimate subcultural
groups, or during a period of rapid social change, there is likely to
be widespread normative ambiguity.

The sectors in my model are also classified according to degree of legality, ranging from legal through legally ambiguous to illegal. Although there is a trend toward consistency between laws
and mores, the two may, and during periods of rapid change do, vary
independently. Accordingly, in contemporary American society, for
each degree of legality, there are all three degrees of conventionality.
Acts which are illegal or legally ambiguous but conventional fall into
two categories. First, there are infractions of antiquated laws which
lag behind changing norms, such as curfew violation, drinking, or
premarital coitus by older adolescents. Second, there are crimes by
respectable and relatively powerful persons, such as police officers,
corporation executives, and presidents. They are classified as

conventional especially when such crimes follow established occupational customs and are sanctioned by professional peers. The contention here is that macrosocial trends in American society had partially or fully legitimated many presidential acts which, in terms of the post-Watergate morality, are crimes. In terms of the present model, many acts which were previously legal or legally ambiguous have now been redefined by Congress, the media, various opinion leaders, and a majority of voters as illegal. Similarly, that which was formerly conventional or normatively ambiguous is now labeled unethical or unconventional.

It seems self-evident that there have been significant redefinitions of legality and conventionality, but to demonstrate precisely what they are presents data-collection problems of staggering proportions. Moreover, the process of redefinition is as yet unfinished and unpredictable, although Ford's pardon of Nixon succeeded in stopping the major drama before its denouement. Accordingly, my suggestions are to be taken as mere hypotheses.

The decisions of judges and juries in the numerous trials of political dissidents, such as Daniel Ellsberg, Angela Davis, the New Haven Black Panthers, the Chicago Eight, and the Berrigans, reveal definitions of legality and conventionality different from those applied to the Rosenberg and Hiss trials and to the judicial punishments of "fellow travelers" in the heyday of McCarthyism. What intervened was a long, disastrous, unpopular war and public revulsion against a corrupt, amoral, power-hungry administration. For part of the society, the unconventional has become at least conventionally ambiguous and, for another, it has become conventional. There have been similar shifts in the definition of legality on the part of judges and lawyers.

In the absence of survey research data, the Articles of Impeachment voted out of the House Judiciary Committee may be our best statement of the new definitions which constitute the post-Watergate morality. The committee supported three articles: obstruction of justice (cover-up of the burglary of the Democratic National Committee), abuse of power, and contempt of Congress in refusing to supply tapes and other evidence to the committee. The secret bombings of Cambodia failed to win a majority as a result of congressional argument that key leaders on Capitol Hill had been kept informed and that Congress itself had a long history of relinquishing its constitutional war-making powers to strong Chief Executives (Newsweek 1974). One might conclude from this that presidential war making without congressional authorization is at most normatively and legally ambiguous, although Congress has passed some legislation curbing the president's power in this area. Finally, the committee failed to report out an article charging the president with income tax evasion and making improper governmental expenditures on his residential properties.

Article I clearly condemns the bugging or burglarizing of the premises of the major opposition party. This effort to destroy the other major centrist or liberal-centrist party has occasioned the most public outrage. Article II is of great interest because it deals with the Nixonian escalation of established traditions of presidental violation of the civil rights of citizens—usually left sectarians and black militants. Here, Chomsky is perhaps correct in his assertion that Nixon's real crime was to harass individuals of power, and to invade their civil liberties, whereas previous presidents had confined themselves to the repression of unpopular minorities. Chomsky points out that FBI memoranda, approved during the Kennedy and Johnson administrations, took for granted that

> the political police have the authority to suppress dis-
> sent, disrupt organizations and undermine their leader-
> ship, foment conflicts, 'neutralize' potential activists
> by deceit, ridicule, fraudulent arrest, or other means
> to be developed under the 'enthusiastic and imaginative
> approach' that agents are 'urged to take . . . to this new
> counter-intelligence endeavor' (Chomsky 1974).

The Second Article of Impeachment voted out of the House Judiciary Committee condemns the attempted politicalization of government bureaucracies in the style of fascist and communist dictatorships. The use of the IRS, CIA, and FBI against political enemies for purposes unrelated to national security and law enforcement are, according to the committee, impeachable offenses. But how much are we protected from future harassment under a broad interpretation of national security?

The crucial question for the future is how far the redefinition of conventionality and legality for political, military, and economic elites will go. We need bold leadership for the "denazification" of our institutions. Ford obviously had no intention of playing this role. With the advent of a new liberal-centrist coalition, the new definitions conceivably will be translated into new institutions. Otherwise, there is danger, as Davis (1974) predicts, that far from dispelling false consciousness, the aftermath of Watergate may be a reinforcement of the myth that the system inevitably works and, then, the most reactionary elements in the power elites may return to business as usual.

NOTE

1. For an explanation of my model, see Himelhoch (1974).

REFERENCES

Chomsky, N. 1974. Watergate and other crimes. Ramparts 12, no. 11 (June): 31–36.

Davis, D. L. 1974. Watergate: government by negotiation. Theory and Society 1: 111–15.

Himelhoch, J. 1974. A psychosocial model for the reduction of lower-class youth crime. In Crime Prevention and Social Control, eds. E. Sagarin and R. Akers. New York: Praeger.

New York Times. 1973. Transcript of former Vice-President Agnew's TV and radio address to the nation. Oct. 16, p. 34.

Newsweek. 1974. The committee takes its bows. Aug. 12, p. 27.

St. Louis Post-Dispatch. 1973. Kennedy won't run for presidency. Sept. 24, p. 1.

11

NEWSPAPER REPORTING OF CRIME AND JUSTICE: ANTECEDENTS OF A MORAL ORDER

John C. Meyer, Jr.

Because most persons have not been the victims of or witnesses to a serious crime, many students of crime have hypothesized that a person's conception of the crime "problem" may be due largely to information derived from vicarious sources such as the mass media (President's Commission, 1967). When this occurs, the individual constructs a "social reality" of crime on the basis of the content imbedded in the various media frames. As Richard Quinney has suggested, "a conception, diffused throughout the society, becomes the basis for the public's view of reality" (1970: 285).

As the term is employed here, "media" refers to those forms of communication serving many receivers (the members of a particularly defined audience) from a single source capable of stimulating attention. Among these communication types are newspapers, magazines, movies, radio, and television. In such modes of communication there exists an impersonal bond between the sending source and receivers of the message—unlike the dynamics involved in face-to-face communication. Because these media are able to serve many persons by directing messages from a single source, a true one-to-many relationship is established.

Although the media messages may be directed at no one in particular, it is possible that an individual's cognitive frame of reference may include the messages received as unique and salient—fitting them into one's past and future in such a way that they make sense in daily life. If such a one-to-one correspondence is established at an individual's level, the media may serve not only to convey but also to legitimate the message content (see Wilkening 1956). If this occurs, the first step has been taken in the construction of a "social reality."

Of all media forms, the newspaper has most often been cited as a prime source for creating conceptions of crime (see, for example, Quinney 1970, Davis 1962, Sheff 1969). In both popular (Holmes 1966, St. Johns 1962) and scholarly literature (Quinney 1970), it has further been contended that the media frame—the context in which the message is presented—may vary from paper to paper such that "one's construction of a conception of crime depends upon which newspaper he happens to read" (Quinney 1970: 282). Figure 1 shows this process in its most simplified form.

As Figure 1 shows, a person's interpretation of both personal experiences as well as mental images of crime and justice may be affected by the kind and quality of crime news reported in the press. In other words, if there is variability in the manner with which crime and justice matters are reported by the press, we might expect that difference to be instrumental in shaping public opinion. This chapter begins to explore this process by seeking to discover whether or not variations among newspapers' reporting styles can be identified.

Although there have been many changes within newspaper publishing corporations during the past few decades, one constant comment voiced by academic and lay observers of the newspaper scene is that the New York Times and the New York Daily News are "different." That is to say, some research evidence points in the direction that the Times is less occupied with crime reporting than the Daily News (Bachmoth et al. 1960, Quinney 1970: 282-83). Indeed, many others aver that the Times and the Daily News hold polar positions vis-a-vis their general philosophies in news coverage. In short, people consider the Times to be more objective in its news reporting style when compared with the Daily News' sensationalistic presentation (Friendly and Goldfarb 1967: 36, Otto 1963: 19).

To determine whether or not these two papers report crime news differently, a sample of matched stories was used. Editions of the Times and News for the period from August, 1970 to October, 1970 served as a sampling frame. Thirty days within that period were then randomly selected. Using the morning editions of both papers for those 30 days, 37 crime stories that presented the same stage of detection or processing were included in the final sample.

Although this procedure strictly curtailed the sample size, such careful delineation of criteria for inclusion may have served as a filter through which, for purposes of the research, no extraneous information might have passed. It also limited the sensational "scoops" that might have otherwise been presented in one or the other of the papers. In all, 9, 20, and 8 stories were selected from the months of August, September, and October, respectively.

To provide some measure of the crimes reported in the sample stories, an analysis was made of the sample offenses. Although the sample was artificially restricted by the strict criteria for inclusion, this analysis presents some insights into press-reporting patterns. It may be that by over- or underreporting certain offenses, the press may generally convey to the public a false impression of the crime picture. Table 2 presents these 37 crimes and compares them with data published in the FBI Uniform Crime Reports for 1970.

FIGURE 1

Impact of Crime Reporting on Public Perceptions

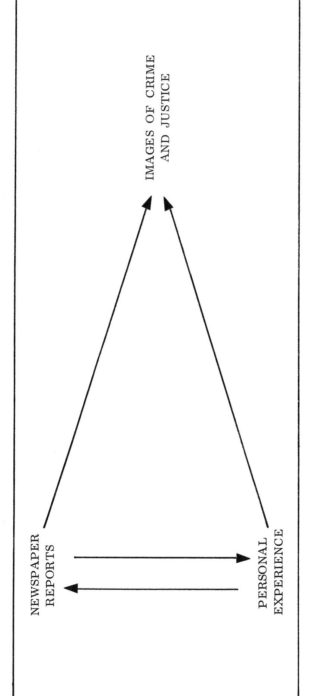

Source: Compiled by the author. Feedback loops have not been drawn from the developing images of crime and justice to the antecedents. It should be understood that such feedback would play an important part in the process shown here.

149

TABLE 2

37 Crimes Reported in the Press for August, September and
October 1970 and FBI Data for Six Index Crimes

	Press-reported Crimes				UCR Crimes		
	Total		Part I Crimes				
	N	%	$\%^a$	Rank	N^b	$\%^a$	Rank^a
Homicide	13	35.1	48.1	1	15,810	0.3	6
Bombing	6	16.2	—	—	—	—	—
Assault	5	13.5	18.5	2	329,940	5.9	5
Larceny^c	3	8.1	11.1	4	1,746,100	31.6	2
Robbery	3	8.1	11.1	4	348,380	6.3	4
Burglary	2	5.4	7.4	5	2,169,300	39.2	1
Disorderly conduct	1	2.7	—	—	—	—	—
Escape	1	2.7	—	—	—	—	—
Auto theft	1	2.7	3.7	6	921,400	16.7	3
Firearms violations	1	2.7	—	—	—	—	—
Drugs	1	2.7	—	—	—	—	—
TOTALS	37	99.9%^{d}	99.9%^{d}	—	5,530,930	100.1%^{d}	—

[a]For six Part I offense classifications which were reported in the press.

[b]From Uniform Crime Reports—1970 (U.C.R. 1971: 6); data are for the six Part I offenses which were reported in the press.

[c]$50.00 and over.

[d]Does not add to 100.0% due to rounding.

Source: Compiled by author.

Of those crimes reported on by the press, only one is relatively minor—disorderly conduct (2.7 percent). It is probable that this one crime would not have been reported except that a noted celebrity was involved. Of the remaining 36 offenses reported, ten separate crime classifications are involved; 27 (72.9 percent) of the crimes fall within six Part I offenses reported by the FBI. Not only, therefore, are the more serious offenses (homicide, assault, larceny, robbery, burglary, and auto theft) more frequently reported in the press, but they also are reported in greater proportion than found in the FBI data—no matter how deficient those data are (rho = -.76)

In this restricted sample of 27 press-reported Part I offenses, 48.1 percent of the stories dealt with homicide while only three-tenths of one percent of the index crimes (within the six index crimes enumerated above) reported by the FBI were homicides. Burglary, the most common of FBI crimes with 39.2 percent of those crimes reported in the sample, was sharply underreported in the press (7.4 percent).

It is clear from these data that newspapers tend to underreport the most frequent crimes (such as burglary) and overreport the least frequent offense—homicide. For the data on media coverage, crimes of personal violence account for a greater proportion of the sample than do crimes against property. "As newspaper men have always known, a good murder is worth a dozen thefts or swindles any day" (Collins 1968: 40).

RESEARCH METHOD AND SAMPLE

Because the research was not primarily concerned with the crimes reported in these stories, each article selected for the sample was analyzed by enumerating every discrete informational bit presented that dealt with the event, the criminal, and the decisions made by the authorities concerning the crime or criminal (see Wilkins 1965a). This procedure was utilized instead of measuring column inches because important information may be contained in, for example, the numerals of an address or the age of a suspect or victim. However, column inches were also measured to provide some continuity in research.

Although the research method used here was particularly well suited for testing nondirectional hypotheses—that is, that differences of any sort exist—specific directional hypotheses were derived from theory and data in the existing literature[1]:

H[1]. J. Holmes, in an early article (1929: 258), noted that conservative papers in New York City tend to print more column inches of crime news than the more sensational papers. Therefore, it was hypothesized that the Times would print more informational bits per article than the News.

H$_2$. Based on Quinney's work (1970: 282), it was hypothesized that the News would print a greater number of informational bits concerning the events and the offender than the Times.

H$_3$. If the Times is more "objective" and comprehensive in its coverage, it was hypothesized that it would tend to print more of the "decisions" made and actions taken by the criminal justice system than the News.

FINDINGS

Table 3 presents the Times and News articles which have been categorized by a procedure discussed by Bryson and Phillips (1975). Although it is seen that there is little difference between the two papers (tau$_b$ = .01), the News did opt for the shorter story. When the data are categorized into two groups (again using the method discussed in Bryson and Phillips 1975), 64.9 percent of the News' stories were less than 350 bits in length while only 48.6 percent of the Times' stories were of that length (x^2 = 1.98, not significant at .01 with 1 df). The minor difference between the papers may be a function of their relative sizes. The News, a tabloid, may simply have proportionately less space available per story than the larger Times.

TABLE 3

Distribution of Crime Articles by Number of Informational Bits

Informational Bits	Times		News		Total	
	N	%	N	%	N	%
0-150	9	24.3	7	18.9	16	21.6
151-250	3	8.1	9	24.3	12	16.2
251-350	6	16.2	8	21.6	14	18.9
351-450	6	16.2	6	16.2	12	16.2
451-600	5	13.5	3	8.1	8	10.8
601+	8	21.6	4	10.8	12	16.2
Total	37	99.9%[*]	37	99.9%[*]	74	99.9%[*]

[*]Does not add to 100.0% due to rounding.
Source: Compiled by author.

Using column inches as a measure, the Times allotted a total of 381 to these stories as compared to the News' 302. However, when pictorial content is considered, the News—"New York's Picture Newspaper"—devoted more of its space than the Times to pictures accompanying these articles—199.75 and 175.0 inches respectively.

The data presented in Table 3, and in Table 4 below, show that the Times did devote a greater number of informational bits to these 37 stories than did the News. However, when using the "t" test for matched pairs, it is not possible to reject the null hypothesis— or accept the research hypothesis—given these data. For the total number of informational bits per story, $t = 2.12$, which is not significant at the .01 level, using the one-tailed test.

Therefore, although these data do not attain statistical significance, in a practical sense at least the "spirit" of H_1 was supported. That is, the Times tended to print longer stories than did the News.[2] When the areas devoted to photographs and illustrations were taken into account, the total space devoted to crime stories was more nearly equal, although the News may have printed proportionately more owing to its smaller page size.

To examine H_2 and H_3, Table 4 summarizes the thirty-seven crimes along the dimensions of event, criminal, and decisions. The nature of sample selection, it will be recalled, is one which severely limited the sample size. This factor must, therefore, be kept in mind when interpreting the conclusions to follow.

An examination of the data dealing with the informational bits devoted to news about criminal events showed that there was no real difference between the Times and the News. That is, each paper devoted approximately half of the total number of informational bits per story to reporting details of the crime itself. The News had a slight edge (51 percent) over the Times (49 percent) but this difference of only two percentage points cannot approach either statistical or practical significance ($t = 1.32$, not significant at the .01 level).

A closer examination shows that the Times devoted more of the total informational bits to the crime in August than did the News; the News, however, reported more than did the Times concerning the criminal event in September; and in October the proportions of all informational bits devoted to the event by the two papers were most nearly equal. And in terms of reporting about the criminal, the same sort of results obtained. While the News devoted two percent more of the informational bits in these thirty-seven articles to reporting about the criminal than the Times, the difference cannot be considered significant ($t = 1.35$, not significant). A monthly examination of the data revealed an almost equal distribution between the two papers. It would appear that when both papers report on the same crime, on the same day, in the same edition, and concerning the same stage of

TABLE 4

Informational Bits in 74 Crime Articles Analyzed by the Data
Presented on the Event, Criminal and Decisions

	Total		Event		Criminal		Decision	
	N	%	N	%	N	%	N	%
Times								
August	1,817	13	881	48	159	9	391	16
September	7,681	55	4,022	52	1,593	21	1,758	23
October	4,737	32	2,057	44	369	8	1,025	22
Total	14,235	100%	6,960	49%	2,121	15%	3,174	22%
News								
August	2,442	21	885	36	213	9	355	15
September	5,825	50	3,578	61	1,246	21	995	17
October	3,417	29	1,532	45	488	14	512	15
Total	11,684	100%	5,995	51%	1,947	17%	1,862	16%

Those informational bits not dealing with the crime, perpetrator or official action are excluded from analysis. This results in the "Total" column not equaling the sums of the other three.
Source: Compiled by author.

processing, there is little difference in the proportion of informational bits devoted to news about the crime or the criminal. Hypothesis 2, therefore, cannot be supported by these data.

Hypothesis 3—that the Times would allot a higher number of informational bits than the News to reporting about decisions—cannot be supported by the sample data ($t = 2.12$, not significant). However, of the three elements under study, the largest spread of percentage points between the Times and the News concerned the reporting of information about official actions (22 and 16 percent for the Times and News, respectively). This difference may, however, have been an artifact of the sizes of the papers. That is, the amount of information reported about decisions may be determined by the amount of available page space set by the editorial policies of the papers. Caution is therefore required interpreting these results.

A monthly analysis shows that the Times consistently devoted a larger proportion of informational bits to official actions than the News. The differences, as can be seen in Table 4, were not large enough to permit conclusive statements to be made. For each month, however, differences are in the direction anticipated by hypothesis 3. All that may be said with any degree of certainty was that the Times appeared to print more of the criminal justice system's activities in the apprehension and processing of alleged criminals than did the News.

SUMMARY AND CONCLUSIONS

This research has, in an exploratory fashion, examined one facet of the contention that newspapers have varying styles of crime reporting. What is problematic for this research is the assumption that there are measurable differences between newspapers which are stylistically different, and that one can assume that a style of reporting runs across all forms of news reported and can be quantitatively measured. To test if, in fact, this difference does exist, the content of seventy-four news stories reporting on thirty-seven events was analyzed. This analysis examined the number of informational bits devoted to reporting about the event, the criminal and the official decisions taken on the matter.

The research has shown that there are no significant differences between the Times and the News when a quantitative measure of the content is used. Of course, further research into the differences in style between these two papers should not simply assume that there are no quantitative differences. The results of this research are based upon data collected from a small sample of news stories. Larger studies are required to validate these conclusions.

What this study does suggest is that one of the most fruitful avenues for future research might be an analysis of the differential impact on the reporting of official actions. It was seen that the largest difference between these two papers was in the space each devoted to the actions taken by officials in the detection and apprehension of criminals.

This may suggest that the public's feeling of well-being is directly affected by the newspaper coverage of the "war on crime" as reported in the newspaper one happens to read. Because so few people are the victims of serious crimes, it may be that the actual fear of crime is created and reinforced by newspaper coverage of crime and what is being done about it. It is a common observation that the news media can create a "crime wave" (Steffens 1931: 285-91). It might be possible that newspapers are, or should be, a crucial factor in the creation of an image of the appropriate official action on crime control. As Felix Frankfurter wrote, "The public derives its opinions about 'the administration of criminal justice' from the kind, the quality, and the volume of newspaper matter affecting criminal justice" (Cleveland Foundation 1922: 518).

If, then, newspapers—and media generally—are creating a picture of society's moral order through their manner of judicial-process reporting, we need to know exactly what that image is. Certainly, aspects of the criminal process, such as corrections (Wilkins 1956b), are not reported in the same volume as the more prominent and, perhaps, more entertaining, elements.[3] What remains is to discover if this difference in reporting has consequences for public images of crime and justice.

The role of the news media has become acutely important in times when "law and order" has become a political rallying point. Perhaps the manner in which crime news, and the activities of the justice process, are reported needs to be studied using an information-system approach. The inputs of the citizenry's conceptions of crime and justice must necessarily be the outputs of a long and somewhat circuitous process of shaping and reporting factual events. The systematic nature of that flow, the impacts of sociopolitical phenomena, and the payoffs of the system's outputs, must be studied as a process if we are ever to assess the impact of the media on the public view of crime and justice.

NOTES

1. The three hypotheses are given in the form commonly referred to as "research hypotheses." What are actually tested are the "null" hypotheses. For convenience, the former are used in the textual discussions. In all hypothesis testing, the level of significance used is .010.

2. This does not imply that I am making short shrift of the statistical test. Quite the contrary! What is meant is that the practical—that is, nonstatistical—significance attached to these data may have "practical" utility in the design of future research along these lines.

3. As is seen in Table 4, only about 20 percent of the content in the sample stories was for reporting on the actions of the criminal justice system. As a rule, feature stories on the operations of the criminal justice system are relatively uncommon in newspapers.

Although this is somewhat true for other areas of reporting as well—although, it may be argued, many areas such as government have regular columns reporting on the latest developments—it is still interesting to speculate on what the effects might be of having a regular feature reporting on criminal justice operations and problems.

REFERENCES

Bachmoth, R. , S. M. Miller and L. Rosen. 1960. Juvenile delinquency in the daily press. Alpha Kappa Delta 30 (Spring): 47-51.

Bryson, K. R. and D. P. Phillips. 1975. Method for classifying interval-scale and ordinal-scale data. In Sociological Methodology—1975, ed. D. R. Heise. San Francisco: Jossey-Bass.

Cleveland Foundation Survey of the Administration of Criminal Justice of Cleveland, Ohio. 1922. Criminal Justice in Cleveland. Cleveland: The Cleveland Foundation.

Collins, P. 1968. Dickens and Crime. Bloomington: University of Indiana Press.

Davis, F. J. 1962. Crime news in Colorado newspapers. American Journal of Sociology 57 (January): 325-30.

Federal Bureau of Investigation. 1971. Uniform Crime Reports—1970. Washington, D.C.: U.S. Government Printing Office.

Friendly, A. and R. L. Goldfarb. 1967. Crime and Publicity. New York: The Twentieth-Century Fund.

Holmes, J. L. 1929. Crime and the press. Journal of Criminal Law and Criminology 20 (August): 258.

Holmes, P. 1966. Retrial. New York: Bantam.

Otto, H. A. 1963. Sex and violence on the American newsstand. Journalism Quarterly 40 (Winter): 19.

President's Commission on Law Enforcement and Administration of Justice. 1967. Task Force Report: Crime and its Impact. Washington, D.C.: U.S. Government Printing Office.

Quinney, R. 1970. The Social Reality of Crime. Boston: Little, Brown.

St. Johns, A. R. 1962. Final Verdict. New York: Bantam.

Sheff, T. 1966. Being Mentally Ill. Chicago: Aldine.

Steffens, L. 1931. Autobiography. New York: The Literary Guild.

Wilkening, E. A. 1956. Roles of communicating agents in technological change in agriculture. Social Forces 34 (May): 361-67.

Wilkins, L. T. 1965a. New thinking in criminal statistics. Journal
of Criminal Law, Criminology and Police Science 56 (September)
277-84.

———. 1965b. The evaluation of penal treatments. Sociological
Review, Monograph No. 9.

PART

THE SYSTEM OF JUSTICE
AND ITS ACTORS

12

THE PROSECUTING ATTORNEY AND THE LABELING PROCESS: AN ANALYSIS OF THE APPLICATION OF OFFICIAL SANCTION

L. Thomas Winfree, Jr. and Lawrence Kielich

Criminological research involving what has come to be called the "labeling perspective" emphasizes the process of defining persons as "criminal-like." Contrary to more traditional approaches to the criminal as someone who breaks the law and is, therefore, somehow different from others, this perspective deemphasizes the criminal act. Moreover, labeling research typically examines either the person or persons being labeled or the persons doing the labeling or, more rarely, both (for example, see Kitsuse 1962, Becker 1963, Lemert 1967, Lofland 1969, Schur 1971, Hagan 1973). While this chapter is primarily concerned with the persons or agencies responsible for the labeling of others, particularly the role of the prosecuting attorney, it does not neglect the role of the persons being labeled. Indeed, symbolic or real actors must be present, for it is their behavior which is reacted to and, in turn, labeled by the labelers. This research investigates the impact of the labelers on the process of defining and labeling actors as deviant.

THE RESEARCH PROBLEM

The labelers represent neither a single group of persons nor a single aspect of the labeling process. That is, the influence of the labelers is felt at all junctures of the process. Initially, however, the labeling process is generally conceived of as a societal reaction to the behavior, real or imagined, of some individual. The primarily

This paper is a revision of papers presented at the annual meetings of the American Society of Criminology, November, 1974, and the Midwest Sociological Society, April, 1975.

unofficial interpersonal aspects of labeling are examined, for instance, in the works of Goffman (1961, 1963). If, for whatever reason, the labelers and the labeled are unable to reduce the dissonance, then an official agency of the community may be asked to intervene. Indeed, the community gives these agencies a mandate to act whenever some behavior is likely to or does result in dissonance. The impact of one such agency, the police, on the labeling process has received considerable attention (Stinchcombe 1963, Piliavin and Briar 1965, Skolnick 1966, Chambliss and Liell 1966). In the courtroom and correctional experience, Goldman (1963), Cameron (1964), Sudnow (1965), Skolnick (1966), and Cicourel (1968) all maintain that certain individuals receive differential treatment in the judicial process. Other writers have demonstrated that the impact of the correctional experience on the attainment and continuance of the deviant label is great (Garfinkel 1956; Goffman 1961, 1963; Green 1961, 1964; Schwartz and Skolnick 1962; Sieverdes 1972). Finally, the role of the prosecuting attorney, an important one in the criminal labeling process, has been the subject of several research projects (Sudnow 1965, Blumberg 1965, Skolnick 1967, Cole 1970, Neubauer 1974).

The current research is concerned with the participation of the prosecuting attorney and his or her office in the labeling process. The authors propose that the adversary role played by the prosecuting attorney is a crucial factor in the process whereby the accused could ultimately be accorded the official status of convicted criminal by the courts. It is generally accepted that persons who in some way are offended by the actual or assumed behavior of another are capable of reacting to that behavior officially and unofficially. In either case, the societal reactions are generally conceived of as early in the labeling process. The police, on the other hand, can react to the behavior proscribed by law as they perceive it or as it is brought to their attention by others. Again, they appear early in the initial process of labeling an individual as a deviant. The courtroom is a crucial point in the labeling process. Prior to and including this juncture, the individual could conceivably be absolved of all guilt and the label removed.[1] However, the court is limited to the cases brought before it and the charges levied.

The influence of the prosecuting attorney is felt at almost all of these junctures. First, the attorney operates under the same mandate as the police and could urge or order the police to enforce laws and statutes against, for example, pornography or sexual misconduct. Or, in the capacity as the attorney for the federal, state, county, or city government, he or she could seek or fail to seek the prosecution of a large industrial concern for violation of antipollution laws. In addition, if a charge is brought, the prosecuting attorney could decide to "make a deal" and let the defendant (a label in itself) "cop a plea" or prosecute to the fullest extent of the law. Finally, and this point is often related to the previous set of alternatives, the attorney could ask the judge for leniency or severity in the sentencing of the defendant. Therefore, it is easy to recognize that the role of the prosecuting attorney in the labeling process is multidimensional.

This chapter represents an attempt to investigate some determining factors in the role of the prosecuting attorney in the labeling process by focusing on three questions. First, what factors are considered by the prosecuting attorney's office in determining which cases will be prosecuted. Of particular concern is a discussion of the defining process engaged in by members of the prosecuting attorney's office in the determination of what constitutes a crime and who is a criminal. Second, once the decision to prosecute has been made, are there factors which influence the type of case presented by the prosecutor? Finally, are the persons in the prosecuting attorney's office aware of their potential impact on the individuals they are instrumental in having labeled as criminals?

METHOD

Data for this study were drawn from a study of the office of the county attorney located in a rural western state. The office of the county attorney is staffed by one full-time prosecuting attorney, two full-time deputies, and several part-time deputies. In addition, there are two full-time secretaries and one part-time secretary on the staff. Finally, the staff is augmented in the summer months by a number of junior and senior law students.

The county attorney has duties in addition to prosecution of the felonies and misdemeanors which occur within his jurisdiction. Routinely, they include the civil activities for the county. In order to facilitate the expeditious handling of all these matters, criminal and civil, the office is organized such that each of the deputies is primarily responsible for certain types of complaints. For example, one part-time deputy prosecutes virtually all drug-related offenses. Another deputy is responsible for all sanity and non-support cases. The county attorney shares the criminal and civil cases with the two full-time deputies. However, the county attorney feels that it is his obligation to try "all the big cases, especially the serious felonies." He believes that to do otherwise would "not give the voters their money's worth since they expect it of me."

The data collection consisted of two phases. The first phase, lasting approximately six weeks, involved nonparticipant observation and unstructured interviews with all members, permanent and temporary, of the county attorney's office. Specifically, two weeks were spent observing the daily work activities of the county attorney. This included not only sitting in on the preparation of cases and courtroom procedures, but also observing plea-bargaining sessions and other extra-trial activities. During this time initial contacts were also made in the offices of the sheriff, district court judges and justice court judges, and in the probation office. The initiation of these contacts was facilitated by the county attorney as he provided the introductions. The remaining four weeks were spent observing and talking with the deputies and law students. The majority of this time involved observing the techniques used by the law students in handling complaints and the liaison between law students and deputies. Besides a daily log, a file of the recurring topics was maintained in order to provide some direction for the more formalized interviews that were to follow.

During this initial stage of the research, it was best to act ignorant on the subjects of the law and criminal justice. The lawyers, staff, and law students, being professionals in this area, went out of their way to assist the poor academician who was "out of his bailiwick." Concern was rarely expressed about what the researcher was doing. Whenever the presence of the researcher became an issue, a simple explanation about a desire to understand the criminal justice system from the prosecutor's perspective would usually suffice. In fact, this answer not only satisfied those curious enough to ask but also opened up new topics of discussion concerning how they thought it ought to function and how it really worked.

The second phase of the data collection consisted of a series of in-depth interviews involving the nine members of the county attorney's staff. The county attorney was interviewed first. At his suggestion, the four law students were interviewed next. Finally, the four deputies were interviewed in as many days. This phase of the research was accomplished in approximately three weeks.

FINDINGS

There appear to be many factors which enter into the dramatization of deviant behavior at the prosecutorial level. In fact, the ones that first come to mind are usually physical evidence and sworn testimony. These are the criteria that are frequently mentioned in criminological and legal literature as the prerequisites necessary to obtain a conviction. However, the current research is not concerned with these factors directly. Rather, those other factors are examined which come to the attention of the prosecuting attorney prior to trial, and the influence of these factors on both his decision to prosecute and the conduct of the trial.

The Decision to Prosecute

At the outset, perhaps the most important factor related to
the process of dramatization is the labeler's definition of the labeled
and the act. That is, what makes a person a criminal and an act a
crime? Law students had very little difficulty in defining a criminal
or a crime. For example:

> A criminal is what the books tell me he is. Right now I
> an a prosecutor, and I do not go entirely on my personal
> feelings, although they do enter into it when I have to
> make a decision. . . . We work with the statutes involved.
> If you cannot demonstrate intent, then he [the defendant]
> is not a criminal. On the other hand, he may be a crim-
> inal in your mind since you know that he committed the
> crime, but he is not a criminal according to statute.

> We have certain statutes. . . . I'm not buying the notion
> that everyone who does a particular act is a criminal. . . .
> I suppose a criminal is one who commits a crime and a
> crime is set up by statute.

From this last statement it becomes apparent that more is involved
in even the law student's definition of a criminal and a crime than
"what the book tells me." Yet at this level there does not appear to
be much differentiation between a criminal and crime. That is,
criminals commit crimes, and a crime is something a criminal commits.

The lawyers in the office operate with much the same basic
definition of the criminal, but the language is sometimes more sophisticated. Some of these definitions included the following:

> [The criminal] would be the guy who commits an act
> against society. The problem that you have is that in
> committing the act it is not a crime . . . unless you have
> act plus intent. Therefore, accidental acts are not crim-
> inal acts. . . . They do not make the person a criminal.

> The criminal is the individual who has abrogated the
> rights of others. . . . He is the actor. . . . But what's the
> cause of the abrogation? What was it that prompted him
> to do that which was wrong? . . . The answer lies in his
> environment, in a lot of things.

One lawyer gave a definition of a criminal without emphasizing intent or questioning the reason for the act. The point of emphasis is, nonetheless, quite interesting:

> You could say that criminals are people who commit crimes, but if you look at the statutes, then probably everybody over 18 has committed a crime. . . . The thing that distinguishes criminals from the rest of us is luck. Criminals get caught. The others don't. . . . What I call criminals are people who habitually engage in antisocial conduct. . . . I distinguish in my mind between people who are basically honest citizens that are somehow brought into the criminal justice field and people who are what I call criminals. And you can see this from their records.

One of the most often mentioned elements in the definition of a criminal was the existence of a criminal record. If the defendant has a criminal record, arrest or conviction, then he or she goes down on the innocent scale and up on the guilty scale. Referring to an attempted murder suspect, a law student stated the following:

> I think that he is guilty of attempted murder, because I don't know whether you're aware that he is facing other charges now. I don't believe that they are in this juris- diction. I don't know whether he stood trial on them or what, but it was for beating up a ten-year-old girl or something like that. And I had access to that information, and they [the jury' didn't.

Another law student referred to a hardened criminal as,

> a person with a fairly long record . . . at least some kind of record is easier to deal with. Particularly with crimes involving physical harm, say like assault or attempted murder. . . . If you have somebody who has committed crimes in the past, this individual is . . . I wouldn't go as far as to say something is wrong with him mentally, but I would say that he doesn't fit in with the rest of so- ciety. And I think that he should even be removed per- manently [from society], or until such a time as he is rehabilitated.

It is apparent, then, that in addition to the length of the defendant's record the type and nature of the previous and current criminal of- fenses are considered by the law interns in the process of the dramatization of criminal behavior. These factors will be examined in more depth later.

The prosecutors, likewise, did not appear to ignore information about a defendant's criminal record prior to the current alleged offense. In fact, not only did the lawyers express many of the same feelings about the criminal histories of defendants as the law interns, they also appeared to be more hardened in these feelings:

> If we have knowledge of the background variables, it does influence our decisions. So often, however, the person we are dealing with . . . we don't know about his past histories until the charges are filed, and we are somewhere down the line . . . and we get the FBI rapsheet or the NCIC (National Criminal Identification Center) report and find out that he has a history of robberies in the past. . . . We definitely go after this guy with full force because he has shown a propensity for the crime. It's no accident or the result of one incident.

Another of the attorneys was not as blunt when discussing past criminal careers:

> Well, an extensive arrest record would cause one to wonder, but that factor alone doesn't provide me with evidence to convict. I can't impeach on the grounds of prior arrests. . . . As for prior charges, although it may produce a certain attitude in the mind of the prosecutor that they guy is guilty, it doesn't do anything as far as the hearing goes. After all, it is not admissible. . . . It's prior records gonna create a question in your mind. What happened to the rest of the crimes?

Or perhaps more simply put,

> With a whole lot of arrests, you can't help but think that where there's smoke, there's fire. . . . It's a fact. A lot of them are guilty, but get away with it.

Finally, with respect to previous criminal histories, sometimes too much information is a bad thing. This seems to be especially true when anything beyond information about previous or current criminal activities is considered by the prosecutors. For example, when asked about the type and extent of information desired by the prosecution, one deputy replied as follows:

> I'm not so sure we would even want any additional infor-
> mation. Now, the reason I say this is . . . uh . . . what
> I'm looking at now is the advocacy role. Once we in this
> office have determined that the guy committed the crime
> and we think we can prove it, it is time to let the advo-
> cacy role take over. . . . I've seen it happen that deputies
> make a very concerted effort to find out the background
> information on the defendant and his view [of the charge].
> And I think that in most cases the prosecutor dropped the
> ball. . . . Even the most hardened criminal has a few re-
> deeming qualities about himself. . . . And if the prose-
> cuting attorney is concerned with these qualities, then the
> advocacy role falls flat on its face. And that is what the
> whole system is based on.

Too much information, then, is conceived of as a threat to the criminal justice system and the trial procedure.

Another factor in the dramatization of the deviant is the type
and nature of the crime committed. That is, the decision to prosecute seemed to be influenced not only by the type of offense, misdemeanors as opposed to felonies, but also the nature of the particular
offense, possession of marijuana as opposed to rape. For example,
when asked if the offense is important, one law student replied,

> The offense should be taken into consideration. . . . I
> would consider a serious crime something involving
> grievous bodily harm. . . . I'm talking about your second-
> degree assault, first-degree, attempted murder, and
> things like that.

However, later on he states that:

> My main objective is not in punishing the guy according
> to the crime. I like to look at the crime and then look at
> the individual. . . . Look at his record . . . his past his-
> tory. . . . Putting a criminal conviction on a man's record
> is a pretty serious matter. . . . Once you get into your
> felonies, it's a real serious matter. I'm real hesitant to
> prosecute. . . . And I must be convinced that a guy is
> really guilty of something serious.

Another law student was more specific in his distinctions between
types of crimes:

I like to break it down into offenses against persons, offenses against property, and . . . possibly offenses against yourself. Offenses against persons is much greater than offenses against property. . . . My third level, offenses against self, is mainly reserved for drug offenders. If he is using drugs and not selling them, that is . . . until he gets so strung out that he is ripping people off to support himself or gets so goofed up that he commits a crime, it's an offense against himself.

While the law students appeared to recognize differences between the nature and types of crimes, they failed to indicate what influence these differences have or should have on the disposition of the case. This finding is not totally unexpected since the actual prosecutorial experience of the interns is extremely limited. In point of fact, only one of the law interns had prosecuted a case at the justice court level. The deputy attorneys, on the other hand, were somewhat more explicit:

The type of crime might have an impact initially. . . . I have charged people with such things as lewd and lascivious and attempted rape before. . . . I think that after the initial shock I don't treat them any differently. . . . You have to consider the average jury member in the charge you seek and how he will respond to it. And in that respect, the crime charged is very important because there are a lot of people who have inner feelings about rape.

Or, as another attorney expressed it,

Put marijuana growing up against rape or some other crime where hospitalization is needed or where someone is killed. I think that society has more interest in that as a crime or so it seems to me. I think that philosophically you can justify prosecution on these grounds better than you can for marijuana growing. . . . They are both against the law, and they are both crimes, but there is a difference.

Perhaps, the overall influence of the crime on the prosecution's case was best expressed by the deputy who stated the following:

At the initial stage of the investigation, I'm bothered by the charge—especially when bodily injury is involved,

like murder or rape. It makes me work all the harder.
But there is a point where I can't let the charge get to
me. That's when I'm in front of the judge or jury. You
can't afford to let the charge get away from you. It can
backfire.

As with the decision to prosecute, there appear to be many
factors which likewise influence the type of case presented and the
extent of the sanction or sentence sought by the prosecutor. The interns indicated that the procedures of law designed to protect society
and the rights of the defendants are closely related to the type of
prosecution. Consequently, even though physical evidence and sworn
testimony are again not directly considered in the analysis, these
elements of the prosecutor's case were frequently mentioned as being
crucial. Yet, the law students were also of the opinion that other
things influence the prosecution of a suspect:

A defendant should not be charged with a crime unless
you are convinced that he is guilty. . . . Well, maybe you
close your mind a little bit once you get to the trial
stage. . . . If you are convinced that this guy did it and
could be convicted . . . well, then, what other course is
open?

It is important to see the complaining witness to convince
yourself that a crime has been committed. . . . It is up to
me to define his evidence as demonstrating that a crime
has been committed.

It's not cold hard evidence that you could use in a trial.
It's evidence that he [the complaining witness] personally
transmits to you, whether written, verbal, or by his de-
meanor, that determines your approach to the case.

Apparently, the zeal with which the law interns approach a
case is potentially affected by factors other than legally admissible
testimony and evidence. At the trial stage they must be convinced
of the guilt of the defendant, and they appear to allow their own subjective evaluations of witnesses, even when "cold hard evidence" is
lacking, to influence their prosecution of a case. Yet the interns
are hardly criminal lawyers. Therefore, it is interesting to note the
techniques used by lawyers prior to and during the trial stage.

The factors involved in prosecution are two-fold. . . .
First of all is he guilty? And, can you prove him guilty?

> . . . The "can you prove it" part goes to your ability to
> overcome defenses. You can know in your mind that he
> is guilty but be unable to prove it because of a lack of
> physical evidence. . . . A third factor, and one we prob-
> ably like to think that we don't use, is what can be gained
> by prosecution.

> Initially, I'm concerned with the rights of the defen-
> dant. . . . I drop my concern with the rights of the defen-
> dant once he has been provided with counsel. The defense
> counsel is then charged with protecting the rights of the
> defendant.

> In my mind once we get to trial he is guilty. I don't feel
> that the case would have gotten that far, in most cases
> anyway. If you don't think that he is guilty and you don't
> think that you can prove it, then you have no business be-
> ing there.

One could conclude, therefore, that prior to and during the trial, the prosecuting attorney must be convinced that he is trying the
right person—that this person has committed a crime and should consequently be convicted. Once the trial is in progress, there are few,
if any, mechanisms allowing for doubt concerning the guilt or innocence of the defendants. These particular observations are reinforced
by statements to the effect that "you can know in your mind that he is
guilty but be unable to prove it" or "in my mind, once we get to trial
he is guilty." Yet as previously indicated, often the prosecutor's decision as to the guilt or innocence of a defendant is based in part upon
inadmissible information and subjective evaluations of the evidence.
It would appear that one major function of information of this nature,
since it could never be used legitimately in court, is to buttress the
prosecutor's case in his own mind. As one intern stated, "If you are
convinced that this guy did it and could be convicted . . . well, then,
what other course is open?"

The Impact of Criminal Prosecution

Even if the guilt or innocence of the defendant is not the issue,
the prosecuting attorneys are aware of what will happen to the person
who is convicted, especially if a jail or prison sentence is involved.
Also, the fact that one is charged and tried could be damaging:

It [prosecution] probably scares the hell out of them.
They are terrorized and terrified of the entire system.
They are one person and they have the whole damn complex working against them. . . . And if I was accused
right now, I'd be scared because it would be me and my
defense attorney against the whole system.

Convicted or not it really must hurt them. Even if you
are not convicted, if the information gets around it could
ruin you, professionally and reputationally.

Or, as another lawyer expressed it,

In the vast majority of cases, it simply is an experience
that leaves the individual with a very negative feeling towards the legal system. . . . I would do damn near anything to stay out of prison, and I think that most people
would. . . . I think that there are any number of people
who presume guilt because a person is arrested. And
any number of institutions ask whether you have been arrested, regardless of whether you were found guilty or
not guilty, the charges dropped, or if it was a case of
totally mistaken identity. . . . In that respect, we have a
great deal of power. An officer can go out and arrest a
person for perfectly groundless reasons and put a blot on
their record. It's clearly very difficult to correct or
clean it up. Once your prints are sent to NCIC and you
have a record, it's there and that's that.

The fact of an arrest or conviction record is not the only thing that
concerns the prosecuting attorneys. They are also concerned about
incarceration and what it does, or fails to do, to the person convicted
of a crime:

Prisons probably don't punish or rehabilitate satisfac-
torily. From what I've read about punishment, it is only
effective when it is administered swiftly and even-handed-
ly. . . . It seems to me that what goes on is neither. . . .
What the system is supposed to do is prevent crime. . . .
To me, some of the penalties have just the opposite effect. . . . Sending offenders to prison is like sending them
to a school of criminals.

For the most part, I think that we are just throwing
people behind the walls. . . . We are going to keep them

out of touch with the rest of us for a while. . . . They're
not going to be in society for a while and they're not going
to be a problem. . . . It does take away his freedom,
away from his loved one, away from the things that he
likes to do. No one likes to be confined. But as for how
they can be rehabilitated, how they can be remolded, how
they can be made what we think are productive members
of society, I don't know. I can say that it [incarceration]
is not the answer.

Although prosecuting attorneys may be out to "get" someone
because they "know" that the defendant is guilty, they realize that
there are defects in the system. It is relatively easy to impute the
label of criminal to a convict or a person with an immense arrest
record. The question is, How do you deal with the others, that is,
with first offenders or low misdemeanants? In the current study, a
concern was usually voiced over the type of crime and the applicability of a deferred sentence. As one law student expressed it,

A deferred sentence would go back to the distinction between the type of crime and the individual you have involved. I think that a deferred imposition is good for the
first offender or the guy who hasn't committed a very
serious crime and looks like he might go straight when
he gets out. It gives him a second chance.

A "second chance" is not the only reason given for deferring
sentence for these types of individuals. In fact, deferred sentences
are frequently only a part of the larger practice of plea bargaining.
This practice allows the prosecution a great deal of latitude in the
dramatization process. For example, it enables the prosecuting attorney and the defendant to exchange a possible criminal conviction
record and prison sentence for a period of probation with no conviction record. In other cases, the recommendation of a reduced sentence is exchanged for a plea of guilty. In both of these instances,
the prosecuting attorney has the somewhat coerced assistance of the
defendant in the dramatization of the criminal behavior; furthermore,
justice is served without a costly jury trial.
The law students had the following to say about plea bargaining:

The main reason for plea bargaining is the large load on
the courts and the many cases that come up before the
county attorney's office. There may even be some serious question as to whether justice is done in cases where
deferred sentences or plea bargaining is engaged. . . .

But plea bargaining goes right along with deferred imposition and it is pretty much up to the discretion of the
county attorney.

Still another student indicated that he had somewhat mixed feelings
about plea bargaining and deferred sentences:

I think that plea bargaining serves its purpose. I don't
think that it is always in the best interest of society. I
think that at times it is. By that I mean, if we have a
charge against a man, and maybe it is not well-founded,
you begin negotiations with your opponent. Perhaps
something, which wouldn't ordinarily, comes out. In
cases like this it is in the best interest of society. At
other times it is abused by the defendant and his counsel.

While the law students expressed concern over whether plea
bargaining, deferred sentences, and reduced sentences were in the
best interest of society, especially since they are abused by the defense counsel and his client, the lawyers were more pragmatic with
respect to these activities. Plea bargaining and related practices
enable the prosecuting attorneys to acknowledge the distinction they
already make between those persons labeled as criminals and those
who broke the law but are not really criminals:

Deferred sentences are great. They come in handy in
plea bargaining. They are also good for the first offenders, people who in my classification are not criminals.
The system would be terribly unjust if it didn't have a
device like that. Deferred sentences are a good way of
giving people a second chance.

In my mind it [plea bargaining] is almost indispensable.
Not because it gets us out of work. We aren't overloaded
in this county or state as they are back east or in California. . . . What it is is a safeguard. If I were a defendant, I would get very excited about plea bargaining.

Plea bargaining can be used for other purposes than reducing
the court load and serving justice without conferring a deviant label
on a person. It can be used as a bargaining tool to obtain a conviction for a state and a reduced sentence for the defendant:

Filing a charge above that indicated by the evidence is
used to provide the county attorney with a lever. I think

> that is done very, very often. I've done it. . . . The
> times I've used it is where I didn't think we had a good
> case, but I didn't really know. . . . A previous history of
> similar offenses, whether convictions or arrests, and
> the facts in the case could legitimize in my eyes these
> actions [the use of an inflated charge].

In conclusion, it is apparent that the prosecutors are aware of the potential impact of a conviction and imprisonment on the defendant. They engage in activities such as plea bargaining in order to avoid these consequences. Yet they also use these same techniques to assist in obtaining a "deserved" conviction. Perhaps another factor, familiarity with the defendant or personal involvement, is involved in this dramatization process. The impact of personal involvement was aptly illustrated by a prosecuting attorney's description of a case soon to be tried:

> I have a friend who is up on a first-degree burglary
> charge, when I know goddamned good and well he didn't
> do it. I'm not handling the case, because I couldn't ethi-
> cally, but I know about it. I read the reports. There is
> no way we can prove first-degree burglary. . . . But I
> would say that it will probably be negotiated to a lesser
> charge. I hate to see it. I hope that he [the defendant]
> doesn't fall into this negotiated-plea trap, because I think
> that if he were tried on first-degree burglary, he would
> get off scot free. There are no lesser and included of-
> fenses.

In an unrelated instance, another deputy noted,

> You know I could charge them with rape or statutory rape
> at the very least. The evidence is there. But I was their
> age once. And I did some crazy things too, but at least
> I exhibited a little better judgment. So, I guess, if they
> plead guilty to a contributing charge, then I'll ask for a
> deferred sentence.

Just as too much information about a preferably anonymous defendant was mentioned as potentially detrimental to the prosecution, it appears that avoidance of personal contacts with the defendant is crucial for the proper dramatization of the deviant label from a prosecutor's viewpoint. In situations in which the prosecutor knows or is associated with the defendant, or has common experiences, the course of the prosecution could be influenced.

SUMMARY

This study represents an attempt to examine the factors that impinge on the role of the prosecuting attorney in the process of labeling a person as a criminal. Three questions were of major concern in the research. First was an interest in delineating those variables which influenced the decision to prosecute. Second was an examination of factors which potentially influence the conduct of the trial. Finally, an interest existed in finding out whether members of the prosecuting attorney's office were aware of the consequence of their labeling.

In summary, the variables considered in the decision to prosecute—that is, in the definition of crime and criminal by the members of the prosecuting attorney's office—consisted of much more than physical evidence and sworn testimony. Such factors as the number of prior convictions, the number of prior arrests, and the type and nature of the current offense clearly affected the definitions of criminality. A large number of arrests or convictions was frequently mentioned as an indicator of a propensity for criminal behavior. In turn, an extensive criminal record was frequently seen as justification for prosecution. The type and nature of the offense were also crucial factors; offenses which created the most public outrage and indignation, rape for example, seemed to require an ardent and unyielding prosecution. Other offenses, such as the possession of marijuana, did not seem to create the same social or legal uproar.

The analysis also revealed that once the decision to prosecute is made, at least three variables influence the course of the prosecution. First, the prosecuting attorney is sometimes faced with cases in which the legally admissible evidence does not support the prosecution's contentions. In fact, the evidence may not even support any lesser and included charges. Nevertheless, the prosecutor "knows" that the defendant is guilty, perhaps for the reasons discussed above. Using the threat of a prison or jail sentence as a lever, the prosecutor may bargain with defense counsel and the defendant for a reduced charge or a suspended sentence in return for a plea of guilty.

In addition to cases which may prove extremely difficult to win at the original charge, the prosecutor may use plea bargaining in cases where a prison sentence or a conviction is not in the best interest of society or the defendant. The accused, in these cases, is usually very different from the habitual criminal offender who has committed some heinous act against society. It would be more difficult to label this person as a criminal; consequently, the prosecuting attorneys make the distinction between lawbreakers and criminals. In such instances, the prosecutor may ask for a deferred sentence or a suspended sentence at the very least.

The final variable considered in the examination of the prosecution's case is familiarity with or personal knowledge of the defendant. There are, as was noted in the analysis, several gradients of this variable. At the very least, it makes prosecution on the original charge difficult. In this respect, it may interfere with the prosecutorial technique of allowing the advocacy role to insulate the prosecutor from the defendant. And at its extreme, it may even lead to an entirely different interpretation of the case by the prosecuting attorney, in the face of physical evidence and sworn testimony to the contrary.

In conclusion, this study contains several implications for both policy and further research. First, in the area of policy, it seems apparent that plea bargaining would profit from standardization and public recognition of the procedure. Currently, it is only quasi-legal (and therefore quasi-illegal) for the prosecuting attorney to engage in plea bargaining. The U.S. Supreme Court has upheld several decisions involving cases in which plea bargaining was involved, but there are no recognized criteria and no judge is obligated to abide by the prosecutor's recommendations. Another possible alternative is the abolition of plea bargaining in favor of some more equitable solution. The federal government's recent Task Force Report on the Criminal Justice System made just such a recommendation. However, the alternative of negotiated pleas is just as tenuous and questionable as plea bargaining. Standardization of plea-bargaining procedures, on the other hand, could lead to a reduction in the misuses of the process by both the defense and prosecution. Furthermore, if the process were explained to the public, perhaps it would not feel that the criminal justice system was "letting some criminals get off scot free." While this paper does not purport to be the decisive work in the area of labeling as used by the members of the prosecuting attorney's office, it has served to focus some attention on how crime and criminality are defined by members of a pivotal and crucial unit of the criminal justice system. In view of the findings of Cole (1970) and Neubauer (1974), it would also appear that there are a great deal of similarities in the actions and activities of prosecuting attorneys regardless of their location. That is, in making their decision to prosecute, the rural prosecutors discussed above, tended to be affected by factors similar to urban prosecutors as reported by Cole and Neubauer. In terms of future research, it would be important to establish whether the findings presented here are applicable to offices and staff of prosecuting attorneys in other rural areas.

NOTE

1. This point is open to debate. See Schwartz and Skolnick (1962).

REFERENCES

Becker, H. 1963. Outsiders: Studies in The Sociology of Deviance. New York: The Free Press.

Blumberg, A. 1967. Criminal Justice. Chicago: Quadrangle.

Cameron, M. O. 1964. The Booster and the Snitch. New York: The Free Press of Glencoe.

Chambliss, W. J. and J. T. Liell. 1966. The legal process in the community setting. Crime and Delinquency (October): 310-17.

Cicourel, A. 1968. The Social Organization of Juvenile Justice. New York: John Wiley.

Cole, George F. 1970. The decision to prosecute. Law and Society Review (February): 331-43.

Garfinkel, N. 1956. Conditions of successful degradation ceremonies. American Journal of Sociology 61 (March): 420-24.

Goffman, Erving. 1961. Asylums. Garden City, New York: Doubleday and Company, Inc.

———. 1963. Stigma. Englewood Cliffs, New Jersey: Prentice-Hall, Inc.

Goldman, H. 1963. The Differential Selection of Juvenile Offenders for Court Appearance. Washington: National Council on Crime and Delinquency.

Green, E. 1961. Judicial Attitudes in Sentencing. New York: St. Martin's Press.

———. 1964. Inter- and intra-racial crime relative to sentencing. Journal of Criminal Law, Criminology and Police Science (September) 55: 348-58.

Hagan, J. 1973. Labeling and deviance: a case study in the 'sociology of the interesting.' Social Problems 20 (Spring): 447-58.

Kitsuse, J. I. 1962. Societal reaction to deviant behavior: problems of theory and method. Social Problems 9 (Winter): 247-56.

Lemert, E. 1967. Human Deviance, Social Problems, and Social Control. Englewood Cliffs: Prentice-Hall, Inc.

Lofland, J. 1969. Deviance and Identity. Englewood Cliffs: Prentice-Hall, Inc.

Neubauer, David W. 1974. After the arrest: the charging decision in Prarie City. Law and Society Review (Spring): 495-515.

Piliavin, I. and S. Briar. 1964. Police encounters with juveniles. American Journal of Sociology 70 (September): 206-14.

Schur, E. 1971. Labeling Deviant Behavior. New York: Harper & Row.

Schwartz, R. D. and J. H. Skolnick. 1962. Two studies of legal stigma. Social Problems 10 (Fall): 133-38.

Sieverdes, C. 1972. An investigation of factors influencing the probation officer's disposition of juvenile offenders. Proceedings of the Alpha Kappa Delta Sociological Research Symposium.

Skolnick, J. H. 1966. Justice Without Trial. New York: John Wiley.

———. 1967. Social control in the adversary system. Journal of Conflict Resolution 11: 52-70.

Stinchcombe, A. L. 1963. Public practice, types of crimes and social location. American Journal of Sociology 69 (September): 150-60.

Sudnow, D. 1965. Normal crimes: sociological features of the penal code. Social Problems 12 (Winter): 255-70.

13

THE RIGHT TO REMAIN SILENT: THE PROBATION OFFICER'S MORAL DILEMMA

Rosalind Reiman

A woman who was convicted of manslaughter and placed on probation supervision at the U.S. District Court was rearrested on a murder charge. The probation officer was immediately notified and, following probation office policy, had the young woman brought to the cellblock in the basement of the courthouse. When she and her probation officer sat down together in a small witness room, she was asked to recount what had occurred. The young woman explained that because of ongoing problems, including both emotional and physical abuse, she had left her boyfriend after a recent bitter fight. She later returned to the apartment she shared with her boyfriend to pick up some clothes, and found him there with his old girlfriend, a 19-year-old woman. The probationer then stated that both her boyfriend and his girlfriend "disrespected" her. She then grabbed a knife and stabbed the 19-year-old woman to death. The probationer explained that she knew this act was wrong but that she could not control her anger.

Several weeks later, the probation officer learned that the probationer was planning to plead "self-defense" and that her boyfriend, who had witnessed the event, was expected to substantiate her plea. In addition to her confession to the probation officer, the probationer initially had made a statement to the police admitting that she had killed without justification, but her lawyer was moving to have this evidence suppressed. The judge who had originally placed this woman

The views expressed herein are those of the writer and not necessarily those of either the U.S. District Court, Washington, D.C., or the federal probation service. The writer would like to express a special thanks to George W. Howard, III, for his invaluable legal assistance, and to Pamela Bryant for her patience and superb typing skills.

on probation in the U.S. District Court had been notified of the arrest and her statement to the probation officer. The probation officer was in a dilemma. Should she go to the prosecutor in the new case with her evidence? If the prosecution was made aware of the evidence she had, could she testify at the probationer's trial? Would her evidence be admissible?

The above incident is true. The problems the probation officer faced reflect pressing legal and moral dilemmas not yet adequately resolved by the courts. The probationer, under no duress, had freely recounted the circumstances surrounding the crime of which she was accused. This woman had often shared her personal problems with her probation officer, viewing her as a counselor first and a probation officer second. Thus, the probation officer's relationship with the young woman clearly demonstrated the ambiguity of the two primary roles of the probation officer—law enforcement officer and counselor. Since the probation officer had played the role of counselor with the probationer for several months, discussing her children, her depressions, her boyfriend, and so on, what role did the young woman assume the probation officer was playing when she asked about the killing? If the probationer saw her probation officer as a counselor when she described the murder, should the probation officer, legally or morally, use her confession against her?

Several court decisions have attempted to answer the question, Is the probation officer a law enforcement officer or a counselor and how do Fifth and Sixth Amendment guarantees apply to probationers and parolees in their dealings with their probation and parole officers? The view of this study is that this is the wrong question. To be effective, the probation officer must play both roles. The question that must be asked is, If both roles are played, when and under what circumstances do the roles change and how can the probation officer do his or her job and still protect the constitutional rights of the probationer? This is the heart of the issue facing federal, state, and county probation and parole officers today.

For the past several years the trend in the federal probation system has been to employ young people with a treatment-oriented conception of probation work. Many of these younger probation officers[*] tend to see themselves as social workers and counselors rather than as law-enforcement officers charged with surveillance

---

[*]The term "probation officer" or "officer" will refer here to both probation officers and parole officers and "probationers" will refer to both probationers and parolees.

of the client. ("Client" is a relatively new term reflecting this change
in emphasis.) It is significant that clients are beginning to respond
to their probation officers as if the probation officers were, indeed,
counselors, and not agents of the criminal justice system. This
response obviously aids the probation officers in giving their clients
needed support and counseling. The problem arises when the probation officers have to exercise their authority as agents of the court
or parole board and gather information for possible probation or
parole revocation. In such situations, statements made by the client
to the probation officer may be used at revocation hearings, or possibly admitted as evidence in a subsequent trial if there is a new
charge. With the testimony of her probation officer, the probationer
mentioned above, for instance, would probably have been found guilty
of second-degree murder, or voluntary manslaughter. Without that
testimony, though she was guilty of criminal homicide by her own
admission, she conceivably could have pleaded self-defense, received
corroborating testimony from her boyfriend, and walked out of court
a free woman. The difficulty is that her confession may have been
the result of her belief that the probation officer was "on her side,"
a belief which may be needed to counsel offenders into law-abiding
alternatives.

Embedded in the above and other similar situations are three
pressing and primary issues that effect much of the probation system:

1. How should the probation officer respond to information
concerning criminal conduct on the part of the probationer—as a law-
enforcement officer or counselor?

2. Under what circumstances may the client prevent the admission of the probation officer's testimony because of the nature of
their relationship and, thus, invoke the Fifth or Sixth Amendment to
exclude such admissions from judiciary proceedings?

3. How will a resolution, if there is one, of these competing
issues, affect the probation officer's dual role as counselor and law-
enforcement officer?

Let's turn now to a consideration of these questions, and their implications for the role of the probation officer.

Are probation officers law-enforcement officers? And, if they
interview clients in custodial surroundings must they apprise them
of their right against self-incrimination and their right to remain
silent? Under the Fifth and Fourteenth Amendments the protection
against self-incrimination leaves to the individual the choice to speak
or remain silent. In Miranda v. Arizona, the Supreme Court, concerned about the circumstances of many of the confessions that had
been obtained by the police, ruled that it is necessary to warn

defendants of this right to remain silent in order to "dispel the compulsion inherent to custodial surroundings" (: 444). The majority opinion in Miranda defined custodial interrogation as "questioning initiated by the law enforcement officers after a person has been taken into custody or otherwise deprived of his freedom of action in any significant way (: 478).

This issue has been before several state courts and contradictory decisions involving the applicability of Miranda to the probation officers have been made. This contradictory state of affairs obviously does not help the individual probation officer who must deal directly with the issue of the applicability of Miranda, if not as a legal concern, surely as a moral concern. A case involving this issue, State of Ohio v. Terry L. Gallagher, was recently brought before the United States Supreme Court but due to an ambiguity in the petitioner's presentation of his case, the court refused to rule on the merits and returned the matter to the State of Ohio for clarification. The State of Ohio reiterated its previous position in support of the defendant, thereby eliminating further appellate review of this case on a federal level. But even if the Supreme Court eventually rules on the applicability of Miranda to the probation officer, such a legal ruling is not likely to dispel the problems that this conflict represents. This is because, at its heart, it is not a problem of law but of the conflicting roles that the criminal justice system asks the probation officer to play: helper and keeper. The particular issue under discussion here is simply a symptom of the failure to resolve this conflict, and it will not be solved until this role conflict is itself resolved.

The issue seems to hinge in part on the definition of what a law-enforcement officer is. This obviously plays a key role in determining the applicability of Miranda to probation officers. In Ohio v. Gallagher, the attorney for the respondent argued that probation officers are indeed law-enforcement officers. He argued that probation officers have the authority to arrest persons under their supervision for "suspected violations," to place detainers on subjects, and in other ways, to deprive persons of their freedom. Therefore he argued the tenets of Miranda should be applied (Brief for Respondent: 5).

It should be noted, however, that the powers granted to, or regularly exercised by, probation officers vary considerably in the various state and federal systems. For instance, it is apparently common for state parole officers to accompany police officers in the arrest of parolees. A Kansas City case involved a parole officer who received information that one of his parolees had a weapon in his possession. This officer passed the information on to the police and then went with them to search his client's home. After the gun was found, it was, in fact, the parole officer who interrogated the man. Instances such as this, and the fact that many jurisdictions allow probation officers to carry weapons, lend credence to the argument that the powers that most probation officers have and the actions that they take are similar to the powers and actions of other law-enforcement officers. If this is true, the probation officer may indeed have to follow the guidelines established under Miranda and may soon be required to apprise clients of their constitutionally protected rights against self-incrimination. Until the United States Supreme Court rules, the probation officer may indeed feel a moral compulsion to give a Miranda-type warning before receiving possibly self-incriminating statements from the client.

The issue of the role of the probation officer as law-enforcement officer is not, however, that easily solved. An argument can and has been made for an opposing opinion. Probation officers have been described as social workers, rather than as law-enforcement officers. A brief filed in support of the State in Ohio v. Gallegher argued that "the function of the probation or parole officer is not akin to that of a police interrogator. The probation officer acts more like a social worker than a policeman, and his goal is rehabilitation of the parolee and not of the securing of confessions to crime." In People v. Ronald W., this point was also made in a brief arguing that "the clearly stated objectives of education and rehabilitation . . . are always paramount in the relationship between the probation officer and the probationer [and] are totally foreign to the elements the Supreme Court addressed itself to in Miranda." Thus, according to this case, the probation officer is not a law-enforcement officer "within the spiritual meaning of Miranda." Two opposing conclusions relating to Fifth Amendment rights flow from this stance of probation officer as social worker. Both were argued before the Court of Appeals of Montgomery County, Ohio, in Ohio v. Gallegher. The state argued that since the probation officer is a kind of social worker and not a law-enforcement officer, the probationer does not have to be warned of the right to remain silent and that what he or she says may be used in court (Brief of Amicus Curiae: 2). The other position, argued by the respondent, is that the relationship between the probation officer and the probationer is a special and unique one, like that of a counselor and client, or a doctor and patient, and that what is said between the two is confidential or "privileged communication," and thus statements made by the probationer to the probation officer cannot be used against the probationer in court.

Drawn from these positions are three possible but opposing resolutions to the controversy concerning the role of the probation officer, and the Fifth and Fourteenth Amendment rights of the probationer:

1. The probation officer is primarily a law-enforcement officer and like other law-enforcement agents must give a Miranda-type warning. Otherwise, what the client says cannot be used against him or her in court.

2. The probation officer is primarily a social worker. Conversations with clients, therefore, are not custodial in nature and are not affected by Miranda. Whatever is said by the client can be used in court.

3. The probation officer is primarily a counselor and what is said between the probation officer and probationer is "privileged communication." What the probationer says cannot be used in court.

Each of these positions will now be considered in detail.

The Probation Officer as a Law-Enforcement Officer

If the probation officer is a law-enforcement officer and therefore bound by the requirements of Miranda, several complications arise. It has been decided in several courts that from arrest through conviction one Miranda warning by a law-enforcement officer is sufficient to satisfy the Miranda requirement. In McGuire v. United States, the United States Court of Appeals for the Ninth Circuit ruled that it was not necessary for law-enforcement officers to repeat the warning even after three days had elapsed from the first warning. When a probationer is charged with an offense, a new warning need not be given if he or she has already been given a Miranda-type warning by an officer of the arresting agency. It could follow, that if the probation officer is a law-enforcement officer, then the warning is not strictly necessary since it has already been given by another law-enforcement officer—the arresting police officer. The court found this to be the case in Gilmore v. People when the confession made to the probation officer was admitted into evidence against the probationer. This argument could conceivably be used to allow confessions made to probation officers to be heard in court even if the U.S. Supreme Court holds that Miranda applies, so long as a previous warning has been given.

Another position states that even though the probation officer is a law-enforcement officer, clients under supervision of this particular law-enforcement officer are "special people" and are in a special legal situation which makes their status quite different from that of the ordinary citizen. Accordingly, some courts have ruled that the client, as a convicted criminal, is entitled to fewer legal

rights than other citizens in their dealings with enforcers of the law.
This might suggest that even if the probation officer is a law-enforcement officer, the probationer is not entitled to a Miranda warning.
In Nettles v. State, the probation officer's testimony about a confession was held to be admissible. The court found that by accepting
probation, the probationer had effectuated a continuous waiver of the
right to be advised of Miranda rights (: 260). The view that probationers possess a peculiar legal status is supported in Morrisy v.
Brewer where revocation of probation is not viewed as part of the
criminal process but instead is seen as an administrative procedure
occurring after criminal prosecution. The "full panoply of rights"
due a defendant does not apply to the probationer if the process of
probation revocation is an administrative rather than an adjudicative
procedure, since the object of an administrative process is not strictly
speaking, a defendant.

Another argument weakening the applicability of Miranda to
the probation officer as a law-enforcement officer was made by the
state in Ohio v. Gallegher. He argued that the probationer is "by
definition a convicted criminal" who has already "been through the
system" and is quite familiar with his or her Fifth and Sixth Amendment rights. This prosecutor maintained that it is therefore unnecessary for the probation officer to re-remind an already convicted
criminal that what is said can and will be used in a court of law.

Even if the probation officer is a law-enforcement officer required to give the client the Miranda warning, the problem of when
the warning has to be given still remains. Addressing a vital element
in Miranda, the state in the Gallegher case pointed out that the Supreme Court held it necessary to give defendants the Miranda warning
in order to "dispel the compulsion inherent in custodial surrounds."
He argued that a probationer at a police station or in a cellblock is
"in very familiar surroundings and in the presence of friends, so to
speak." Therefore, since the client is quite at home and not at all
intimidated as an individual would be who was experiencing a first
arrest, there is no rationale for an explicit Miranda warning from
the probation officer (ibid.).

Even if the probation officer is deemed to be a law-enforcement
officer, problems still remain if incriminating statements are made
in other than custodial surroundings. The problem of self-incriminating statements from clients is a daily problem for the probation
officer. Clients invariably report minor illegal acts. There is probably not one probation officer in any federal or state system who has
not been informed by a client that the client had engaged in the illegal
act of possessing marijuana. Some clients voluntarily admit to the
use of harder illegal drugs such as heroin, cocaine, or preludin.
Some may even admit to offense such as shoplifting or maintaining

employment while receiving welfare payments. The type of crime may vary depending upon what is considered "acceptable" illegality, but the fact remains: clients are continually confessing to crimes. Although not legally required, is there a moral obligation on the part of the probation officer to warn clients that what they say may be used against them? If the client should be warned, then under what circumstances or how often should this warning be given? Once a year? once a month? At the beginning of each visit? Is the officer under a moral or legal obligation to report all these admissions of illegal acts to the Court? If not, what of the situation in which a client reports a serious violation after the probation officer has allowed the establishment of a pattern of minor confessions without reporting them.

Finally, with respect to the Miranda-precipitated right to counsel, under what circumstances should a probation officer have to advise the client of his or her right to counsel before receiving information concerning a new offense? If the probation officer is a law-enforcement officer and must follow all the precepts of Miranda, it would appear that unless the client waived his or her right to counsel each time a new offense was discussed, the client could insist on having counsel present.

It seems clear, that if the probation officer's role is defined as that of a law-enforcement officer, problems still remain since the guarantee of Fifth and Sixth Amendment rights cannot be as easily engineered in the case of the probation officer as it can with the police officer. Some have argued, however, that if the probation officer is a kind of social worker these conflicts do not arise.

The Probation Officer as Social Worker

If the probation officer is primarily seen as a social worker rather than a law-enforcement officer, then a Miranda-type warning would be unnecessary in most situations, since social workers do not give their clients such a warning. However, it would follow then that whatever is said to the probation officer/social worker could be used in court. An exception might be argued when the "social worker" enters the "police-dominated atmosphere" of a cellblock or jail and begins asking questions. The client might feel compelled to answer and possibly confess. Even outside of custodial institutions there may still be a "quasi compulsion" inherent in the relationship between the client and the officer. In United States v. Deaton, it was argued that the probationer was under "heavy psychological pressure" to answer inquiries made by his or her probation officer, pressure "perhaps even greater than when the interrogation is by a law enforcement

officer. It is unclear whether the source of this pressure was seen
as the prior counselor-client relationship or the underlying fear that
the client has of the probation officer because of the officer's ability
to influence a judge or parole board. Although in its Miranda decision the Supreme Court had in mind the use of a different kind of
pressure (brute force, atmosphere of power, promises of leniency,
etc.), there may be a kind of pressure inherent in the relationship
with a probationer that is just as compelling. To simply say that the
relationship between the probation officer and the probationer is essentially that of social worker and client and, therefore, not subject
to Fifth or Sixth Amendment procedural safeguards, would ignore
the "cellblock atmosphere" of some of those interviews, the actual
power that the officer has over the probationer's fate, and the nature
of many probation officer-probationer relationships. Perhaps this
could be dealt with by applying to the probation officer-probationer
relationship the concept of "privileged communications," applied in
other instances of counselor-client relationships. This leads to consideration of the third alternative.

Communication Between Probation Officer and
Probationer as "Privileged"

If the probation officer is primarily a social worker or counselor, then inherent in the relationship of counselor to client may be
the right of "privileged communication." In such a situation the client could prevent the admission of any adverse information by claiming the same protection of confidentiality that adheres in lawyer-client
or therapist-patient relationships. Certainly no probation officer
establishes a counselor-patient relationship with every probationer.
There are, however, numerous instances where these relationships
do evolve and those are obviously the ones in which the problem herein discussed is most acute. The issue is whether or not the probationer who enjoys such a relationship with the probation officer
should be allowed all the privileges normally associated with the
doctor-patient relationship.

If the probationer were allowed the right to privileged communication, it would greatly complicate the probation officer's role
as an agent of the court and parole board. By federal statute, for
example, the probation officer has a duty to determine whether the
probationer is conforming to the restrictions and obligations imposed
by the court. Information regarding the probationer's compliance
with the conditions of probation—the restrictions on employment and
travel, new arrests, residency, and so on, are usually obtained from
the client. To hold that that type of communication is not privileged,

but other admissions are and thus cannot be reported to the court, would confuse both the client and the probation officer. If it were argued that all communications between probation officer and client are privileged, the probation officer's role as a law-enforcement officer is completely obliterated, and any obligations the probation officer has to the court are severed. This would have the effect of putting the probation officer in the position of violating federal statute and of working solely for the probationer. Since the issue of privileged communication has been raised in the courts, it is important that some legal ruling be made to help clarify this sensitive area.

CONCLUSION

Each of the three views just discussed have been argued in various courts around the country. Each poses new problems and new legal and moral issues further complicating the already complex role of the probation officer. The argument that the probation officer is simply a law-enforcement officer completely ignores the supportive, concerned, helping role that most probation officers also play and must play to realize the goals of rehabilitation. To say, however, that the officer is actually a social worker simply working for the rehabilitation of the client, is a position that is incompatible with the law-enforcement aspect of the probation officer's duties. An individual who may search his client's home, carry a gun when he sees his client, request a warrant for his client's arrest, participate in his client's arrest, and who has the power to recommend that the client go to jail, can hardly be described as merely a social worker. Although not all probation officers necessarily perform all these acts, many do, and all perform some.

The probation officer is therefore neither purely a law-enforcement officer nor purely a social worker. And that is the crux of the problem. Probation officers invariably play both roles—that of a law-enforcement officer and that of a social worker. This duality of conflicting roles is inherent in the job. And it is the very fact that these two roles are contradictory and often switch without the client being aware that they have switched, that presents the legal and moral dilemma to the conscientious probation officer.

The primary role the probation officer played with the woman described in the beginning of this paper was that of a social worker. The major communication during her early months of supervision involved children, housing, emotional concerns, and the like. As soon as the probationer was arrested, however, the probation officer's role as social worker became deemphasized and replaced with the role of law-enforcement officer. The probation officer then began to perform in an official capacity to obtain information for the court in order to determine whether probation should be revoked. Realistically, the probationer had little way of knowing that the roles had changed so drastically. It may very well be that when the probationer confessed to the probation officer, she was still responding to her probation officer as if she were her social worker rather than a law-enforcement agent for the U.S. District Court.

This situation is not a solitary incident, but rather one dramatic example of numerous conflicts created by the ambiguity of the probation officer's role. The following few suggestions are just those, and cannot hope to solve a problem what is so much a part of the conflicting demands made upon the probation officer by the judicial system.

The relationship between the probation officer and the probationer is a unique one and presents unique problems. Since the probation officer is neither a law-enforcement officer nor a social worker, but both, and since these roles intertwine and the emphasis may switch without notice, the nature of the probation officer's role itself creates the need for protection of the rights of the probationer. This protection however should not destroy the probation officer's capacity to do a meaningful job. It does appear that when a client has been rearrested the probation officer must legally give the client a Miranda warning. This is the time of the most dramatic change in role and the probationer should be so advised. Since probationers and parolees have, by definition, already been through the system and are usually quite familiar with the court processes, legal matters, and their legal rights, it does not appear to be necessary for them to have an attorney present if they choose to answer questions about the new offense. They are indeed "in familiar surroundings" and it is enough that they are reminded of their probation officer's present official role. To suggest that clients should be warned on a regular basis that what information they voluntarily give their probation officer may be reported to the court tends to ignore the client's experience with the court system. Most probationers and parolees are very much aware of the probation officer's power and obligations with respect to revocation. A regular official warning although morally sound, would also make counseling sessions with the client difficult if not ludicrous. A probation officer who meets a client for the first time may want to remind him or her that admissions of illegal acts are made at the client's own risk, but even this warning is usually unnecessary since the client is quite adept at sizing up the probation officer and learning what is and what is not acceptable behavior.

These few suggestions of how to deal with the complicated issues I have outlined are not meant in any way to dispose of the problem. It does not seem, however, that a United States Supreme Court ruling will make all things clear. The problems will continue since the roles of the probation officer as a law-enforcement officer and social worker fluctuate depending upon the philosophy and whims of each individual office, the court or parole system involved, and the particular situation he or she must confront. The system seems to want two relationships and two roles—a supportive and trusting relationship inherent in the counseling role, and an adversarial relationship inherent in the custodial and surveillance role of the probation officer as agent of the court. As has been pointed out, these two roles are not only often contradictory but by their very nature may jeopardize the constitutional rights of the client. The roles of the probation officer and the rights of the probationer must be more carefully defined. The thin and shaky legal line that the probation officers now walk has to be drawn more clearly. Spelling out the legal responsibilities so that the rights of the probationers can be protected may help to create a real basis of trust between officer and probationer. It has been argued that by being placed on probation or parole, the client has given up some rights. It is unclear which of these rights have been given up and what role the probation officer plays in the denial of those rights. It is clear that in playing the role of social worker the probation officer may be setting the client up to be deprived of privileges to which the client is legally entitled. On the other hand, to the probation officer personally committed to helping the client, the conflict between the role of social worker and law-enforcement officer is bound to be a source of a continuing moral dilemma.

This moral dilemma is particularly exacerbated when above all, one is concerned with protecting the safety and interests of the community at large. It was argued by the state in the Gallegher case that "even conceding the harm to criminals of admitting at the trial, confessions related to their probation officer, when balancing the interests between these criminals and the public, who is harmed more greatly when voluntary and reliable statements such as these are suppressed or prevented from coming into existence (Brief for Petitioner: 17). Or, as stated most clearly by the prosecutor in the Gallegher case, "the Constitutional safeguards were designed for the protection of the innocent, not the freeing of the guilty.

The probation officer must therefore be concerned with not only the protection of the rights of the probationer, but also the protection and safety of the probationer's community. This last concern, although only mentioned now, must be the overriding concern of the probation officer. Keeping the interests of the larger community in mind, however, does not make the legal issues clear or the job of the probation officer easier. Instead, it adds to the complexity of each issue confronted and, therefore, also placed the probation officer in situations that are, more often that not, legal and moral dilemmas.

REFERENCES

Brief for Petitioner, Ohio v. Gallagher, 74-492: 17.

Brief for Respondent, Ohio v. Gallagher, 74-492: 15.

Brief of Amicus Curiae by State of California, Ohio v. Gallagher, 74-492: 2, 3.

Gilmore v. People, 457 P. 2d 828 (Colo. 1970).

Maguire v. United States, 396 F. 2d 237 (1968).

Miranda v. Arizona, 384 U.S. 436 (1966).

Morrisy v. Brewer, 408 U.S. 471 (1972).

Nettles v. State, 248 So. 2d 259 (Fla. Dist. Court of App. 1971).

Ohio v. Gallagher, 425 U.S. 257 (1976).

People v. Ronald W., 302 N.Y.S. 260 (1969).

State v. Leakas, 442 P. 2d 11 (Kansas 1968).

United States v. Deaton (5th Cir. 1972), 468 F. 2d 541; cert. denied, 410 U.S. 934.

18 USC 3655.

14

SCIENTIFIC DISPLACEMENT OF PERSONAL RESPONSIBILITY

Harold E. Pepinsky

INTRODUCTION

In September, 1974, an American President pardoned his immediate predecessor from criminal liability for acts the latter committed during his term of office. President Ford reasoned that former President Nixon had been punished enough for his transgressions (by being forced to resign from office), and that the pardon was the "right thing to do."

By contrast, within a year of the pardon, President Ford proposed federal legislation to "get tough" on street crime, mandating prison terms for convicted felons (Time 1975: 10). In so doing, the President echoed the advice of social science "experts" in the field of criminology.

His reluctance to subject Nixon to the penalties of criminal law—let alone the reluctance of Congress to conclude there was sufficient evidence that Nixon had committed "high crimes and misdemeanors" to support impeachment—stands in stark contrast to the routine conviction and imprisonment of defendants in American criminal courts. With no hearing in eighty percent of American criminal cases, and the remainder generally leading to short trials, findings favorable to defendants seldom result; defendants are routinely convicted of crimes with little fuss or bother. Presidential support for a higher rate of incarceration for convicted defendants comes in a country which already has twice as high a rate of incarceration as Canada, two or three times that of most European and Asian countries (and nine times the Netherlands' rate), matched only by a few countries like Poland (Waller and Chan 1974: 58). A few examples of other cases further illustrate the contrast.

A part-time county public defender is rumored to be defrauding clients in his private law practice. It is several years before the man is tried and convicted of felony fraud. Loss of the right to practice law is initially deemed sufficient punishment for this defendant, who is given several years' unsupervised probation with no term of incarceration. It is only after a couple of years that the sentencing judge, finding "inconsistencies" in the findings that underlay the original sentence, imposes a six-month jail term.

A federal parolee, with a prior record of robbery and forgery, never before known to have committed burglary, is caught trying to break into a post office to steal money orders. There is no loss and no damage. This defendant had for some time been unsuccessful in obtaining employment, and was badly in need of money to support a wife and newborn child. In a short hearing, the defendant, who has pleaded guilty, is sentenced to five years in prison (and serves two before parole).

A defendant with a record of several prior burglaries is caught taking a television set from his mother-in-law's home. The mother-in-law refuses to cooperate in prosecution. The defendant has a steady job, and his employer is prepared to retain his services. There is evidence that the theft was the product of a quarrel with the then-estranged wife of the defendant, but the wife is prepared to forgive all and take the husband back to live with her and their children. In a trial and disposition that takes no more than fifteen minutes, the defendant is sentenced to two months in jail, and loses his job as a consequence.

These examples reflect the common distinction in American courts between routine conviction and incarceration of street criminals on the one hand, and special consideration given "respectable" defendants on the other. The difference is well documented in criminological literature (see, for example, Robin 1970).

The distinction has struck many American observers as being outrageous. Quinney's (1974) work has received as much attention as have any of this category. A fascinating aspect of the bulk of this criticism is the dominance of anger at the escape of the social elite from state punishment over anger at the ease with which agents of the state subject anyone to punishment at all. The social science finding of class discrimination in court proceedings is beginning to have a substantial impact on court practice, in the form of a major increase in prosecution and conviction for "white-collar" crime (see McCarthy 1975).

To take for granted that class discrimination in processing of criminal cases is a natural outgrowth of an economic order is to beg an important question: Psychologically, how do people manage to inflict conviction and incarceration on any class of people routinely without intolerable pangs of conscience? A sense of compassion for the fate of a fellow human being apparently constrained President Ford from accepting personal responsibility for tolerating the incarceration of his predecessor in office. If a family member maliciously destroyed one's prized possession, one would be hard put to accept personal responsibility for locking the other away for a period of months or years in retaliation, even though the loss was dear. How is this sense of compassion, which makes it so difficult to take responsibility for punishing another person, subdued sufficiently for police, prosecutors, judges, court services officers, and even many defense counsel to cooperate freely in facilitating the incarceration of such large numbers of criminal defendants? Though such cooperation is taken for granted by Americans, it is rather remarkable that officers of courts—many of whom are undoubtedly generous and compassionate on a day-to-day basis—can readily ratify long-term deprivation of liberty for numerous criminal defendants—equating the loss of a television set, for example, with a couple of months in jail.

ABDICATION OF PERSONALITY RESPONSIBILITY

A display of compassion toward a wrongdoer has an essential element: acceptance of personal responsibility for deciding the other person's fate. By contrast, unmerciful infliction of punishment on another generally seems to require that the occasion for punishment be the responsibility of someone other than the inflicter alone. This appears to have been the case in the laboratory (see Milgram 1973), where deference to someone else's authority facilitated the infliction of punishment. Similarly, attribution of responsibility to others has coincided with routine infliction of punishment on criminal defendants by officers of court.

The abdication of personal responsibility for punishing criminals has a long history in Western law. In trial by ordeal, the decision to inflict punishment was believed to rest in heavenly hands, and human agents were merely passive instruments of the meeting of that responsibility (see Aubert 1959: 5-7). At common law, punishment of offenders came to rest on a finding that defendants were responsible for their own undoing. As some defendants were found mentally incapable of incurring responsibility for criminal punishment, classes of people came to be exempt from criminal liability: first, children and then, the insane. Ideally, the responsible offender could be held to advance notice of the penalties prescribed by law for his or her conduct, so that the penalty could be assumed to be the defendant's free choice. Convicts bore the responsibility for incurring punishment "under law"; officers of the court accepted responsibility only for showing compassion in grants of mercy, as in "the enormous attrition in felons brought to public notice" in Elizabethan England (Samaha 1974: 45-66).

Abdication of responsibility for punishment of offenders was rendered a far more complex task by the impact of positivist criminology beginning in the nineteenth century. It became widely recognized that different convicts merited various kinds of criminal sanctions. Untreatable offenders needed to be diagnosed for permanent isolation from society. The sentencing of treatable offenders needed to be more flexible, to allow both for efficacious rehabilitation and for minimization of wasteful incarceration once rehabilitation had been accomplished. For some of those who could not legally be held responsible for crimes, responsibility for care and treatment devolved on state officials. The range of dispositional alternatives open to choice by officers of the court increased tremendously to permit the exercise of discretion in determining length of incarceration, in the use of alternatives to incarceration, or in the use of civil commitment of those who could not be held legally responsible for their crimes.

While it might once have been credible that justice was done merely by meting out a sentence fixed by law to anyone who took on the responsibility of committing a crime, it has become increasingly apparent that the sole responsibility of a defendant for determining the punishment for each crime ended with the defendant's conviction. At that point, manifest responsibility passed to officers of the court—primarily to judges—to decide which sentence out of a number of alternatives should justly be imposed. The growth of the technology for classifying convicts for state supervision on criteria other than the crimes they had committed has increased the burden of responsibility on officers of the court in yet another way. Visions of making people better members of society led to increasing reliance on court processes, and court caseloads expanded accordingly. Court officers, other than judges, have taken on increasing roles in figuring out what should be done with defendants. It has come to pass that police officers, prosecutors, defense counsel, and court-services personnel are all asked to help make dispositive decisions as to what sentences defendants shall receive, and even to exercise discretion as to what offense to charge a defendant with. This feature of case disposition is common knowledge among American criminologists.

Less obvious is the fact that the development of such responsibility on officers of the court is scarcely reversible. Some have called for a return to the simpler days of correlation of sentence to offense committed (American Friends Service Committee 1971, National Advisory Commission 1973: 42-65). But devolvement of such heavy responsibility for discretionary disposition of cases onto officers of the court has removed the foundation of tradition as to which disposition is the one merited for commission of any particular crime. People can no longer agree on how to translate abstract principles of retribution or just deserts into operational terms for each offense. The dilemma of court officers—how to balance political demands for intolerance of a mounting crime problem with the heavy burden of personal responsibility for punishing human offenders—is increasingly troublesome and difficult to escape.

SCIENTIFIC DISPLACEMENT OF RESPONSIBILITY

Social scientific technology, the source of the burden of responsibility on officers for deciding when and how to impose incarceration, simultaneously provides an escape from the burden, that is, the means by which that responsibility can be displaced. It has become a truism that those administering American criminal justice "must seek knowledge and admit mistakes," to which end:

> All operating agencies of justice urgently need the close
> contact with academic thought that could be achieved
> through use of faculty consultants; seminars and institutes
> to analyze current problems and innovations; advanced
> training programs for judges, police administrators, and
> correctional officers; and more operational research
> projects and surveys conducted in conjunction with agen-
> cies of justice (President's Commission 1967b: 291).

A cycle of dependence on the application of social science technology results. Research findings point to extralegal criteria used in criminal justice decision making. These criteria commonly take the form of inferences, from information provided by other officials, as to how the latter would expect subsequent decisions to be made. Direct interaction and involvement with clients is rendered practically superfluous. Pepinsky (1976) has confirmed it in the classification of calls by police dispatchers to patrolmen to make offense-reporting decisions. In addition, Gottfredson et al. (1973) found a lack of interaction with clients in the use of case records in parole decision making, while Sudnow (1965) has reported it in the use of arrest reports by prosecutors and public defenders in plea bargaining. This phenomenon is a kind of goal displacement (see Blau 1955: 231-49) in which conventions are established among decision makers to act as passive ratifiers of others' decisions instead of relying on personal standards to make independent case dispositions.

Demonstration of the ability of social scientists to make this kind of inference of implicit decision-making policy leads to the inevitable social criticism encountered by most public officials and, furthermore, makes criminal justice decision makers receptive to social engineers' offers to establish information management systems. Typically, the engineers adopt one of two strategies. One strategy is to make preexisting decision-making patterns more efficient, as in the Prosecutor's Management Information System (Sullivan and Work 1973), or the general stochastic network modeling of the criminal justice system in Champaign County, Illinois (Hogg et al. 1975). The other strategy is to recommend a single principle for use in sentencing, as in the latest fad for "shock" sentencing of young first-time convicts (see Ritchie and McGraw 1975). The officials have come to rely on the constraints imposed by the social engineers as authoritative bases for decision making (in the guise of "professionalism"), while the social engineers rely on officials' decision-making criteria as authoritative bases for selecting constraints. The choice of bases for decision making is cyclical and the responsibility for making the choice tend to be displaced from everyone.

The rise of social-engineering practitioners in criminal justice is a recent addition to the role played by some physicians (notably some psychiatrists) and some members of the rising social-work profession. David and Sheila Rothman have been compiling a detailed account of the role of medical and social-work professionals in criminal justice during this century (for a preliminary report, see Rothman 1975). They find that the people subjected to state jurisdiction and the length of confinement of people in total institutions have, until recently, grown mainly on the authority of these "experts." These experts have differred from the social engineers who have risen to prominence during the last few years, for the medical and social work experts claimed special competence not only to decide what should be done to whom, but to do it themselves. Here, at least, there has been no displacement of responsibility. Instead, the treatment specialists have applauded their own efforts to help—rather than punish—those diagnosed as having mental diseases or defects. Lately, a number of critics have argued that this is a distinction without a difference, that what is called "treatment" is a more intrusive version of criminal justice punishment with no demonstrable benefits to clients or to society. In the course of this criticism, the Maryland Institution for Defective Delinquents (also known as "Patuxent") has received special notoriety (see, for example, Wilkins 1975).

Partly out of disenchantment with the results of the multitude of efforts on treatment of offenders, and partly out of the spirit of the "Great Society" in the middle 1960s, the role of the social scientist as a criminal justice engineer was raised to national political prominence with the sponsorship of the President's Commission on Law Enforcement and Administration of Justice (1967b). There were some notable earlier attempts at social engineering, such as Ohlin's (1951) study setting parole criteria, but the President's Commission carried the relationship between social scientists and criminal justice officials much further. This writer recalls a conversation with a lawyer who was centrally involved in putting the commission together. He had started, he said, with the presumption that there were a lot of social scientists around the United States who knew exactly how to respond to the American crime problem. He was soon disabused of that presumption.

Nevertheless, with heavy social science input, the commission generated a series of reports laden with recommendations about how to respond to crime, from the field of measurement to the realm of corrections and to special sets of recommendations on the use of science and technology and on responses to organized crime. The commission even had the first three of the now commonplace victim surveys conducted (President's Commission 1967a), in which some social scientists presume to be measuring, as nearly as possible, the "true" nature, scope, and trends of the crime problem. These surveys have quite literally been taken as definitions of the needs of law enforcement, as in the case of the Law Enforcement Assistance Administration (LEAA) grant, arising out of a victim survey in Pueblo, Colorado, to develop "target hardening" measures in that community (Inciardi 1976). In the extreme case of victim surveys, the cycle of abdication of responsibility is extended beyond criminal justice officials to include community residents-at-large.

As illustrated by the Prosecutor's Management Information System and other examples mentioned above, relationships between social scientists and criminal justice agencies have since proliferated, often supported by LEAA funding. It has now become commonplace for criminal justice officials to have social scientists instruct them as to how official decisions should be made.

CONCLUSION: CRIMINAL JUSTICE WITHOUT COMPASSION

It has been suggested, as by Cahn (1955), that the capacity to depersonalize victims promotes crime. The same may be said for promotion of widespread punishment of offenders. By abdicating personal responsibility for the fate of those one "treats," infliction of punishment (such as incarceration) is facilitated. The parallel between the expedience of responding to crime and the expedience of committing crime is not lost on offenders (see, for example, "Frisco" 1972). If criminal justice decision making in general, or court processing of defendants in particular, is to set a moral tone of intolerance for crime, decisions there must exemplify a quality of justice imbued with compassion.

Predominantly, the impact of social science technology on the treatment of defendants has been one of suppression of compassion. Compassion inheres in acceptance of personal responsibility to another for one's treatment of that person, and the application of social science technology has tended to displace such responsibility, eroding affective ties between criminal justice officials and their clientele. A moral principle underlying criminal justice decision making is growing more apparent—do unto others before they do unto you, and try to confine them from doing it back; take before being taken; strike before being struck; be depersonalized and objective in getting what you need at others' expense. Increasingly, the criminal justice system, with the help of social science technology, is coming to ratify the very moral philosophy it is supposed to suppress. The dedication of applied social scientists to help the criminal justice system to run efficiently and rise above criticism carries a cost. Self-report studies since that of Wallerstein and Wyle (1947) have indicated that practically every American can be found to qualify for criminal sanction. We have not nearly exhausted of the pool of potential candidates for incarceration and other forms of treatment. As efficiency of criminal justice decision making is increased, the capacity of the system increases accordingly. It is the job of officials to use that capacity. The increased overhead of giving more services to more clients tends to compensate for decreased time and expenditure in handling any individual case. Continued growth in the size and expense of the officially recognized crime problem can be expected as a consequence.

Max Weber (1946) once suggested that it was the proper role of the scientist to raise questions about social policy rather than to attempt to answer such questions for others. As Weber put it: "To let the facts speak for themselves is the most unfair way of putting over a political position" (1946: 146). It is likely that there would be increased acceptance of personal responsibility among criminal justice decision makers if social scientists would limit themselves to raising questions and doubts, instead of attempting to provide an authoritative technology of efficient resource utilization. Such a commitment in applied research, called a "strategy of search" by Empey and Luback (1971), is not as common as it might be. If official decision makers could be encouraged to accept more responsibility for what they do to others, and were moved to greater compassion for officially suspected or convicted offenders in the process, perhaps they might discover that handling interpersonal conflict in a just way does not require one of the highest rates of incarceration in the world. And, in American criminal justice, more "quality" might be put back into the meaning of "justice" after all.

REFERENCES

American Friends Service Committee. 1971. Struggle for Justice. New York: Hill and Wang.

Aubert, V. 1959. Chance in social affairs. Inquiry 2 (Spring): 1-24.

Blau, M. 1955. The Dynamics of Bureaucracy. Chicago: University of Chicago Press.

Cahn, E. 1955. The Moral Decision. Bloomington: Indiana University Press.

Empey, T. and S. G. Lubeck. 1971. The Silverlake Experiment: Testing Delinquency Theory and Community Intervention. Chicago: Aldine Publishing Co.

"Frisco." 1972. A prisoner's views on scientific penology. In Criminal Life: Views from the Inside, eds. Davis M. Petersen and Marcello Truzzi. Englewood Cliffs, N. J.: Prentice-Hall, Inc.

Gottfredson, D. M., L. T. Wilkins, P. R. Hoffman, and S. M. Singer. 1973. Parole Decision-Making—Summary: The Utilization of Experience in Parole Decision-Making, A Progress Report. Davis, California: NCCD Research Center.

Hogg, G. L., R. E. DeVor, and R. J. Luhr. 1975. Analysis of court systems via generalized stochastic network simulation. In Proceedings of the Sixth Annual Conference on Modeling and Simulation. Pittsburgh: Instrument Society of America.

Inciardi, J. A. 1976. The role of criminal statistics and victim survey research in planning and organizing for more effective law enforcement. In Victims, Criminals, and Society, ed. Emilio Viano. Washington, D.C.: Visage Press.

McCarthy, C. 1975. White-collar crime. Washington Post, Apr. 11.

Milgram, S. 1973. Obedience to Authority: An Experimental View. New York: Harper & Row.

National Advisory Commission on Criminal Justice Standards and Goals. 1973. Courts. Washington, D.C.: United States Government Printing Office.

Ohlin, L. E. 1951. Selection for Parole. Dubuque, Iowa: William C. Brown, Inc.

Pepinsky, H. E. 1976. Police offense reporting behavior. Journal of Research in Crime and Delinquency 13 (January): 33-47.

President's Commission on Law Enforcement and Administration of Justice. 1967a. Field Surveys I-III. Washington, D.C.: United States Government Printing Office.

———. 1967b. The Challenge of Crime in a Free Society. Washington, D.C.: United States Government Printing Office.

Quinney, R. 1974. Critique of Legal Order: Crime Control in Capitalist Society. Boston: Little, Brown and Company.

Ritchie, J. and R. C. McGran. 1975. Report challenges shock probation's success: correction officers' strikes delay findings. Ohio State University Lantern (June 3): 1.

Robin, G. D. 1970. The corporate and judicial disposition of employee thieves. In Crimes Against Bureaucracy, eds. E. O. Smigel and H. L. Ross. New York: Van Nostrand Reinhold Company.

Rothman, D. J. 1975. Behavior modification in total institutions: an historical overview. Hastings Center Report 5 (February): 17-24.

Samaha, J. 1974. Law and Order in Historical Perspective: The Case of Elizabethan Sussex. New York: Academic Press.

Sudnow, D. 1965. Normal crimes: sociological features of the penal code in a public defender's office. Social Problems 12 (Winter): 255-76.

Sullivan, W. A. and C. R. Work. 1967. The role of the prosecutor in the urban court system: the case for management consciousness. Journal of Law, Criminology and Police Science 58 (June): 173-81.

Time, Inc. 1975. The crime wave. Time, June 30.

Waller, I. and J. Chan. 1974. Prison use: a Canadian and international comparison. Criminal Law Quarterly 17 (December): 47-71.

Wallerstein, J. S. and D. J. Wyle. 1947. Our law-abiding law-breakers. Probation 25 (March-April): 105-12.

Weber, M. 1946. Science as a vocation. In From Max Weber: Essays in Sociology, trans. and eds., H. H. Gerth and C. M. Mills. New York: Oxford University Press.

Wilkins, L. T. 1975. Putting "treatment" on trial: efficiency, equity, and the clinical approach to offenders. Hastings Center Report 5 (February): 35-48.

15

COMMITMENT OF JUVENILES: A CRITICISM OF THE USE OF CONSENT DECREES AS A MEANS OF INVOLUNTARY CIVIL COMMITMENT BY SOME JUVENILE COURTS

Alphonso Jackson

INTRODUCTION

The purpose of this article is to provide an in-depth analysis of problems raised by a particular method of disposition employed by some state juvenile courts. This narrow area involves broad questions relating to the need for procedural protection for children in their contact with the juvenile court system.

Because of the narrowness of the problem involved, it is necessary to begin with general overview of the juvenile court system and then proceed to a more detailed discussion of involuntary civil commitment authorized by statute for both adults and children.

The theory underlying the juvenile court system, stated briefly, is that children, though legally capable of distinguishing right from wrong, should not be punished for their wrong actions because they cannot have the requisite experience to assess the consequences of their acts. Therefore, the purpose of the juvenile court is not to ascertain guilt or innocence in order to determine a punishment, but to determine the extent of a child's antisocial acts and then to select a counseling program that is in the best interests of the child. Also, courts have relied upon the fact that juvenile proceedings are civil and not criminal in origin and, therefore, they may deny children constitutional protections that are provided adults.

THE ADMINISTRATIVE SYSTEM AND PROCEDURES

Court workers in a juvenile division are usually divided into departments all of which are directly responsible to a judge. These departments usually consist of an administrator, juvenile and hearing officer, and the legal department. The other departments are usually the neglect and delinquency units. Each has an intake department where new cases are given a preliminary screening.

Authorization for Consent Decrees

In juvenile cases, a consent decree is a method of disposition in which no petition is filed;[*] jurisdictional facts are admitted, but the court does not take jurisdiction; and the parents consent to the disposition recommended by the court.

Consent decrees in the juvenile court are authorized by statutes, which gives the court the power to make a preliminary inquiry into any situation regarding a juvenile after receiving, in writing, a statement that indicates that the child falls within the jurisdiction statute. As an example, Section 211.081 of Missouri Revised Statutes provides, "On the basis of this inquiry, the juvenile court may take such informal adjustment as is practicable without a petition or may authorize the filing of a petition by the juvenile officer." Some juvenile courts have interpreted provisions of this nature to include the authorization of consent decrees. In many jurisdictions, where no formal petition is filed, cases may be continued without any finding being made, even after there has been a hearing on the merits of the delinquency complaint. Alternatively, some juvenile courts may choose to proceed under other jurisdictional provisions such as neglect, dependency, or mental health. If jurisdictional provisions other than delinquency are employed, legal arguments surrounding mental incompetency are avoided and the main attention is directed to the juvenile's need for treatment. The interpretation follows the report of the President's Commission of Law Enforcement and Administration of Justice which states:

> A juvenile court should make fullest feasible use of preliminary conferences to dispose of cases short of adjudication. Juvenile courts should employ consent decrees wherever possible to avoid adjudication while still settling juvenile cases and treating offenders (1967: 84-87).

The question then becomes, Where are consent decrees used? They are used to place the child under informal supervision, to temporarily transfer physical custody from the parents to a foster-home situation, and to require the parents' financial contribution if the child is removed from the home. Consent decrees may come out of an informal hearing or an agreement between parents and a social worker.

---

[*]"Petition" refers to a court document which alleges that a juvenile has committed a crime.

A Case Analysis of Consent Decree Procedures

By tracing a case through the court structure, it is possible to see more clearly the relationships among individuals and procedures. When a delinquency referral is first received, it is sent immediately to delinquency intake where it is screened by a social worker. A day or two prior to the evidentiary hearing, the file is sent to the judge, commissioner, or heating officer assigned to hear the case, who then has an opportunity to review the file prior to the hearing.

At the hearing, the facts relevant to each allegation of the petition are ascertained through questioning of the child and the witnesses. If the allegations are found to be true, the court takes jurisdiction over the child. All pertinent facts regarding the disposition of the case are discussed, and the court then enters an order of disposition. If the case has been heard by the commissioner or the hearing officer, a recommendation is entered for disposition which then must be approved by a judge. Once the disposition is made and approved, the file is sent on to the appropriate department. For example, if supervision is ordered, the file is sent to one of the supervisory units, where it is assigned to a social worker who then takes charge of the case and works with both the child and family. If a case has been screened for an informal hearing, the docket clerk sets it on a docket and then routes the case to the individual who will hear it. Once a decision has been made, the file is again routed to the appropriate department. For example, if the disposition is to be voluntary supervision by consent decree, the file is sent to one of the supervisory units for assignment to a social worker.

As pointed out earlier, cases may be disposed of without any type of hearing. One of these dispositions is a consent decree without a hearing. For example, suppose a child is already under voluntary consent supervision and is again referred to the court. The worker supervising the child may decide, with the parents, that short-term placement in an open institution is desirable. If so, the worker will then draw up a consent decree signed by the parents placing legal and physical custody of the child with the desired institution. If the judge approves the decree, the child goes to the designated institution. This method of disposition is also used to commit children, involuntarily, to mental institutions without a hearing.[1]

HISTORICAL ARGUMENTS FAVORING CONSENT DECREES

Historically, traditional arguments in favor of procedures such as outlined above have included:

1. Mental-health facilities often refuse to take either adults or juveniles with a court record;

2. Correctional institutions are reluctant to handle mentally disordered juveniles;

3. Parental cooperation is necessary in the treatment of juveniles, especially those who are mentally disordered. Therefore, procedures that place the largest emphasis on parental cooperation are the best;

4. A juvenile should not go through a competency hearing because it is harmful at that age.

Many mental-health facilities, both private and public, refuse to accept the mentally disordered juvenile who has a court record. These mental-health facilities are somewhat reluctant to become involved in legal matters. They have maintained that mentally disordered delinquents are disruptive to their rehabilitation treatment programs. Therefore, the less formal contact the juvenile has with the court system the better are his chances of receiving treatment. The emphasis upon parental cooperation is necessary in the treatment of juvenile delinquents, especially those with mental disorders. If parental cooperation can be relied upon, the mental-health facilities will be able to treat the child in out-patient facilities, thus maintaining their inservice rehabilitation program.

ARGUMENT AGAINST CONSENT DECREES

Statutory

The first argument against consent decrees is statutory. It is based on the finding of a quasi-jurisdictional relationship between the court and the child by the use of consent decrees as authorized under statute. In Morgan v. United States, Chief Justice Hughes stated:

> That those who are brought into contest with the government in quasi-judicial proceedings aimed at the control of their activities are entitled to be fairly advised of what government purposes and to be heard upon its command. . . . The requirements of fairness are not exhausted in the taking or consideration of evidence, but extend to the concluding part of the procedure as well as to the beginning and intermediate steps.

General Fairness

Another argument against consent decree commitments to mental institutions is based on general fairness. In <u>Kent</u> v. <u>United States</u>, the Supreme Court held "that the hearing [in juvenile proceeding] must measure up to the essentials of due process and fair treatment." Note that <u>Kent</u> did not present a constitutional question, but the decision contained suggestions of the court's feeling about the constitutionality of certain juvenile court procedures. It is this concept of fair treatment that is violated by consent-decree commitments to mental institutions. Kenneth Davis has stated that "the American legal profession focuses too much on fairness of administrative procedure as a process of controlled discretion. Consent decrees, by their very nature, are discretionary exercises of administrative power by the juvenile court" (1969). If one accepts Professor Davis's contention that procedural protection, short of trial-type procedure, is to determine what protection should be offered juveniles in commitment proceedings.

Due Process

Since <u>Kent</u> v. <u>United States</u> and <u>In Re Gault</u>, the due-process clauses of the Fifth and Fourteenth Amendments have applied to proceedings in state juvenile courts. The <u>Gault</u> case involved a juvenile who had been accused of making lewd and indecent remarks to a woman over the telephone. Gault was never informed of his right to counsel and privilege against self-incrimination, neither Gault nor his parents were given notive of the specific accusation against him, and he was never confronted by the complaining party. Gault was found guilty under the statute for using vulgar and obscene language. Because Gault had been before the court previously for being in the presence of another boy who had stolen a wallet, the court found him to come under the statutute as a "child who habitually so deports himself as to injure or endanger the morals or health of himself or other." Gault was placed in the custody of the State Industrial School until the age of twenty-one unless sooner discharged.

The Supreme Court's opinion asserted that the juvenile commitment involved was a "deprivation of liberty. It is incarceration against one's will, whether it is called 'criminal' or 'civil'." Stating that the distinction between a civil and criminal proceeding is moot when an individual's fundamental right to liberty is at stake, the court held that the power of the state to exercise <u>parens patriae</u> was not unlimited. Due-process safeguards must be applied when civil proceeding endangers the right to liberty.

Thus, in reversing the Arizona State Court decision, the Supreme Court held that delinquency proceedings that may result in commitment of a juvenile to a state institution must meet four due-process tests:

1. A juvenile charged with delinquency, and his parents, must be given written notice of "the specific charge or factual allegation" in advance of any hearing to adjudicate the merits of the charge; this notice must be "sufficiently in advance" of scheduled court proceedings.

2. Before a hearing of this nature may be held, the due process clause of the Fourteenth Amendment requires the juvenile and his parents be notified of the child's rights to be represented by counsel retained by them, or, if they are unable to afford counsel, that counsel will be appointed to represent the child.

3. The constitutional privilege against self-incrimination is applicable in hearings of this nature and the child must be advised that he does not have to testify.

4. Absent a "valid confession," an adjudication of delinquency at a hearing of this nature cannot be sustained without sworn testimony of witnesses who are available for confrontation and cross-examination.

The most significant aspect of the Gault decision was the court's holding that all procedural guarantees applicable to adults charged with crimes also apply in juvenile delinquency proceedings. The court echoed its view, as stated in Kent, that "We do not mean . . . to indicate that the hearing to be held must conform with all of the requirements of a criminal trial." The fact that, in both Gault and Kent, the Supreme Court was dealing with the jurisdictional part of the procedures involving juveniles does not rule out their application to the problem of consent-decree commitments. The major difficulty with consent-decree commitments derives from the fact that there are too few controls placed on the court. The disposition of commitment to the state mental institutions comes before any legal determination that jurisdiction exists. The fact that the Gault case involved a commitment to a correctional institution rather than a mental institution did not stop the court from the holding applied to all juvenile commitments to state institutions. All the institutions under the administration of the state are state institutions, and, therefore, Gault applies to commitments to the state mental-health institutions. It is easy to see that consent-decree commitments do not meet the four due-process requirements for juvenile commitments set out in the Gault decision.

Should juveniles alleged to be mentally disordered be considered juveniles or individuals undergoing involuntary commitment procedures? The recognition that involuntary, civil commitment procedures may result in the deprivation of a person's fundamental right to liberty and

greatly influence the course of his or her future life has led to the
incorporation in some jurisdictions of due-process safeguards. Although many are still minority views, their acceptance is desirable
in order to insure adequate protection of individuals affected by the
commitment process.

One basic element of due-process safeguards is the "defendant's"
right to notification of the nature of the charges against him. This
right to notice is well established in both civil and criminal proceedings. Yet, some state commitment statutes either fail to require
such notice or require that only minimal information be provided.
Recently, the trend has been to discard this approach. A few courts
have held that due process may not be offended by a temporary confinement without notice where immediate action is necessary for the
protection of society or the person; however, such confinement cannot
continue beyond prescribed limits without notice to the individual of
other available rights, such as the right to a hearing or the right to
counsel. Regardless of whether temporary or indefinite commitment
is at issue, the allegedly mentally ill person must be provided adequate and timely notice of the action before such commitment proceeding can commence. According to the court in Lassard v. Schmidt,
notice of an impending commitment proceeding must be sufficient in
terms of information provided—not just the date, time, and place;
is must also include the basis for detention, the right to counsel and
to a jury trial, the standard upon which the individual may be detained,
the names of the examining physicians and all others who may testify
in favor of continued detention, and the substance of the proposed
testimony.

Therefore, providing a juvenile due process of law when a
commitment to a mental institution is the favored disposition would
involve, at least, those criteria set out in the adult involuntary commitment statutes. It is clear that consent-decree commitments do
not meet any of these due-process requirements.

Equal Protection

This argument against consent-decree commitments to state
mental institutions rests on the constitutional guarantee of equal protection. Stated simply, this guarantee holds that the law may not
treat persons in the same situation differently. In State v. Gregari,
it is said:

> Legislation is void as contravening the equal protection
> guarantee if it makes an act a crime when committed by
> one person but not so when committed by another in a like
> situation.

In Gault, Justice Black, in a concurring opinion, advanced two arguments in favor of procedural guarantees for juvenile delinquents:

1. That Gault was entitled to all rights he was asserting which are enumerated in the Bill of Rights. [Justice Black's rationale was that Gault was charged with a crime under Arizona law and ordered by the court to confinement for up to six years, and that the Bill of Rights enumerated the guarantees of persons charged with crimes, and these guarantees are made applicable to the state through the Fourteenth Amendment.]

2. That had Gault been an adult, he would have been given all the guarantees of the Bill of Rights; to do otherwise because he was a juvenile was to deny him equal protection of the law in violation of the Fourteenth Amendment.

Commitments to mental institutions do not involve an act which is classified as a crime, but a mental status which is classified as legally incompetent or "mentally disordered." The argument runs that, if one person with a specific mental state is committed to a mental institution under a statute, and another person with the same mental state is adjudged competent under the same statute, then the first person has been denied the equal protection of the law. This is directly applicable to consent-decree commitments of state mental-health institutions in which psychiatric and psychological reports are used as evidence. Psychiatrists and psychologists who have examined the child have provided sworn testimony as to the mental condition of the child. In consent-decree commitments, only a mental status report made within the preceding year is required. Therefore, a child whose mental status would not permit his commitment in a formal proceeding can be committed by a consent decree. Thus, all the requirements of equal protection should be present in the juvenile commitment by consent decree procedure.

A PROPOSED ALTERNATIVE

What does general fairness require in juvenile commitments to mental-health institutions? The Supreme Court of Missouri stated in State v. Dickman that, as a general rule, no person should be adjudged insane or mentally incompetent without a hearing. Defining persons, in this holding, to include juveniles, the Missouri Supreme Court would surely hold that some kind of hearing is necessary before a juvenile may be committed to the state Division of Mental Health.

Should juvenile procedures follow adult procedures? In Gault, the Supreme Court stated that due process requirements is as follows:

We do not mean to indicate that the juvenile hearing must measure up to all the requirements of a criminal trial or administrative hearing, but we do hold that the juvenile hearing must measure up to the essentials of due process and fair treatment.

Gault recognized that there could be a difference in the way juvenile delinquents and adult criminals are handled. In McKeiver v. Pennsylvania, the Supreme Court held "that a jury trial in the juvenile court's adjudicative stage is not constitutionally required." The court noted that the Sixth Amendment right to a jury trial was held to be applicable to states through the Fourteenth Amendment in all criminal cases. But, it still held that a jury trial in juvenile court is not a constitutional requirement. Although the juvenile court had failed to attain earlier goals, the court doubted whether granting the right to a jury trial would remedy those defects.

The question still facing juveniles courts is deciding standard for determining whether a particular right is one of the "essentials of due process and fair treatment." For juvenile proceedings, the court in McKeiver held "that fundamental fairness, as established in In Re Gault and In Re Winship, is the applicable due process standard in juvenile proceeding." What are the particular procedural safeguards which will make juvenile proceedings fair? In McKeiver, the court stated that rights accorded to juveniles should be reflected by the accuracy of fact finding in juvenile proceedings. This does not necessarily entail all of the procedural safeguards given to adults.

Is a formal hearing necessary? In McKeiver, the court emphasized that juvenile courts should be allowed to use procedures that are different from those used in adult courts. Also, it stated that juvenile proceedings do not have to replicate adult criminal proceedings in the name of due process. Sections of the Uniform Juvenile Court Act make provisions for informal adjudication of juvenile cases and set forth the following criteria:

1. Jurisdictional facts must be admitted and stated.

2. The juvenile and the juvenile's parents must be given counsel and advice that is in the best interest of the child and the community.

3. The parents and the child must consent in writing to the disposition made informally with the understanding that they can have a hearing if they so desire.

4. There must be a three-month time limit for any disposition made by consent decree.

These criteria for consent decrees provide a higher degree of fairness than the procedures now used by Missouri and other state juvenile courts. However, they are questionable criteria for commitment to a state mental-health institutions, especially the three-month limitation. This is not to say that the principles of general fairness require the same strict criteria required by due process in adult criminal proceedings. Some of the procedures suggested by Professor Davis with regard to administrative proceedings appear to be applicable here. The child should receive notice of adjudication, should be allowed to hear the evidence, and should be given a chance to explain his or her actions and state what procedures would be in the child's best interest. All of this should be done before a hearing officer, someone who is able to determine objectively the best interests of the child. In this way the minimum standard of fairness is met, and the child is less likely to feel "railroaded" into a mental institution.

CONCLUSION

The lengthy process of interpretation of the role of due process in juvenile proceedings, which started with Gault and led to McKeiver, will certainly continue. In these two cases, the court made the following evaluations of juvenile delinquent proceedings: (1) that the adjudication of juvenile delinquency proceedings are similar to the criminal fact-finding proceedings; (2) that some of the constitutional protections which exist in state criminal proceedings will be applicable to juvenile delinquency proceedings; (3) that the provisions of the Bill of Rights will be applied to delinquency proceedings on a case-by-case basis; (4) that these constitutional safeguards will be applicable when the delinquent is faced with the possibility of confinement in a state institution; and (5) that delinquency proceedings will not necessarily replicate adult criminal proceedings.

The most important point of the Gault decision is that the court held that all procedural guarantees which are applicable in cases of adults charged with crimes are applicable to juvenile proceedings. Although in Gault the Supreme Court was addressing itself to the jurisdictional part of the procedures involving delinquency, this does not rule out the application of these safeguards to the problem of consent-decree commitment. The fact that the Gault case involved a commitment of a juvenile to a correctional institution rather than a mental institution did not stop the court from applying its principles more broadly by holding that Gault applies to all juvenile commitments to state institutions. All the institutions which come under the administration of the state are state institutions, and therefore the Gault decision applies to the state mental-health institutions. The consent-decree commitment used in a number of states does not meet the due-process requirement set ou in Gault for juvenile commitment. Therefore, consent decree-commitment should be disallowed and the due-process requirement set out in Gault and Kent should be accepted. As a comment in the Mercer Law Review stated, "If we must discriminate against children, let's at least be fair about it" (Comment 1969: 406).

Therefore, even in light of Gault and McKeiver, a juvenile should be accorded all procedural safeguards given in an adult criminal proceeding particularly when faced with the possibility of a lengthy confinement. Today, there are only a few states which provide for a jury trial and then only when it is demanded by the juvenile or his parents. Another state provides for a jury trial only upon appeal. Yet, another state refers the delinquent to the district court for trial by jury and after trial the case is remanded to the juvenile court for disposition. It must be noted that the different approaches in cases probably meet constitutional standards of the Sixth Amendment by merely requiring that accused persons have a right to an impartial jury. Also, these procedures more than likely meet the requirements of due process under the Fourteenth Amendment.

There is no question about the need to protect the delinquent when coming in contact with the juvenile court. Therefore, the same safeguards accorded the adult criminal proceedings through the Fourteenth Amendment should be accorded the juvenile. There is no room for the use of consent-decree commitments, which deny juveniles their constitutional rights of due process and equal protection.

APPENDIX

1. The case studies used as examples of each of these types of commitments are taken from the files of a Missouri juvenile court (St. Louis County) as an illustration of the procedures used by the court in each form of commitment.

CASE STUDY #1

This boy was committed by his parents to St. Louis State Hospital Youth Center in 1967 when he was 13. In 1968, he ran from the Youth Center to his home. Youth Center discharged him upon his parents' request. During November and December of 1968, he committed various delinquent acts and finally came to the attention of the court.

Because of the nature of his offenses (unprovoked assaults, truancy, molestations, and voyeurism) and his record of prior commitment, the court had him evaluated at Youth Center. The psychiatric and psychological reports indicated a severe mental distrubance. A petition was filed, and the case was set on the docket in February, 1970. At the hearing the child was represented by court-appointed counsel from the Public Defender's Office. Present at the hearing were the child's parents, an aunt and uncle, a minister, the child and his counsel, a psychologist from Youth Center, a social worker from the court, the legal officer from the court, the child's victims, and various police officers. After taking testimony from everyone present, the court found the child to have committed the acts alleged in the petition and, in the matter of disposition, found the child to be mentally disordered and committed the child to the state Division of Mental Diseases. The parents were in complete agreement with the commitment. The child was sent by the state Division of Mental Diseases to Fulton State Hospital where he was placed in the area reserved for the criminally insane. In late 1970, the child applied for a rehearing under section 202. 837 before the juvenile court. The rehearing was granted and the court obtained the services of an independent psychiatrist, a psychologist from Fulton State Hospital, the legal officer from the court, and the child's minister. All were allowed to testify. In the opinion of the independent psychiatrist, the child was in need of further care and treatment. No objections to this were raised. The court found the child to be in need of further care and treatment and remanded him to the custody of the state Division of Mental Diseases.

In this case, as in all juvenile commitments, the child was committed under section 211. 201 (1), which states that if a child is under the jurisdiction of the court and the court finds that the child is epileptic, mentally deficient, or otherwise mentally disordered, the court may commit the child to the state Division of Mental Diseases. Jurisdiction is determined by section 211. 631 which lays out very broad jurisdictional grounds, as do must juvenile codes. In this case, there was no difficulty in finding jurisdiction because the court found that the child had committed acts that would be considered crimes if committed by an adult. The statute sets up no standards by which a child is to be found judged, leaving the procedures to the discretion of the Court. In Case Study #1, the procedure chosen by the court directly paralleled the adult commitment procedure set out in section 202. 807. That statute calls for notice to all interested parties, representation by counsel of the alleged insane person, opportunity for all interested parties to testify, and testimony of at least one doctor who had examined the patient no more than 20 days prior to the hearing. A

further indication that the court in this case was following the adult
commitment statutes is the fact that the juvenile code does not provide
for a rehearing on the initiative of the committed child. The adult
commitment procedures do so provide, and in this case they were
followed, even as to allowing the child's petition for rehearing to be
based specifically on section 202. 837, the rehearing provision.

The second case study is an example of an informal hearing
resulting in a consent-decree commitment to the State Division of
Mental Diseases. This hearing was held before the commissioner,
but the same procedures would be used in a similar hearing held before the hearing officer.

CASE STUDY #2

This child was voluntarily committed to St. Louis State Hospital
Youth Center by her parents in 1966 for evaluation. She ran away
from there several times until, in 1967, she was released to her
parents and continued in outpatient care. She was enrolled in the
Special School District in St. Louis County, and the court initially
became involved because the Special School District reported her as
truant. In 1967, her court involvement was limited, to several visits
with a worker in the Short-Term Counseling unit. In early 1968,
she ran away from her home and again came to the attention of the
court. At this time she was readmitted to Youth Center for evaluation and upon her release was brought before the commissioner for
an informal hearing. Present at this hearing were the child, her
parents, and the worker from the Short-Term Counseling unit who
had originally seen her at the court. Testimony of the child and her
parents was taken and the various reports and recommendations of
the doctors at Youth Center were studies by the commissioner. The
parents agreed to sign a consent decree committing the child to the
state Division of Mental Diseases. The consent order was approved
by the judge, and the child was placed at Youth Center by the state
Division of Mental Diseases.

The procedures followed in this case are not as strict as those followed in the first case study, and certainly did not follow adult commitment procedures. However, there was notice given of the hearing,
medical reports and recommendations that were less than a week old
were used in the final determination and there was an objective third
person, the commissioner, to make the final determination.

The third and final form of commitment to the state Division
of Mental Diseases is a consent decree without a hearing. There is
no doubt that this type of decree serves a useful purpose in the court
system. It provides for swift disposition of many minor matters for
which a hearing is not only unnecessary, but also undesirable. There
are many areas where it should not and cannot be used. One of these
is commitment to state Division of Mental Diseases. The court has
interpreted sections 211.201 and 211.081 together to mean that a
juvenile may be committed to the state Division of Mental Diseases
by a consent decree either after an informal hearing or without any
hearing. The following case study is a typical example of a consent-
decree commitment to the state Division of Mental Diseases.

CASE STUDY #3

This 15-year-old child was placed in St. Louis State Hospital Youth
Center by her parents. She was referred to the court for running
away from Youth Center and brought to the detention facility. She
had never been under the jurisdiction of the court. Her parents refused to accept her back into their home and the child refused to return voluntarily to Youth Center. At a conference held between the
child, her parents, and the deputy juvenile officer, the parents signed
a consent decree committing the child to the state Division of Mental
Diseases. At this time the child was 16. The judge approved the
commitment and the state Division of Mental Diseases sent the child
to Fulton State Hospital.

Procedurally, there are many differences between commitment by
hearing and consent commitments without a hearing. The most obvious difference is the place in the court structure in which each occurs. It can be seen that a consent-decree commitment bypasses all
of the functional departments and places the responsibility for the
decision of jurisdiction and disposition on one social worker and the
parents of the child. Certainly, the decisional process is shortened
considerably, but the question remains whether or not this reduction
is actually a short circuiting in which the child's rights to due process
under the 14th Amendment are sacrificed for expediency. This question can be answered only after a determination that the social worker
making these decisions is competent legally or practically to do so.
The question then becomes whether the legislature wished to provide
for a judge to hear juvenile cases? And if a social worker is to be
practically competent to make these decisions, must he or she have
a grounding in legal as well as social principles?

REFERENCES

Burdick, P. 1968. Uniform juvenile court act. Pennsylvania Bar Association Quarterly 40: 47.

Carver, L. H. and P. A. White. 1968. Constitutional safeguards for the juvenile offender: implications of recent supreme court decisions. Crime and Delinquency 14 (January).

Comment. 1969. America's most discriminatory laws and courts. Mercer Law Review 20: 400-13.

Davis, K. 1969. Discretionary Justice. Baton Rouge: Louisiana State University Press.

Donovan, J. A. 1969. The juvenile court and the mentally disordered child. N. Kak. Law Review 45: 222-25.

Dorsen, N. and D. Rezneck. 1967. In re Gault and the future of juvenile law. Family Law Quarterly 1, 3: 9-31.

Douglas. 1968. Juvenile courts and due process of law. Juvenile Court Judges Journal 19: 9-14.

Fester, E., T. Countless, and E. Snethen. 1970. Separating official and unofficial delinquents: juvenile court intake. Iowa Law Review 55: 864-70.

In re Gault, 387 U.S. 1, 12-57.

Kent v. United States, 383 U.S. 541. 541-543 (1967).

Kittrie, N. 1969. Can the right to treatment remedy the ills of the juvenile process. Georgia Law Journal 52: 848-49.

Lassard v. Schmidt, 349 Fed. Supp. 1078 (E.D. wis. 1972), vacated and remanded on other ground, 414 U.S. 473 (1974) (per curian), modified, 379 Fed. Supp. 1376 (E.D. Wis. 1974).

Lefstein, N., V. Stapleton, and L. Teitelbaum. 1969. In search of juvenile justice: Gault and its implementation. Law and Society Review 3 (May): 491-562.

McKeiver v. Pennsylvania, 403 U.S. 528. 529-540.

Morgan v. United States, 304 U.S. 1. 18-20 (1938).

Paulsen, M. G. 1966. Kent v. United States: the constitutional context of juvenile cases. The Supreme Court Review 167.

Popkin, A. B., F. Lippert, and J. Keiter. 1972. Another look at the role of due process in juvenile justice. Family Law Quarterly 6, 3: 233-49.

President's Commission on Law Enforcement and the Administration of Justice. 1967. The Challenge of Crime in a Free Society. Washington, D.C.: U.S. Government Printing Office.

Reasons, C. E. 1970. Gault: procedural change and substantive effect. Crime and Delinquency 16 (April): 163-71.

Sheridan, W. H. 1962. Juvenile court intake. Journal of Family Law 2: 143-56.

Skoler, D. 1968. Counsel in juvenile court proceedings—a total criminal justice perspective. Journal of Family Law 8: 243.

State v. Dickman, 157 S.W. 1019 (1913).

State v. Gregari, 3 Southwest 2d 747, 748 (1928).

Weinstein, N. and C. Goodman. 1967. The Juvenile Court Supplement to Chapter 17 of the Missouri Family Law Digest.

16

AUTHORITARIAN ORGANIZATIONS AND THE CORRUPTION OF JUSTICE

Richard A. Ball

Any reasonable consideration of the processes involved in the corruption of justice must begin with working definitions of "corruption" and "justice." One who attempts such working definitions may expect to encounter immediate and vigorous dissent, since to define central terms differently is actually to threaten the "reality systems" of those who see the problems from other perspectives. Thus, for example, we have the persistent and still unresolved argument over the definition of "white-collar crime." Perhaps we can be helped by a recognition that the real issue is not whether a definition is "correct," but rather the advantage of employing one definition over others.

"Corruption" has been defined in many different ways (Gardiner and Olson 1974). Usually, there is an emphasis upon misuse of authority. Generally, this misuse of authority is traced to reasons of personal gain, although it is admitted that the gain need not be monetary. The frequent implication is that the problem can be traced to the "bad apple" who is contaminating the barrel and whose removal will set things right (Gardiner and Olson 1974: 277-82). In contrast to this viewpoint, this chapter argues that "corruption" goes far deeper than we wish to admit and suggest that the fundamental ethical problem is one of institutionalized injustice. Perhaps the barrel itself is rotten. If that is the case, even the best apples are likely to be contaminated.

What is "justice"? Rawls (1958) has probably come as close as anyone to an acceptable working definition, equating justice with "fairness." A similar definition is offered by Frankena (1962: 26) who refers to "a point of view which is fully free, informed, and rational, transcends both ourselves and our actual society, and is committed to a respect for the good life of every individual." The truth is that our specific definitions have evolved over several thousand years and will likely undergo considerable changes in the future. Today, concepts of justice are closely associated with concepts of law; and the implementing agencies are collectively referred to as the criminal justice system.

Viewed sociologically, law is a complex built of two primary social phenomena: ethics and power (Timasheff 1937). The balance of ethics and power through law makes social justice possible. What is less clearly understood is the extent to which social justice makes possible continued human interaction and viable social systems. It is in this sense that Fuller (1969) has described "customary law," law which is not the result of official enactment, as a latent specification of the underlying ground rules governing social interaction in a given social system. Without these ground rules, human interaction itself becomes problematic.

The vital balance between ethics and power is, however, more delicate than it appears. If we recognize that justice is really a process rather than an abstract principle, it becomes apparent that the key to social justice through law lies in a focus upon implementation. As Dewey (1971: 506) has said, a given legal arrangement is what it does. "Without application, there are scraps of paper or voices in the air but nothing that can be called law" (: 508). Max Weber, who treated the development of law as a function of the historical trend toward "rationalization" of custom, stressed the rise of bureaucratic organization as a technique for such rationalization and foresaw the possibility of humanity captured in an "iron cage" of its own making. The bureaucratic implementation of law represents a problem precisely because the bureaucracy represents a concentration of power without an ethical tradition. The concentration of power results from the collection and coordination of resources far beyond the scope of those in the hands of private individuals. The ethical poverty of bureaucracy springs from the fact that, historically, ethical thought developed in terms of personal behavior, it is not immediately applicable to the functions of incumbents of large-scale organizations who feel that they are merely "following orders" or "carrying out policy." The result is an inherent tendency toward authoritarianism. Bureaucracy means that law, in theory a balance of ethics and power, tends to be corrupted as it is applied.

BUREAUCRACY AND AUTHORITARIANISM

Authority administered bureaucratically is forever in danger of authoritarianism. The bureaucratic model of organization may be described as an "ideal type" in the sense of a pure form which may be approximated in greater or less degree by real organizations. First set forth by Weber and later elaborated by Ellul (1964) and Crozier (1973), the model is characterized by a manifest focus upon the rational pursuit of goals to be obtained by systems of regulations, procedures, and specifications administered in impersonal terms through a hierarchical structure based on formal competence. As Weber recognized, the prototype of contemporary bureaucracy is the military organization, particularly as exemplified in the nineteenth-century Prussian state. Communication is highly formalized through specific reporting channels. Power is tied to the authority of an office rather than a particular individual and is brought to bear down a chain of command. Ranks, often indicated by insignia, are also evident in patterns of differential privileges and forms of deference. In an effort to cope with the new organizational problems produced by the industrial revolution, the new large-scale production units tended to adopt the bureaucratic mode with its hierarchical structure and its emphasis on order and discipline as techniques of management. Thus it is that modern organizations, be they educational institutions, welfare systems, or criminal justice agencies, tend to reflect a mixture of military-industrial models.

Although some might dispute the term, these models remain essentially authoritarian (Argyris 1964) in terms which can be described in detail. The implementation of law through such organizations represent an institutionalization of corruption. Just as institutional racism, built into social systems, can proceed without any personal prejudice whatsoever, institutionalized corruption can proceed among those whose personal ethical and moral standards are no lower than those of the typical citizen. Dramatic stories of ineffectiveness, bribery, brutality, and the manipulation and usurpation of power are only the surface manifestations of a deeper structural corruption. Gardner (1968) has referred to this latter as a "dry rot" characteristic of many contemporary institutions. The answer is not to "turn the rascals out," to "professionalize" the officials or to develop systems of "accountability," for it would appear that the fundamental problem of corruption of justice is rooted in the organizational modes now employed to administer the law. This is the problem which must be understood: Quis custodiet ipsos custodes?, Who shall guard the guardians?

A reinterpretation of Smelser (1971) will allow us to guide our understanding of institutional corruption through several key questions. The first has to do with the manner in which ethically questionable behaviors are made organizationally acceptable: By what processes is corruption of justice actually legitimized by our criminal justice agencies? Legitimization is to a considerable extent built into the powerful tendency toward authoritarianism which is so characteristic of the bureaucracy. To some extent, this is a result of the hierarchical structure itself and the emphasis upon discipline and subordination of personal attitudes and interests to organizational policy. One becomes accustomed to these patterns; they are seldom questioned. Bureaucratic structures foster a detachment, and one result

is a drift toward "dehumanization," a process which may be defined
as a failure to recognize in oneself and others the full complement of
human qualities (Bernard et al. 1971: 105). There is evidence that
the bureaucratic detachment of the functionary is achieved through
psychological defense mechanisms including denial, repression, de-
personalization, isolation of affect, and ethical compartmentalization
(Argyris 1964). The results include increased emotional distance
from other human beings and a diminished sense of personal responsibility for the consequences of one's actions. Traditions of personal
ethics are rendered "inoperative," for as Aristotle says in his Nicho-
machean Ethics (Book V), "to act unjustly is to do harm to someone
voluntarily, and voluntarily means knowing the person affected, the
instrument and the manner of injury." Bureaucracy shields one from
such knowledge. This "denial of responsibility" tends to "neutralize"
ethical and moral restraints (Sykes and Matza 1957) in such a way
that one may believe deeply in justice but implement unjust policies
as an organizational "duty." As has often been pointed out, conventional morality tends to break down in the absence of identification
with the victim.

Not only do these organizations operate so as to legitimize
possible corruption, but careful study frequently reveals specific
policies which provide tacit authorizations for the violation of ethical
norms and legal principles. Here we come to the second question:
How is this corruption actually authorized? The authoritarian preoccupation with order which is so characteristic of bureaucracy leads
toward organizational rigidity of a particular sort. Organizations
established as means to implement legal ends become ends in themselves as focus shifts from the original mission toward an emphasis
upon status and career enhancement through identification with a
strong (that is, large and powerful) organization with an expanding
budget and increasing opportunities for promotion. Thus, the old
argument that the end justifies the means arises. In the typical
bureaucratic system, the means are likely to become the ends. Each
organization is staffed by incumbents who comprise a collective subterranean "technostructure" with goals of its own (Galbraith 1967).
Image fabrication and "empire building" tend to dominate the concerns
of high-ranking incumbents while those lower in the organization become increasingly alienated (Argyris 1964). Official goals tend to
be oversimplified by the industrial emphasis on indexes of "productivity" which quickly become fetishes rather than guides (Ellul 1964).

Once we have seen how organizational processes have legitimized and authorized ethical and legal violations, we can turn to the
third question: By what organizational process is corruption mobilized? Here one will discover additional organizational processes
which actually operate to push incumbents toward the questionable

practices which are covertly legitimized and authorized. Through a typical socialization process (Michael 1973), newcomers are taught the covert operating rules, including the fact that there are some things which must be done because there are no alternatives if one is to "get the job done." Sanctions, both subtle and direct, are employed to set straight the "idealists." Transfers are employed as control devices to ensure conformity to the subterranean operating rules. In all of this the newcomer is taught to recognize a critical distinction between "us" and "them." The stigmatized group is systematically stereotyped; contact with "them" is minimized except when it is possible to ritualize the contact is such a way as to reinforce the bias by demonstrating to the neophyte just how undeserving they are and how "realistic" one must become about their motives. The newcomer is taught to displace his frustrations and resentments from the superordinates in the hierarchy above him and to use the stigmatized groups as a convenient scapegoat. It is learned that if one will not "go along," one at least owes it to one's peers to be tolerant of their behavior. Finally, there is considerable evidence that the newcomer to the organization, having experienced a certain self-disgust at the initial powerlessness and moral confusion, will tend to project it onto others (Michael 1973: 191).

Next, there is the major structural question: By what processes is corruption actually organized? First, there is the fact that bureaucratic operations are structured in such a way that any incumbent can perceive only a limited portion of the entire operation. Although able to ignore, or even participate in, questionable practices within the organization, the bureaucrat, trained to minimize the risk of error by reliance on codified procedures, tends to develop "trained incapacity" to act positively without the protections of "red tape." Meanwhile, there is a distinct tendency for the powerful organization, rather than adapt to changes in the environment with which it must deal, to seek to control that environment and impose its will. This tendency is greatly facilitated by a social psychological process of "groupthink." Operations are structured in such a way as to defend the organization in its illustion of moral invulnerability. Organized pressure is applied to internal critics in such a way that their dissent is itself organized in "domesticated" fashion. Dissent of this sort may be tolerated so long as the critics (1) do not voice their doubts to "outsiders" and (2) keep their criticism within organizational bounds by never challenging the fundamental assumptions upon which the organized corruption rests. Such groupthink depends upon a fear of disapproval, a shared illusion of unanimity of judgment based on silence, a stereotype of the "others" as beneath moral concern and an unquestioning sense of the inherent morality of the organization (ibid.) Self-appointed "mind guards" operate to protect policy from overly sensitive scrutiny and are often well rewarded for their efforts (ibid.).

The phenomenon of groupthink functions to further disperse the sense of ethical and moral responsibility. All decisions are "group decisions," and a great deal of effort is expended in shared efforts at rationalization (ibid.). The ethically questionable behavior has been legitimized and subtly authorized, actors have been mobilized, and the sub rosa processes have been effectively organized. Afterwards, there is the final question: Just how is corruption rationalized by the organization? Of extreme importance here is the tendency to appear to higher loyalties (Sykes and Matza 1957). If the supreme value is "social order," then it is a simple thing to link the well-being of the society with the well-being of a particular organization within it and to argue that this particular organization must be defended and strengthened at all costs. Once this link is accepted, there is a tendency to believe that the organization in question can do no wrong. There is a tendency to point to other organizations which are alleged to be much worse or to insist that these organizations would do even more evil if they were allowed the opportunity. One of our most difficult problems lies in the equation of authoritarianism with a dictatorship based upon a cult of personality and an all-powerful political party. Unfortunately, modern bureaucratic processes supported by a public relations front make possible a faceless, technocratic "friendly fascism" of a type with which we are ill-equipped to cope because of its familiarity (Gross 1970).

Criminal "sociopathy" has been defined as "a defective quality of interpersonal relationships with a deficiency of human identification and so of ethical and moral values" (Sanford and Comstock 1971: 22). In just this sense, contemporary bureaucratic organizations, to the extent that they manifest the characteristics described above, can be said to show distinctly sociopathic tendencies. Is this true of the criminal justice system? It may be worthwhile to examine police, courts, and correctional organizations separately and in a bit more detail. What we discover is that particular patterns vary somewhat from one system to another, but the general characteristics which can be described in connection with each can be applied in broad terms to all.

Police

Police organizations have been developed in terms of the bureaucratic model described. Thus, it is especially important that we attend to the paramilitary nature of police organizations (Sherman 1975: 368-70). The importance attached to the uniform, the badge, the weaponry, and the rank system signify a preoccupation with threat and the assumption that this most salient of system problems can be dealt with in terms of power through imposed order. The underlying assumptions as to the nature of man and society are essentially Hobbesian—the image of a latent war of "all against all" which must be suppressed by constant vigilance. Thus,

> the structural model most frequently advocated and utilized in American police endeavors was first implemented in the Anglo-Saxon world by the Metropolitan Police Act, which established the London "bobbies" in 1829. This model follows closely the tenets of the classic organizational theory, which is an ideal-type based on pre-twentieth-century organizations. In spite of the tremendous changes in society, its culture and values, no significant changes have occurred in the approach to police organization and management since 1829 (Angell 1971: 186).

The preoccupation with real and imagined threats leads to the organizational defensiveness common throughout the criminal justice systems of advanced industrial societies. One result is a pattern of organizational regression toward the feudal mode commonly associated with threat systems. Different writers have remarked upon the feudal characteristics of many police departments (Sherman 1975: 368). Here the pattern is one of personal politics by which the local vassal affiliates himself with another who, by virtue of his institutional political skills, can carve out an informal fiefdom within the official structure. Such a feudal pattern is historically and organizationally a patchwork which tends to develop with the collapse of integrative systems based on a communal ethic in the absence of viable universalistic standards justly applied.

The resulting organizational problems are ubiquitous. First, there are serious communication problems. Information flowing toward the top is filtered so as to protect and enhance the positions of those who can affect the communication (Sherman 1956: 371). Thus, it is unlikely that organizational policy can be developed based on an accurate assessment of the problem. Moreover, communications flowing downward in the form of orders, directives, and regulations are bent to the point of redefinition so that the eventual application reflects the structural and social-psychological interests of the infrastructure rather than the policy as initially promulgated. To complicate matters, bureaucracy emphasizes the avoidance of risk, and the feudalistic tendency leads to the promotion of those who are successful in this and are able to demonstrate loyalty to others in a position of authority.

Angell (1971) has pointed to three major consequences which deserve to be considered. First, the bureaucratic structure of contemporary police tends to foster attitudes among the members of the organization which are inconsistent with the democratic values espoused by modern, industrial societies. Secondly, the organizational form requires and supports incumbents who demonstrate immature personality traits reflecting a regressive authoritarianism. Finally, this model tends to be "unable to cope with significant environmental change, overreacting with apathy on the one hand or hostility on the other. Such organizations can be relatively successful in a stable environment, but like the mighty dinosaur, they are poorly suited to the flexible response patterns demanded by the rapidly shifting problems of the late twentieth century. The consequent internal corruption is a persistent problem. Although the so-called "meat eaters" who "aggressively misuse their police power for personal gain" obtain the extremely lucrative payoffs, the Knapp Commission (1975: 138) found them to represent a small percentage of all corrupt policemen encountered in their investigations. The vast majority of corrupt policemen were merely "grass eaters" who did not deal in large payoffs at all. Nevertheless, the commission correctly concluded that these policemen were the heart of the problem, both because "their great numbers make corruption 'respectable'" and because they encourage an organizational "code of silence that brands anyone who exposes corruption a traitor" (Knapp Commission 1975: 139).

Courts

Judicial systems are not free from the corrupting features of contemporary organizational structures. The profession of law has itself been so subtly coopted that Blumberg (1967) compares legal practice under present circumstances to a confidence game. Despite the legal theory of the adversary system, less than 10 percent of the convictions in criminal cases results from the actual application of formal adversary proceedings, and even when a "trial" is held, evidence suggests that it is essentially a perfunctory legitimation of pretrial findings and decisions arrived at administratively (Blumberg 1967: 16-17). The legal concept of due process tends to give way to the organizational pressures for productivity and career advancement. Again, we find the tendency of the system to serve its own infrastructure rather than the public. Blumberg (1967: 18) goes so far as to refer to the court as a "closed community" of judges, attorneys, and assorted personnel and suggests that "the simple explanation is one of an ongoing system handling delicate tensions . . . requiring almost pathological distrust of outsiders bordering on paranoia."

The cooptation of law may be clearly observed in connection with plea bargainings, in which, as Sudnow (1965) has shown, crimes are actually classified and handled by standards of bureaucratic convenience rather than by legal principles. There is, in fact, a working presumption of guilt which flies in the face of legal abstractions thought to govern due process. Beneath the legalistic trappings, we find a highly developed sub rosa system with emphasis upon a good "show" which rests upon ceremonial "fronts" (Blumberg 1967). Most of this "game" is designed to advance the interests of the closed community or judicial infrastructure, as can be seen in the fee-fixing strategies employed. In keeping with the bureaucratic pattern of transforming all ends in terms of its own interests, once promising innovations such as probation become mere bargaining points, with administrative convenience more salient than rehabilitation. Blumberg summarizes as follows:

> Sociologists and others have focused their attention on
> the deprivations and social disabilities of such variables
> as race, ethnicity, and social class as being the source
> of an accused person's defeat in a criminal court. Large-
> ly overlooked is the variable of the court organization it-
> self, which possesses a thrust, purpose and direction of
> its own. It is grounded in pragmatic values, bureau-
> cratic priorities and administrative instruments. . . .
> Organizational goals and discipline impose a set of de-
> mands and conditions of practice on the respective pro-
> fessions in the criminal court to which they respond by
> abandoning their ideological and professional commit-
> ments to the accused clients, in the service of these
> higher claims of the court organization. . . . The client,
> then, is a secondary figure in the court system as in cer-
> tain other bureaucratic settings. . . . (1967: 17).

The usual bureaucratic emphasis upon productivity has tended to become not only the index of a prosecutor's ability to manipuate the system to produce convictions but is now increasingly praised as indicative of court "modernization" (Cannon 1974: 121). There is a particular irony here, for the movement toward the bureaucraticiza-tion of the courts may be leading us toward even more serious problems as we attempt to solve the basic problems of bureaucracy by more of the same. It is true enough that our courts are administra-tively archaic, inefficient, and prone to confusion and fiscal waste (National Advisory Commission 1973). As with police systems, a distinctively feudal pattern has been exposed (Blumberg 1972). The inadequacies of the organizational framework have become more apparent with the rapid increase in court workload. Moreover, there is a particularly embarrassing problem, for although the common bureaucratic response to increased input is to increase staff support, the judiciary cannot rely too obviously upon this tactic since it makes patently obvious the shift of responsibility from judges bound by legal traditions to bureaucrats bound by organizational imperatives.

Van Ness (1973) has displayed some sensitivity to these complex issues in his dissent from the report of the National Advisory Commission on Criminal Justice Standards and Goals. The commission, recognizing inefficiency and "the discretionary nature of administrative processing" as constant sources of injustice, has emphasized that, "One thread common to many of the standards is an attempt to utilize and improve the informal, essentially administrative, processes that affect the flow of most criminal cases through the court system" (1973: 2-3). This seems to say not only that the informal bureaucratic processes must be acknowledged but that they must be strengthened by further formalization. Is this the answer? Given the nature of contemporary bureaucracy, the typical result of such management information systems and planning-budgeting operations has been to magnify past injustices (Argyris 1970: 6) or to encourage bureaucratically safe modifications which produce merely an illusion of real change (Michael 1973: 135). In view of these facts of organizational life, the attempt of the commission to increase court efficiency—through foreclosure of collateral attack on convictions, restrictions on the right of appeal, and use of six-member juries—may pose some real dangers. Social justice is an evolving legal concept and not an administrative regulation. Criminal law must be free to grow. Collateral attack, although "wasteful" of time and fiscal resources, has contributed significantly to the development of law. Surely the commission does not mean to stifle the socially necessary development of criminal law for the sake of administrative order. And as for gains of efficiency which might result from restrictions on the right of appeal, one must agree with Van Ness that "the plain intent of the standards is to make it more difficult for a person to challenge the validity of a conviction (1973: 320). Although such a move may contribute to administrative efficiency and enhanced productivity by eliminating many "frivolous" appeals, the commission itself has recognized that it was not able to define these terms. Finally, Van Ness (ibid.) would appear to be correct in his assertion that the six-member jury, by easing the burden of proof resting on the state and by making a hung jury less likely, is far from a mere choice between what the commission terms "archaic traditionalism" and "modern administrative procedures." All in all, the revisions suggested by the commission would seem to provide for more, rather than less, justice. Unless the larger issues of bureaucratization are confronted, the result of the revisions may be quite different from the intent of the reviser.

The public defender was once an admirable innovation designed to advance the cause of social justice but, in that case again, too little thought was given to the real nature of the system and the likely outcome of the apparently progressive addition to the basic court structure. One simply assumed ethical conduct on the part of the public defenders. The facts of life were never faced. As recent studies have begun to clarify the cooptation pressures at work, the power of the underlying systemic processes has become more and more obvious:

> The morality of the courts is taken for granted. The P. D. assumes that the D. A., the police, judge, the narcotics agents and others all conduct their business as it must be conducted and in a proper fashion. That the police may hide out to deceive petty violators; that narcotics agents may regularly employ illicit entrapment procedures to find suspects; that investigators may routinely arrest suspects before they have sufficient grounds and only later uncover warrantable evidence for a formal booking; that the police may beat suspects; that judges may be "tough" because they are looking to support for higher-office elections; that some laws may be specifically prejudicial against certain classes of persons—whatever may be the actual course of charging and convicting defendants—all of this is taken, as one P. D. put it, "as part of the system and the way it has to be." And the P. D. is part of the team (Sudnow 1965: 256).

Corrections

For present purposes, correctional systems may be typed in three major categories: hierarchical, differentiated, and autonomous (Steele and Jacobs 1975). Despite the apparent diversity, the essential model is bureaucratic. Corrections tends to be organized in terms of "coercive structures" with a primary goal or order and with compliance patterns of an "alienative" nature (Etzioni 1961: 3-39). But since coercion does not provide a really satisfactory means of control in this context, the result is the "corruption of authority" through subterranean reciprocities (Sykes 1958). The infrastructure of informal reciprocities provides only enough organizational integration to maintain a corrupted equilibrium based on a precarious truce.

There is no shortage of examples of the familiar tendency to convert ethical reforms into organizational control strategies which advance the interests of the incumbents. Both the indeterminate-sequence and behavior-modification techniques are cases in point. Authoritarian organizations tend to maintain their characteristic informal systems by policies of subtle intimidation, manipulation, and suppression of any negative environmental feedback to which they might have to adapt. Designed as a reasonable means to the end of rehabilitation, indeterminate sentences now hang over the heads of prisoners, to be used to stifle legitimate complaints and punish the bearers of bad news. Designed as the most empirically effective means of shaping human behavior in socially desirable directions, behavior-modification techniques have been transformed into control devices used to condition prisoners toward compliance with organizational directives. In neither case do we find among policy makers a realistic awareness of the manner in which contemporary organizations operate to systematically corrupt innovative policies.

The greater the failure of criminal justice policy, the more coercive the total system and the greater the emphasis placed upon power. Ethical concerns take a back seat. Under conditions of hostility and low trust, all involved in the system will tend to adopt competitive behavior strategies (Michael 1973: 191). In such a situation, the fundamental advantage of organized social life, effective social cooperation, is lost, and the Hobbesian struggle emerges in an institutionalized form. A basic prisoner subculture springs up around roles representing power relationships relative to the most significant deprivations suffered at the hand of the organization. The results are well known but not officially admitted:

> A system evolves in which both inmates and guards assume roles that allow guards to act "as if" they are actually in control of the prison. In the final analysis, the amount of authority exercised by guards is no more than the amount granted by the inmates. The inmates allow the guards to remain ostensibly in control as long as the inmate power structure is allowed to function sub rosa. It is advantageous to both groups that the fiction be maintained.

> The inmates, of course, realize that the free community will not tolerate their running the institution openly, so they settle for the next best thing—the appearance of order (Murton 1976: 65).

This "appearance of order" is gained, however, through an institutionalized "zero-sum" game. Commonly found in authoritarian settings, such a counterproductive strategy means that system itself becomes a rigid form in which one person's gain is always another's loss. There is no real basis for "positive-sum" interaction in which cooperation leads to improvements all around. This reality is also reflected in high turnover and lack of commitment on the part of staff members and in ritualistic manipulations, insulated interactions, and communication distortions of an almost surrealistic character (Manocchio and Dunn 1970). Meanwhile, the organization, true to its prototype, operates through a coercive policy of personal accountability, a practice which amounts to little more than an institutionalized scapegoating by which a staff member is held responsible for developments over which he may have no real control (McCorkle and Korn 1954). Both prisoners and staff are corrupted by this system (Sukes 1958, Etzioni 1961, Murton 1976).

The importance of a realistic analysis of these organizations lies in the view it can cast on the ethical and moral dilemmas of an approach which argues for more of the same. To take but one example, Schwitzagebel (1971: 600) has recently proposed that coercive monitoring techniques be employed with chronic recidivists. These monitoring systems would be implanted beneath the skin, allowing a twenty-four-hour-a-day "relationship" with the central system even "beyond the usual geographic barriers." As Murton (1976: 207) has pointed out, Schwitzgebel, himself a distinguished professor of law, manages to dispose of even the civil rights issues by proposing that the monitoring devices be used only "with voluntary participants (such as inmates seeking release from an institution)" (Schwitzgebel 1971: 608). As to the prisoner, he concludes that "the system extends rather curtails his rights within present correctional practice (1971: 605). Similar proposals have been more recently advanced by Smith (Murton 1976: 269) and by Ingraham (: 269-70). A reasonable familiarity with the bureaucratic tendencies of correctional systems will force us to a fuller awareness of the real implications prior to taking such steps.

TOWARD A MODEL OF ORGANIZATIONAL ETHICS

If it is true that latent processes of corruption are an inherent consequence of the contemporary organization of the criminal justice system, then we must undertake a fundamental reappraisal of that system. Fortunately, realistic organizational analysis has developed quite rapidly in the past decade. Empirical research suggests that new organizational models must be developed.

The transition to a service-based economy in a postindustrial society of increased professionalism will require that we transcend the organizational systems developed upon military-industrial models designed to fight a "war on crime." In keeping with this transition, we must learn to view police, court, and correctional systems as information-processing systems which develop decisions rather than as production systems manufacturing output units. The need is for open organizations structured for effective problem scanning and decision making. This will require that the hierarchical form be modified by the use of shifting "task-force" systems in which authority is derived from knowledge and competence with respect to a given problem rather than official bureaucratic status (Bennis and Slater 1968). Current defensive policies must give way to policies derived from free information flow. Emphasis upon organizational discipline must give way to emphasis upon problem solving. Environmental adaptability must be designed into these systems.

What we need are not only organizations capable of finding the right answers, but organizations capable of discovering and reacting to the right questions (Drucker 1954). Such systems can be defined as learning systems (Michael 1973) which are flexible and open with an internal capacity for modification based on a rapidly changing social environment. They may make possible some resolution of the ethical and moral dilemmas of organizational life. As we have already seen, Frankena (1962), having explored the evolving concept of social justice, concludes that the best working definition emphasizes "a point of view which is fully free, informed and rational." The authoritarian systems which we have described above do not foster a point of view which is "fully free," but rather a narrow, defensive, and stereotyped view of social reality. Nor can one characterize the prevalent point of view as "informed;" it is, instead, the product of systematic communication distortion and information rejection. Learning systems might provide the "free" and "informed" point of view from which Frankena insists that social justice can be derived. As for the rational nature of the result, it has been said that genuine human rationality is synonomous with the capacity and willingness to learn.

Freund (1962: 107) has stressed that law attains justice only when actually applied in terms of standards of consistency, equality, predictability, fair shares, social utility, equitable distribution, and the satisfaction of reasonable expectations. Anything else is corruption of the law. In terms of our argument, it is particularly interesting to find Freund suggesting that a legal realism requires means by which legal abstractions, on the one hand, can be related to application of law, on the other. The answer would appear to lie in a wedding of principles of jurisprudence with the kind of organizational analysis necessary to solve concrete problems and guide toward new directions. Learning systems are based not on a principle of superior knowledge or strength but upon a superior capacity to learn in a "fully free, informed and rational" manner. And it must be emphasized that there is nothing particularly "soft" or "weak" about the sorts of organizational models proposed (Argyris 1970: 85). They represent a new conception of power. In the new conception, the capacity of an organization to accomplish its missions is seen to depend upon its capacity to confront the truth. Such systems offer the possibility of a new synthesis of ethics and power.

Systems designed for adaptability through an open information-processing system has been described by Bennis and Slater (1968) as "organic-adaptive" models. They require that a certain degree of structural uncertainty and role ambiguity be accepted. Where traditional bureaucratic organizations have tended to cover mistakes, the "newer" models must reward a strategy of "error-embracing" (Michael 1973) by which organizational misjudgments are sought out as opportunities to learn from failures. These models will make social-psychological demands which necessitate the development of greater interpersonal competence among police, court officials, and correctional personnel. Here the chief problems lie in the recruiting and socialization of those who will staff the organizations envisioned. Unless these problems are solved, old habits will likely reassert themselves. At the moment, there is evidence that the relatively authoritarian systems of criminal justice implementation tend to attract individuals who are drawn by the appearance of order and strength and certain basic misconceptions about the nature of the mission. The disillusionment of the rookie police recruit drawn by the image of a tough front, backed by a badge and a gun, is notorious, for it is soon discovered that the great bulk of the job involves human relations and that professional restraint and reasonable flexibility may be the major weapons.

A variety of new techniques appear to be of considerable help in the process of socialization for interpersonal competence. One of these is role playing, a means by which social and emotional distance is bridged through identification with the problems of various groups with which the new professional must deal. Sensitivity training and encounter-group techniques offer additional possibilities so long as they are not themselves bureaucratized. All of this can make the current trend toward "professionalization" of criminal justice personnel a means of system transformation. The genuine professional has always been distinguished from the "organization man" by his commitment to service governed by thoughtful, ethical concerns.

Through specific system modifications such as "job enlargement," it should be possible to remove the ethical blinders which now insulate incumbents from larger concerns. At the same time, "positive-control" management techniques provide a means of operation based less on those punitive sanctions which alienate staff and stifle organizational development (Argyris 1964: 275). The use of "devil's advocates," information-disclosure policies, and programs which foster public participation can be of use in opening the organizations. These alterations are aimed at the development of "synergistic" systems providing a matrix for "positive-sum" games in which all "players" gain (Boulding 1970: 25).

Angell has pointed toward the development of new models in his recent discussion of police organizations:

> The following model is an attempt to develop a flexible, participatory, science-based structure that will accommodate change. It is designed for effectiveness in serving the needs of citizens rather than autocratic rationality of operation. It is democratic in that it requires and facilitates the involvement of citizens and employees in its processes. . . .
>
> The controls in this system are varied, in contrast with the single chain of command control required by classic concepts. . . .
>
> First by eliminating formally assigned supervision and by providing officers with more control over their own jobs, it should increase the morale and effectiveness of employees. . . .
>
> The decentralization of these groups will give citizens more influence in policy decisions. . . .
>
> It provides for increased communications and more adequate information about perceptions and expectations of the various actors in the system. It provides employees with the authority and responsibility necessary for attaining professional status. It facilitates citizen involvement and organizational responsiveness, the hallmarks of democratic institutions (1971: 200-01).

If the critical problems of organizational ethics are to be solved, such changes must be envisioned for our courts. Through the tradition of legal realism, we focus on theories of jurisprudence based upon what is actually happening rather than what is supposed to be occurring. From this perspective, procedural tendencies toward authoritarianism, careerism, organizational fetishism, and system rigidity become matters of grave concern to the law itself. Formal legal education must give more attention to the varieties of real ethical dilemmas faced by prosecutors, defense attorneys, and judges who find themselves enmeshed in questionable but well-entrenched systems. We must integrate current efforts toward the development of courts so that citizens can find an easier process, and judges will regard information flow as a virtue. If social justice, rather than "efficiency" or "productivity," is the aim of reorganization, the court must be structured after the model of the learning system and not as a production unit. In order to be in the best position to make an ethical decision, a judicial system whose officials are fully aware of what they are doing, in human as well as legal terms, is needed. In some parts of Europe, judges are expected to have concrete experience in the prisons to which they will be sentencing offenders. It is not too much to suggest that prosecutors and defense attorneys should also become familiar with the realities faced by those who come before the court.

Some of the principles underlying a new correctional model have been described by Steele and Jacobs (1974) in their discussion of "autonomous" correctional systems. The advantages of such organizations include small size, manageable staff, and a minimum of "professional treaters" (Steele and Jacobs 1974: 159). The possibilities of the newer model, even within an institutional setting, may be illustrated by the C-Unit Project at California's Deuel Vocational Institution. This project has been specifically described as an attempt to develop a "problem-solving community of prisoners and staff" (Studt, Messinger, and Wilson 1968). What is particularly interesting about the C-Unit experiment is the finding that even a relatively successfully program will tend to "succumb to pressures for functional integration with other units demanded by the hierarchical prison system" (Steele and Jacobs 1974: 159). Here again are the problems inherent in a piecemeal approach. Do we continue to allow innovations to be reabsorbed into the bureaucratic regime, or do we reorganize the total system?

The traditional bureaucracy has become an obstacle to corrections. Newer developments, such as halfway houses, work-release programs, and probation subsidies appear to represent positive steps, but these too may be corrupted by the control tendency. It is instructive to observe that few of our most successful innovations have been developed within present organizational structures. This is true largely because of the bureaucratic mentality which focuses upon "tightening up" the organization, so as to present an authoritative image of tough competence to handle problems, which results in a failure to consider nonbureaucratic solutions. As Murton has put it:

> But since the official reformer often believes that organizational structures, per se, hold the key to reform, he may concentrate on structure exclusively and

consequently bargain away real reform in exchange for a more sophisticated bureaucracy. It is with this "progress" of bureaucratic structuring that reform measures wane, change is hindered, and achievement is thwarted by state agencies that lend to perpetuate themselves rather than to serve the needs of the citizenry.

<u>When the creature controls the creator, the creation becomes corrupted</u> (1976: 101-02; emphasis in original).

Little can be done to solve the ethical and moral problems inherent in the criminal justice system so long as we are unwilling to alter the system. The closed, bureaucratic structure fosters secrecy, distortion, corruption, and injustice, but it protects its members, rewards their loyalty, and provides them with a reasonably secure career. It should be clear by now that the fundamental problem is not simply the abuse of bureaucracy but the authoritarian tendencies inherent on the organizational model itself. The system is particularly adept at avoiding basic change. When it attempts to deal with a recalcitrant environment, it tends to approach the issue in terms of more complete control, rarely questioning its own ethical and moral positions. Standard reactions include systematic denial of negative environmental feedback, "tightening up" the chain of command and communications channels so as to filter problems before they reach higher echelons, and harassing the bearers of bad news. Problems, which should be seen as challenges demanding adaptive responses, are treated as embarrassments to be suppressed by tactics which shift focus from one symptomatic crisis to another and avoid the basic problems (Michael 1973).

The result is that the criminal justice system, as it now functions, tends to further corrupt those on the side of illegality even as it corrupts those who join the system on the side of the law. What the times urgently require are developments which can assist us in gaining control over our own institutions. Piecemeal innovation is not a substitute for a totally new concept of organizational goals and means. There are no panaceas here, but it seems clear that a concerted movement toward democratic, organic-adaptive learning systems offers one of our few real hopes for a system capable of translating the concept of social justice into social reality.

REFERENCES

Angell, J. 1971. Toward an alternative to the classic police organizational arrangements: a democratic model. Criminology 9, 2-3 (August): 185-206.

Argyris, C. 1964. Integrating the Individual and the Organization. New York: Wiley.

――――. 1970. Intervention Theory and Method: A Behavioral Science View. Reading, Mass.: Addison-Wesley.

Bennis, W. and P. Slater. 1968. The Temporary Society. New York: Harper & Row.

Bernard, V. W., P. Offenberg, and F. Redl. 1971. Dehumanization. In Sanctions for Evil, eds. N. Sanford and C. Comstock. New York: Jossey-Bass.

Blumberg, A. S. 1967. The practice of law as a confidence game: organizational cooptation of a profession. Law and Society Review 1 (June): 15-39.

――――. 1972. The criminal court as organization and communication system. In Criminal Justice: Law and Politics, ed. George F. Cole. North Scituate, Mass.: Duxbury Press.

Boulding, K. 1970. A Primer on Social Dynamics. New York: Free Press.

Cannon, M. 1974. The federal judicial system: highlights of administrative modernization. Criminology 12, 1 (May): 10-24.

Crozier, M. 1973. The Stalled Society. New York: Viking.

Dewey, J. 1971. My philosophy of law. In The Great Legal Philosophers, ed. Clarence Morris. Philadelphia: University of Pennsylvania Press.

Drucker, P. 1954. Practice of Management. New York: Harper & Row.

Ellul, J. 1964. The Technological Society. New York: Vintage.

Etzioni, A. 1961. A Comparative Analysis of Complex Organizations. Glencoe: Free Press.

Frankena, W. K. 1962. The concept of social justice. In Social Justice, ed. Richard B. Brandt. Englewood Cliffs, N.J.: Prentice-Hall.

Freund, P. A. 1962. Social justice and the law. In Social Justice, ed. Richard B. Brandt. Englewood Cliffs, N.J.: Prentice-Hall.

Fuller, L. 1969. Human interaction and the law. American Journal of Jurisprudence 14: 1-36.

Galbraith, J. 1967. The New Industrial State. Boston: Houghton Mifflin Co.

Gardiner, J. A. and D. J. Olson. 1974. Theft of the City. Bloomington, Ind.: Indiana University Press.

Gardner, J. 1968. America in the twenty-third century. New York Times, July 27.

Gross, B. 1970. Friendly fascism: a model for America. Social Policy 1: 44-53.

Knapp Commission. 1975. Police corruption in New York City. In Criminal Law in Action, ed. William J. Chambliss. Santa Barbara: Hamilton.

Manocchio, A. and J. Dunn. 1970. The Time Game: Two Views of a Prison. New York: Dell.

McCorkle, L. W. and R. Korn. 1954. Resocialization within walls. Annals of the American Academy of Political and Social Science 293: 88-98.

Michael, D. W. 1973. On Learning to Plan—And Planning to Learn. San Francisco: Jossey-Bass.

Murton, T. 1976. The Dilemma of Prison Reform. New York: Holt, Rinehart and Winston.

National Advisory Commission on Criminal Justice Standards and Goals. 1973. Report on Courts. Washington, D.C.: U.S. Government Printing Office.

Rawls, J. 1958. Justice as fairness. Philosophical Review 67: 164-94.

Sanford, N. and C. Comstock. 1971. Sanctions for Evil. San Francisco: Jossey-Bass.

Saari, D. J. 1970. Modern Court Management: Trends in the Role of the Court Executive. Washington, D.C.: U.S. Government Printing Office.

Schwitzgebel, R. K. 1971. Development and Regulations of Coercive Behavior Modification Technique With Offenders. Rockville, Md.: NIMH Center for Studies in Crime and Delinquency.

Sherman, L. W. 1975. Middle management and police democratization: a reply to John F. Angell. Criminology 12, 4 (February): 363-77.

Smelser, N. 1971. Some determinants of destructive behavior. In Sanctions for Evil, eds. N. Sanford and C. Comstock. San Francisco: Jossey-Bass.

Steele, E. H. and J. B. Jacobs. 1975. A theory of prison systems. Crime and Delinquency 212 (April): 149-62.

Studt, E., S. L. Messinger, and T. P. Wilson. 1968. C-Unit: Search for Community in Prison. New York: Sage.

Sudnow, D. 1965. Normal crimes: sociological features of the penal code in a public defender office. Social Problems 13: 255-76.

Sykes, G. 1958. The Society of Captives. Princeton, N.J.: Princeton University Press.

Sykes, G. and D. Matza. 1957. Techniques of neutralization: a theory of delinquency. American Sociological Review 22: 664-73.

Timasheff, N. S. 1937. What is "sociology of law"? American Journal of Sociology 63: 225-35.

17

JUSTICE IN THE PRISON: A DEVELOPMENTAL ANALYSIS

Peter Scharf

INTRODUCTION

This chapter seeks to offer a new perspective towards the problem of prison justice. With Kohlberg's theory of moral reasoning as a conceptual base, a methodology will be suggested for categorizing prison justice structures as well as a means to score inmate perceptions of prison moral climate. These perceptions of moral climate are here considered to be critical in the process of inmate moral change and rehabilitation. A project in the Connecticut prison system, which has operated as an intentional Just Community with a measure of success during the past six years, is given as an illustrative case

PERSPECTIVES ON THE DEFINITION OF PRISON JUSTICE

The traditional literature on imprisonment has (perhaps uncritically) assumed a functionalist perspective both towards the problem of prison justice and that of moral socialization and learning. Sykes (1952), Cressey (1960), and Grosser (1960) all implicitly assume, in their analyses of prison life, a functionalist moral view of prison practices and accept a norm socialization view of moral learning. The normative assumptions of this perspective, of course, follow the sociological and philosophical work of Durkheim (1906). Durkheim assumes that the morality of social institutions must be viewed relative to particular cultural norms. Also, he suggests that norms are taught primarily through the immersion of individuals in particular referent groups with specific normative frameworks (Merton 1956).

The functionalist perspective has been critiqued from a number of sociological and criminological positions. For example, Marxist sociologists (Gouldner 1972) have criticized functional theory for its conservatism and ahistoricity. They have, however, implicitly accepted the functionalist postulate that social collectively is the ultimate judge of moral truth (though for Marx it is the economic rather than the cultural collective). Similarly, while critics have questioned the content implied in Durkheim's view of moral learning (that schools should teach the cultural norms of particular societies), they have accepted, almost blindly, Durkheim's notion of moral learning as the internalization of moral norms.

In order to challenge this traditional perspective towards prison justice as well as the norm socialization view of moral learning, we have collaboratively adopted Kohlberg's theory of moral reasoning, education, and justice to the problem of imprisonment. Kohlberg suggests that concepts of justice and law develop through a progression of invariant stages; each higher stage of law and society is progressively more differentiated and morally adequate than are antecedent stages; these stages of justice and law are implied in his general theory of moral growth and development (Kohlberg 1967). This theory, documented by twenty years of cross-cultural and longitudinal research, posits six stages of moral development, evolving sequentially in all societies.

Social institutions play a critical role in determining both the rate of moral growth and the final stage of moral reasoning. Broadly speaking, institutions that encourage open dialogue, moral conflict, and democratic interaction are associated with rapid sociolegal development. Individuals placed in roles with the responsibility for maintaining group and institutional norms often develop advanced moral thinking. For example, student leaders tend to show more mature thinking than do other students (Kohlberg 1967). Similarly, gang leaders forced to morally dialogue with, and to role-take the perspective of, gang members tend to be more morally mature than are gang followers.

This theory offers both an alternative to and a critique of functionalist perspectives towards justice and learning. In his theory, Kohlberg violates one of the cardinal axions of functionalist sociology. As opposed to Durkheim's theory of cultural and moral relativism, Kohlberg suggests that there is a set of universal moral principles which ideally can be agreed to from any cultural perspective. While, for Durkheim, moral norms differ from society to society, and social action may only be judged relative to a particular social group (Durkheim 1938), Kohlberg argues that, in fact, there are universally valid, general criteria by which moral ideas, institutions, and actions may be rationally evaluated.

This position is justified in two ways. First, using empirical data in each of seven cultures, Kohlberg observes a common sequence of moral development. Although traditional societies' development

TABLE 5

Kohlberg's Stages of Legal Justice Perspectives

Stage 1	Law conceived in terms of concrete prescriptions. Wrongdoing implies automatic punishment.
Stage 2	Law defines guidelines as to what will be tolerated by authorities. Laws have no moral value, except as is instrumentally useful to particular individuals.
Stage 3	Laws constitute a shared consensus as to right action. The law has force as an expression of group opinion and feeling.
Stage 4	Law is defined in terms of fixed generalized laws or rules. Laws are to be obeyed in order to preserve social order and to maintain respect for society and its institutions.
Stage 5	Law is seen as being defined from legitimate, voluntary social contract. Laws are valid when symbolically agreed to and when they perform utilitarian functions.
Stage 6	Law is seen as embodying implied justice principles of social contract. Illegitimate laws seen as not prescriptively valid.

Source: Derived from Kohlberg et al. (1974).

is slower than that of modernized ones, the same invariant sequence is found to exist. Second, he offers philosophical support to his claim that each higher stage is in fact more morally adequate than the lower stages. For example, he argues that the Stage 5 utilitarian principle ("greatest good for the greatest number") is a more adequate moral principle than the Stage 4 collective-welfare ("greatest good for the collectivity") moral argument. Similarly, adapting the elaborate arguments of Rawls (1972), he offers that his Stage 6 principles of justice and ideal reciprocity are more adequate moral formulations than are Stage 5 conceptions of justice.

In addition, the theory suggests that the functionalists confuse the content of moral norms with their structure. While functionalist interpretations accurately point to acceptance of inmate norms in the prison, they fail to show how these norms are understood by inmates. Thus, while Sykes (1958) cites the dictum "don't rat" as an example of the inmate ethic, he fails to offer explanation of the different meanings the norm might have for different inmates. Thus, in one study performed in a traditional prison (Scharf 1971), we found some inmates holding a Stage 1 notion of the "rat ethic" ("I'll get stomped if I rat out another inmate"), while another inmate offered that the dictum implied "that inmates must not betray other inmates if they are to survive as a group" (Stage 4). Finally, Kohlberg's theory of moral development implies that while the functionalist model explains which norms are held by particular societies, they offer little insight into the reasoning processes used by individuals to interpret these norms.

OPERATIONAL JUSTICE STRUCTURES:
METHODS AND PROCEDURES

In the present research, the Kohlberg system was introduced to the study of institutional moral atmospheres in two conceptually discrete, but interrelated ways. First, an attempt was made to sociologically assess the justice structures of correctional institutions. It was hypothesized that correctional institutions were marked by implicit justice structures which allocated rights, duties, rewards, and punishments to inmates and staff. Often, the formal system of rules and regulations did not accurately reflect the actual "operational justice structures." Instead, informal and implicit definitions of justice relationships more accurately reflected the actual justice relationships in the setting.

The justice structure of a particular setting in revealed through systematic observations of justice practices and through consensual validation of the "operational justice structures." The methodology requires intensive interviewing as well as observation of ongoing justice practices to infer the moral logic underlying the distribution of rights, rewards, and punishments. The justice structure, once defined, may be defined through reference to a justice structure-typology developed by the author and loosely paralleling Kohlberg's system. The key difference between Kohlberg's system and ours is that, while Kohlberg attempts to score the justice of individual moral thinking, we seek to type collective prison justice structures:[1] Type 1, Coercive Power Orientation; Type 2, Personal Exchange Orientation; Type 3, Informal Norm Agreement; Type 4, Structured Norm Agreement; Type 5, Principled Agreement. Elaborated definitions of types may be found in Appendix 1.

JUSTICE: THREE PRISONS

Three prisons were chosen for our study: a traditional custody prison, a prison using behavior modification, and one using a complex network of psychotherapy.

Observations of the traditional prison justice structure indicated that inmates had no fixed civil rights. Liberty of political expression, freedom of movement, property rights, and rights of assembly were all restricted by prison officials. "Privileges" granted by staff were subject to arbitrary revocation. No "moral appeal" by inmates, to demand that rights be honored, was possible. Inmates, through their role definitions, were systematically excluded from decision-making powers.

Prison rewards were often "doled out" automatically by impersonal bureaucratic rules (for example, job pay, work release, and good time). Other rewards, however, such as admission to the honor block and job preferences, were "manipulated" by prison authorities as an exchange to secure cooperation among key (powerful) inmates. This was an important means of social control, defined as such by prison staff.

Punishments were largely decided automatically, sometimes for infractions of fairly innocuous rules (such as exchanging library books). Punishment often involved segregation in the "box" (a segregation cell where inmates were kept in the dark, given a "restrictable" diet and nothing to read but the Bible and Reader's Digest). The discipline board hearings involved little effort to ascertain inmate guilt or innocence, and no attempt was made to explain to the inmate the reasons for punishment. Some episodes of punishment represented acts of personal retaliation by guards.

Rights, in the prison using behavior modification, were defined in therapeutic contracts with prison counselors. Inmates were coerced into choosing contracts which would be acceptable to prison staff and which "paid" easily earned points. Discipline decisions were generally based almost entirely on staff behavioral reports on inmate actions.

Release and institutional rewards were administered by the prison point system. Release was achieved when the inmate accumulated 7,187 points. Privileges were bought through the payment of "funny money" (that is, a shower cost 50 prison dollars). Inmates engaged in broadly practiced "point frauds" such as counterfeiting and embezzlement of prison dollars. Similarly, inmates consciously "gamed" staff recording their behavior by appearing to complete behaviors which they openly scorned and, in fact, did not do. For example, inmates were observed carrying toothbrushes to the bathrooms which, in fact, they did not use.

Punishments operated through the fining of inmates as well as through traditional prison discipline procedures. A fight might cost an inmate as many as 3,000 points, equivalent to three months' overtime. Many of the inmates perceived such fines as "coercive punishment" rather than as an absence of reward, as intended by the behavioral therapists running the prison.

The psychotherapy prison similarly utilized a system of staff-inmate contracts to define inmate rights. Inmates were more free to define the terms of these contracts than in the behavior-modification prison. The freedom of movement granted to the inmates was far greater than in either the custody or behavior-modification prisons.

Rewards tended to be dispensed through the staff's evaluation of the inmate's therapeutic progress. Thus, inmates who appeared to "gain insight regarding their problems" tended to be given greater privileges (for their greater maturity) than more recalcitrant inmates. Release depended partly on the inmate's therapeutic progress as perceived by both himself and staff members. At one parole hearing, when asked why he should be released, an inmate responded, "Because I understand myself now and know why I did what I did."

Punishments tended to take into account both the motives as well as the psychological context of the offense. For example, we observed a discipline hearing involving a fight between two inmates. One inmate diagnosed as a neurotic was sent to his counselor. The second was diagnosed as "an asocial aggressive" and was immediately transferred to the "adjustment cell" ("punitive-custody cell").

The operational justice in the three settings may be categorized according to typology suggested above: Justice in the custody prison primarily was Type 1 in that there was almost no public rationale for justice decisions other than "do it or it's the 'box'." While there were Type 4 bureaucratic standards, these were manipulated often in dealing with troublesome offenders, and administrators rarely appeared to feel bound by them. The behavior-modification prison seemed to invite Type 2 implicit contracts with inmates, albeit with a Type 4 justification. Inmates were, in effect, told what the rewards would be for conformity as well as what the price would be for disobedience. This, some officials reasoned, would result in a more harmonious prison community as well as aid inmates in adjusting to societal expectations. The psychotherapy prison assumed a Type 3 normative orientation. This norm of treatment seemed to be used in making most justice decisions. Thus, inmates were supposed to "act mature," as staff were expected to "be concerned" with the inmate's rehabilitation.

THE PERCEPTION OF PRISON JUSTICE:
SUBJECTS, INSTRUMENTS, AND METHODS

The researchers sought to relate these prison operational justice structures to inmates' perception of moral atmosphere. Our concept of moral atmosphere (or perceived prison justice) depends on a body of psychological research conducted by Kohlberg et al. (1975). They suggest that individuals tend to prefer the highest stage ideas they are able to comprehend. Typically, comprehension is limited to one stage above an individual's dominant moral stage. Ideas below an individual's stage tend to be rejected as morally wrong or just "plain silly." Thus, a "positive" moral atmosphere is one which is accepted as just by a large percentage of inmates.

To test this hypothesis, the researchers developed a measure, called the Moral Atmosphere Scoring System (M.A.S.S.), to score inmate perceptions of prison justice. Inmates are given a two-hour, transcribed interview to elicit their views of prison rules, roles, rewards, rights, and punishments.

Twelve predominantly Stage 3 inmates were selected in a stratified (by stage) random sample.[2] These more mature inmates were used because our theory predicted that they would reject justice practices which operated at a logic below their own (that is, at Stages 2 and 1).

Trained interviewers were used in gathering the data for the study.[3] Interviews were recorded on tape and later transcribed. Trained scorers from the Laboratory of Human Development at Harvard University analyzed the transcribed data. The interviews were scored blind, and scorers had no identification with the experimental project. An interjudge reliability of .81 was achieved among Moral Atmosphere raters. A .92 reliability was achieved by the Moral Judgement scorers.

RESULTS

The results of the study indicate tentative confirmation of our hypothesis. The three institutions were found to differ in terms of acceptance and rejection (as determined by the acceptance-rejection code on the M.A.S.S.).

The punitive-custody prison was characterized by extremely negative perceptions. Overall, less than 10 percent of the inmate atmosphere perceptions were coded as "accept." Even Stage 3 inmates perceived the setting as Stage 1 or Stage 2. Characteristically, other inmates were perceived in Stage 2 exploitative categories.

Other inmates were "ripped off, punked or taken." Staff were perceived in punitive Stage 1 terms. Their authority was largely seen in their ability to throw inmates in the "box" or to delay their parole. One inmate, when asked why they had prisons, responded that there was a plot to "get the guards and captains off of welfare."

The behavior modification prison was perceived only slightly more positively. Less than 20 percent of the inmate perceptions were coded as "accept." Characteristically, many of the inmates perceived the point system as a scheme "to bribe you into being a good little patsy." Inmates saw staff as "not caring about you." Rules were often described as "silly and Mickey Mouse." Inmates rarely perceived the reasons for "taking away points . . . or giving you points." Parole, which was based, in part, on achieving a certain number of points, was seen as an exercise in which inmates sought to "play the game" in order to get out quicker.

The Transactional Analysis prison was the most positively perceived prison in the group. More than 60 percent of the inmate perceptions were coded as "accept." Inmates, on the whole, saw staff as being supportive and "really caring" about the ward. Rules were typically seen as fair in that they "were for both the staff and the ward." The discipline was characteristically seen as positive in that the counselor "really explained to you what you had done and really tried to help."

The results seem to support the original hypothesis. The two settings characterized by predominantly Type 2 (exchange) modes of justice were seen far more negatively than was the psychotherapeutic setting with a Type 3 (shared, informal norm agreement) justice structure. This seemed to support the empirical findings of the Kohlberg et al. study which offered that individuals tend to accept ideas above their own stage and reject ideas below their own stage. The mixed Stage 2 and Stage 3 inmates tended to see the punitive-custody and behavior-modification prisons negatively, perceiving their justice structures below their own stage of thinking. The same Stage 2 and Stage 3 inmates, on the whole, tended to accept the psychotherapy prison with its emphasis on mutual support and concern.

These results may be illustrated by a comparison of the perception of rules by three reasonably comparable nineteen-year-old Stage 3 inmates, each arrested, for a second time, for breaking and entering. Jim, at the custody prison, for example, typically perceived prison rules as coercive, and he vehemently rejects their justice, legitimacy, as well as their use:

Q. What are some of the rules here?

A. No running in the hallways, no talking while you are watching TV, so many books in your cell, so many

TABLE 6

Perceptions of Prison Rules

Prison/Type of Justice	Accepts[a]	Ambivalent[b]	Rejects[c]
Custody/Type 1	1	2	9
Behavior modification/ Type 2	2	2	8
Psychotherapy/Type 3	8	2	2

[a]Judged as accepting the rules of the institution.
[b]Judged as conflicting with, ambivalent to, or ambiguous towards prison rules.
[c]Judged as rejecting the prison rules.
Source: Compiled by author.

magazines, you can't have this in there. You can't have
a picture on your wall, you have to put it in a square.
You have this square on your wall and you can only put
pictures in this long square. You can't put them nowhere
else. They have this really fucked-up thing for fighting,
like if you are attacked, I might be attacked, I still go to
the hole for fighting, you know, and it is really fucked up.

Q. Are some of the rules unfair?

A. A lot of them are; some of them make sense to a degree. I don't mind a rule to a degree, but it depends
which way you are going to enforce it. Some people enforce it all the way, as strong as possible as they can.
Like I was over the hospital once and I was there for
back trouble, and the medic told me to stay in bed, well,
I didn't constantly stay in bed for 5 straight days, but
one day I walked out of my cell to get my food and the
guy gave me a report for it. It's stupid. Okay, I was
supposed to stay in bed, but still and all, I broke the rule.

Q. Who makes the rules here?

A. I guess they come from ——, from the commissioner; and the warden probably has a lot to do with it, too;
the superintendent.

Q. What is good about the rules here?

A. I myself, I don't abide by the rules; I don't need
them, but you've got to have them; there are so many
fools, so many little kids here, it is ridiculous. They
abuse things. I can't contradict the whole system,
everything, because I can see why a lot of it is happening
like that. There are so many people, and a lot of people
abuse it, you know.

Q. What were they thinking about when they made the
rules here, do you think?

A. Discipline.

Q. What do you mean by that?

A. I think they deliberately made some of them just to
bust your balls; the whole lesson thing, you know.

Bill, in the behavior-modification prison, perceives the rules
as being used to get inmates to conform to the administration's policies. Besides insuring obedience, they are seen as trying to shape
the offender's behavior after release. Similarly, to the custody
prison they are seen as "illegitimate," if not quite as harsh:

Q. What are the rules like here?

A. Unfair rules. Like they got a point system. It's a
regular program; you got to make points, for school, and
they have pool tables and things like that. Like pool,
most guys, if they are going to do something, they play
pool; but if you want to stay up late at night, the less
points you get; you detract points from it.

Q. How is it unfair?

A. Well, it's not the way it should be. It should be
something like, you know, like you do your time without
messing up, and we will give you less time. You get out
before your time is up. Like, I got two years and I am
going to get out in 18 months, instead of the whole two
years. And go back to my family. Instead of being
locked up a real long time, because they ain't going to
make me work.

Q. Who makes the rules here?

A. Staff and the people up front.

Q. Do you know how they are made? Do you know what they are thinking about when they make them?

A. They are thinking about ten-year people, like Louis ... like be puppets, I will pull the string and you jump to it. And if you don't, I will pull your strings for not doing it and put you someplace where you can't do nothing.

Q. What do you think about that?

A. I think that is like turning people into animals, you know. You know, how you train a dog, to obey your rules. An animal.

Q. What is wrong with that?

A. Some people, they are like what they are, and by people always changing, people trying to change you to make you something that they want you to be. And not something that you want to be.

The psychotherapy prison inmates seem to accept the legitimacy of the institution's rules. Most perceived the rules as benign and necessary. Les, for example, offers:

Q. Can you tell me some of the rules you have here?

A. You can't go in people's bed area because they are afraid you are going to rip them off, and you can't smoke in school and you got to be in small groups; just little things like that, you know. You got to be in at special times at night. You got boundaries, that you can't go out of certain areas.

Q. What kind of rules do you run head on into, hassle you?

A. I don't come up against any rules here, I just kick back and do what I am supposed to do.

Q. What is fair rule?

A. Just here. Like they have a rule that you can't be in another person's bed area. When I first got here I was getting ripped off because I didn't have no lock on my locker and I think that is a fair rule because they are protecting someone else's property. Just rules that are protecting other people.

Q. Do you think some of the rules here are to protect you?

A. Yah, some of the rules here are to protect me. Someone might come in my bed area and try to stab me.

Other inmates, however, perceived the rules as almost as manipulative as those in the other two institutions. Sam, a very aware, mature inmate, offered:

Petty rules, you know. It's like a conditioning program. Condition you like to an 8-to-5 job or something; that's what they figure you are going to need when you get out of here. . . . I don't think they are actually looking at me. They are just looking at everybody on the halls. . . . I am just a number here . . . you play the game and make them think you are programmed and get out. You are part of the silent majority and if you do things, like smoke marijuana, keep it under your hat.

IMPLICATIONS

Our research in the area of penology has offered two operational definitions to clarify the concept of prison justice. First, we have suggested that prisons may be broadly categorized as to their level of operational justice. Also, we have offered a beginning methodology to score inmate acceptance or rejection of the prison's moral atmosphere or the perceived level of justice.

During the past six years the author, along with colleagues Lawrence Kohlberg and Joseph Hickey, have sought to apply these concepts to develop a mode of therapy described as "justice as therapy." In June 1971, we were invited to collaborate with the staff and inmates of the Connecticut Correctional Facility at Niantic to develop a new governance structure and therapy program for the prison.

During the summer months, inmates, guards, and administrators met in what we called a "constitutional convention." Here, rules were proposed for what we referred to as a "model cottage." Though negotiations were painful, the convention agreed to clearly define limits for a proposed democratic framework. Inmates would control internal discipline, propose furloughs for members, and define program objectives and activities. All prison offenses, excepting major felonies, would be referred to a "cottage community meeting."

For the past six years, decisions have been made through a democratic format created in the convention. A community member can call a meeting at any time. When a "cottage-rules offense" is discovered, the community meeting acts as jury to determine guilt or innocence. If a "discipline" is in order it is referred to a "discipline board" which includes two inmates and one staff member, both of whom are chosen at random. Routine issues involving such matters as work assignments, love triangles, or interpersonal conflict are dealt with through open dialogue and discussion. Rarely, but not exceptionally, the community deals with issues of contraband, assault, and attempted escape. "Cottage rules" are redefined every twelve weeks in a "marathon meeting." Often there are further negotiations, with administrators, as to the types of issues which the "cottage" democracy may act upon.

To illustrate the "community meeting" system, I offer an example of inmate and staff decision making. A female inmate named Terry had assaulted another woman named Pam. (Earlier in the week, the group had expelled an inmate named Linda for a similar assault, in similar circumstances.) Both inmates had repeated histories of violent behavior both in the prison and "on the streets." The group had to consider that, an hour before the assault, Terry had approached a staff member and asked to be "locked in her room." She said she "felt her anger building up" and that she was "afraid of what she might do to Pam," who had rejected her in a homosexual relationship. The staff member had refused to lock Terry up, saying she should be "able to deal with her emotions."

Ellen[*]: What about Terry. Should she leave?

Barbara: All I know is Terry tried to beat up Pam. Then she should leave, too.

Jean: Yah, it's physical violence.

Tony[*]: How can we throw Linda out and leave Terry here?

_____

[*]Ellen and Tony are staff members.

Ellen: If we are going to be fair don't we have to deal with the thing on a group basis? Look, we have a rule in the constitution on violence.

Jessica: But Terry asked Betty[*] to put her in the infirmary and give her medication. She told you what would happen!

Ellen: I see that, but does that excuse what she did to Pam?

Jackie: I don't know. It's hard. I see that we should be flexible about it. If she told the staff, then that puts the weight more on the staff than on her.

Debby: But still, Terry can't go around pulling on people's hair and knocking them down. She should go, too. How can you kick Linda out and talk this shit about Terry. It's the rule.

Jackie: But it's different. Terry was out of control. Like when I was doing Banks and shit, I knew what I was doing. But there's other things like that guy in the men's thing that went crazy and beat his father. That's crazy. He needs help. Like Terry.

Jerry: I agree. In society, doesn't being crazy kind of excuse you? Like they put crazies in Norwich [Mental Hospital]. Not here in Niantic.

Ellen: I don't know what we are going to do with you, Terry, I see what you are saying about telling staff when it's too much for you to handle, but still, there's the thing of fairness with Linda.

Bobbette: Is there something else we can give her? You know, that she would feel as bad as if she left. Like "Lockup"? That might help her to think?

Jackie: But "Lockup" don't do nothing for you. Just gets you crazier. . . .

---

[*]Betty is a staff member.

The community seeks to establish itself as a new moral reference group. It is hoped that inmates will increasingly judge their
actions in relation to the moral consensus of the cottage community.
To accomplish this, the leaders of the group attempt to point out
contradictions between an individual's moral statements and actions.
In one meeting, for example, a staff member was reprimanded for
"not showing concern in doing her job." Similarly, the group punished
an inmate for not reporting an escape because this showed she "didn't
really care about the community."

The approach differs from conventional prison-milieu therapy
(such as those adopted in the Daytop prison program, the Dr. Max-
well Jones-inspired hospitals at Henderson and Dingleton, or the
American Patuxent Prison) in several respects.

Unlike most group psychotherapy, the goal of the present
project is the encouragement of rational thought rather than self-in-
sight. The inmates are being asked to govern their minisociety in a
more just manner rather than just reflect upon their "hang-ups."
This difference in emphasis helps avoid many of the problems implicit in "insight" therapies. Residents are not "diagnosed" or
"treated." There are no assumptions that lead to the inmates being
defined as more "sick," "antisocial," or "neurotic" than the average
citizen. Also, release is not dependent upon the psychiatrist's cer-
tification of the inmate's "cure" or rehabilitation.

The focus on the ideal of justice implies that the project is
concerned with rectifying the injustices of prisons as well as with
stimulating the rehabilitation of prisoners. As much of our effort is
aimed at a reconstruction of the law as it is in reshaping the thinking
of the offender. In the context of Anthony Burgess' A Clockwork
Orange, we would seek to alter the power of Dr. Brodsky (the slightly demonic, behavioral therapist) as well as the reasoning and actions
of "poor Alex," the "psychopath" subjected to the dreaded "Ludvico
Therapy."

Finally, the program limits the power of the professional
therapist. Psychological skills are taught to the correctional officers
and inmates who maintain the program. This makes the program
cheaper to run than conventional custody or treatment programs. In
six years, there have been only three escapes and almost no serious
acts of violence. The absence of professionals in the program makes
it more difficult for staff members to exempt themselves from the
judgments of the group, or to deny the legitimate moral claims of the
inmates.

The prison project has proven successful in several respects.
Younger inmates have been found to change dramatically in terms of
moral thinking: the average change has been one-half a moral stage
over a nine-month period). Initial recidivism (return to prison) rates

are roughly half that of state norms for groups matched for age, race, and crime.[4] Finally, the program has been extended to a "community-based" facility using the same governance principles as the Niantic unit.

CONCLUSION

Our research observations and experiences with the Just Community program suggest the importance of the concept of social justice in prison research. Our work offers a means of evaluating prison programs in categories which apply to the core goals of corrections: the maintenance of social justice and the reintegration of the offender into society. In an era in which prison therapy has been almost uniformly condemned, it offers new meaning to the ideal of rehabilitation. By ensuring justice, which is accepted by offenders and staff members as fair and is collectively maintained by all members of the prison community, the ends and means problem of conventional programs is avoided. What is just may well be what is ultimately rehabilitative. We need not choose between a just prison which does not educate and a setting which seems to rehabilitate but does not respect the offender's valid moral claims. In our notion of "justice as therapy," we seek at once to reorder the basic moral structure of the prison as well as to offer the inmate a new form of education based on a developmental notion of moral learning.

This type of program is one appropriate to the core ideology of a constitutional society. The founders of the Walnut Street Reformatory saw the restoration of the offender into political and community life as a crucial goal of the prison (Morris 1974). They believed the prison had to demonstrate a commitment to the ideals which the system of justice was sworn to protect. If society wishes to respect democratic justice, it is obligated to offer it in practice as well as in ideology. Only by providing a means to democratically and fairly resolve conflict within the prison can we hope to guarantee the inmates basic rights and protections as well as offer the opportunity for his or her reeducation and reintegration into the community.

APPENDIX 1

Types 1 and 2: Personal Modes of Justice

Type 1: Coercive Power Orientation

"Justice" is personally delegated by the powerful. The strong, the powerful, determine right. There are no common rules or definitions to which these powerful superordinates are bound.

The orientation is towards coercive force. There is no basis for agreement between subordinate and superordinate agents other than the compliance of the weak to the strong. Power exerted unilaterally by the strong defines the right.

Authority is invested in the powerful. Authority is not defined by fixed expectations or rules. Rules for lower subordinates tend to be arbitrary and prohibitive, and they have no application for superordinate members.

Type 2: Personal Exchange Orientation

"Justice" is defined through exchange and negotiation between individuals. There are no norms which are "commonly" accepted as defining the right beyond individual instrumental interest.

The primary orientation is to the instrumental interest of individuals within the organization. These interests are achieved through exchange and negotiation with particular social members. There are few accepted rules or customs which regulate these transactions.

Authority is maintained through bargaining with individuals. There are no fixed rules that are regularly enforced. Compliance is induced through individual negotiations (bribes, graft, payoffs, and so on). Rules tend to be stated as "things that one is allowed to get away with."

Types 3 and 4: Collective Justice Modes

Type 3: Informal Norm Agreement

Through shared tradition, customs, ideology, or stated goal, office holders are bound to common standards with subordinate figures. Shared informal norms is primary orientation. These mutually orienting norms provide a basis for adjudication of conflict between lower subordinate and superordinate figures. Lower subordinates may appeal to customary, traditional, or ideological norms and may insist that superordinate figures maintain consistency with these informal standards.

Authority is bound by shared expectations as to conduct. There is consensus as to how a "normal" staff member should conduct himself. These standards remain informal and uncodified. "Rules" remain in the customary mode. There is "implicit" understanding of standards which should govern interaction. Conflicts are resolved through reference to the "customary," "traditional," or ideologically correct solution, rather than reference to rules or laws.

Type 4: Structured Norm Agreement

There are common rule standards. Rules are codified and public. Rules provide a basis for adjudication of conflicts of claims. Rules regulate interaction of superordinate as well as with subordinate figures.

Primary orientation is to fixed, codified rule standards. Rules are justified in terms of a genuine order-maintaining function. Fixed common rules define justice practices and transactions.

Authority is defined through codified procedures. Rules define interaction between office holder and subordinate. Rules apply to authority figures. Lower subordinates may appeal over superordinate figures to rule structure. Rules are generally exhaustive, clearly defined, and categorical in nature. Rules differ from Type 3 informal standards in their codified formality, universality of application, and in their functional justification in terms of order maintenance.

Type 5: Principled Orientations

Type 5: Shared Principled Agreement

There is shared consensual process to determine the right. There is a differentiation between justice and administrative functions; that is, there is a moral standard which is applied beyond administrative rules. There are collectively agreed-upon principles which adjudicate conflicts among rules and norms.

The primary orientation is towards "principles" of welfare and contractual agreements of right (or prerogative) and procedure. Institutions are bound to maintain individual rights and to guarantee due process. Freedom is bound to be maximized consistent with freedom for others. There is a consent component to basic institutional arrangements.

There is authority based on mutual contract. Contract implies that authority maintains an agreed-upon ethical basis of law as well as to enforce specific rules. The rule structure is subordinate to a more abstract contract which applies justice criteria to particular rules.

NOTES

1. Detailed methodology is described by Scharf (1977).

2. The inmates were randomly chosen within a pool of conventional-reasoning inmates.

3. Several of the interviewers were former inmates from federal institutions. It was felt that former inmates with no affiliation with the experimental project would have the best chance of acquiring candid interviews from the subjects.

4. A careful research program designed to measure the program's effects on recidivism is now in progress.

REFERENCES

Cressey, D. 1960. Contradictory directives in complex organizations: the case of the prison. Administration Science Quarterly 4: 1-19.

Durkheim, E. 1938. The Rules of Sociological Method. Glencoe, Ill.: Free Press.

Gouldner, A. 1972. Coming Crisis of Western Sociology. Glencoe, Ill.: Free Press.

Grosser, G., ed. 1960. Theoretical Studies in the Social Organization of the Prison. New York: Social Science Research Council.

Kohlberg, L. 1967. Stage and sequence. In Handbook of Socialization Theory and Research, ed. Golslin. New York: Rand McNally and Co.

Kohlberg, L., J. Rest, and E. Turiel. 1975. Comprehension and Moral Learning. In Collected Papers in Moral Education, L. Kohlberg, ed. Cambridge, Mass.: Moral Education Research Foundation.

Kohlberg, L., K. Kauffman, P. Scharf, and J. Hickey. 1974. Just Community Approach to Corrections. Cambridge, Mass.: Moral Education Research Foundation.

Merton, R. 1956. Social Theory and Social Structure. Glencoe, Ill.: Free Press.

Morris, N. 1974. Future of Imprisonment. Chicago: John Wiley.

Rawls, J. 1972. A Theory of Justice. Cambridge, Mass.: Harvard University Press.

Scharf, P. 1971. Atmosphere of the prison. Address to American Psychologists Association.

Sykes, G. 1952. Society of Captives. Princeton, N. J.: Princeton University Press.

PART
IV

LEGALITY, MORALITY, ETHICS AND CRIMINOLOGICAL RESEARCH

18

VIOLENCE AND VALUES: THE IMPACT OF EVERYDAY REALITY ON CRIMINOLOGICAL RESEARCH

Raymond J. Michalowski

INTRODUCTION

The causes and control of violence have always been major concerns in modern criminology. These concerns, however, have focused upon what history has rendered a relatively narrow range of violent behaviors. While the common-law offenses of murder, rape, robbery, and assault may adequately represent the scope of potential violence in preindustrial society, they are but a portion of the violene available to a complex, postindustrial world. Yet, it is primarily these common-law offenses which continue to receive the bulk of attention given by modern criminologists to the problem of violence.

Traditionally, criminologists have held that the appropriate focus of criminology is behavior designated by law as criminal. If nothing else, this perspective has the advantage of easily meeting the criteria generally deemed necessary for a scientific study of crime. Reid (1976: 4-5) demonstrates quite clearly the methodological attractiveness of a legalistic approach:

> If empirical investigations comparing criminals and
> noncriminals are to be made, it must be possible to de-
> velop operational definitions of those terms. The defini-
> tions must be precise and unambiguous and capable of
> measurement.

For those agreeing with this perspective, the failure of criminologists to study forms of violence not prohibited by criminal law is of little significance, and certainly no cause for criticism.

In recent years, however, this legalistic approach to the study of crime has been heavily criticized by radical criminologists. There are two dominant themes reflected in this criticism. First, allowing the law to determine the subject matter of criminology makes the discipline subservient to the political economy which determines both the content of the law and the nature of its enforcement. The relationship between the political economy and the content and enforcement of law, they argue, should be the focus rather than the determinant of criminological research. Second, the methodological purity claimed for the legalistic approach is adequate only to a positivist definition of science, and such sociological positivism is inadequate to the development of a structural sociology capable of dealing with power and interests.[1]

Rather than law and its violations as a starting point, radical criminologists argue that the basis of criminology should be a definition of crime as any behavior violating politically defined human rights (Schwendinger and Schwendinger 1970). Unlike legalists, radical criminologists can find much to criticize in the approach of traditional criminology to the study of violence; the radical perspective leaves criminology free to include "imperialism, racism, capitalism, sexism and other systems of exploitation which contribute to human misery and deprive people of their human potentiality" under the heading of violence (Platt 1974: 6).

While it is possible to critique criminology from a "human rights" definition of crime, one need not go beyond a legalistic approach to find anomalies in the traditional approach to the study of violence. The criminological literature abounds with research and theory concerning murders, rapes, robberies, and assaults while comparatively little is written about the marketing of known dangerous drugs, the violence resulting from gross traffic negligence, illness resulting from violations of air and water pollution standards, and the death and injury resulting from violations of building, fire, mine, and industrial safety codes. Yet these mala prohibita acts can result in real harm and are prohibited under the criminal law of various jurisdictions. Given these two characteristics, they are no less crimes of violence than the common-law offenses most frequently studied. While it may not be significant from a legalistic perspective that criminologists seldom study forms of violence not prohibited by law, it is significant that some types of legally proscribed violence receive noticeably less attention from criminologists than others.

There are a multitude of factors, many of them political, which influence the types of behavior most heavily studied by criminologists. The content of substantive and procedural laws, the enforcement and sentencing practices which influence the availability of both victims and offenders for study, the powerlessness which deprives some offenders of the right not to be studied, and the greater willingness of public agencies to fund certain types of research—all are products of political processes. Insofar as they have a substantial impact upon the content of criminological research, they are certainly valid focuses for an inquiry into the nature of criminological research. However, this chapter will examine the differential emphasis given by criminologists to various forms of criminal violence, not from the perspective of political determinants, but from the perspective of socially shared belief systems.

The view presented here is that behavior sets are generally surrounded by belief systems and their constituent cognitive orientations which, while they may not be causal, do play an important interactive role in supporting and maintaining a world view within which the behaviors make sense and can continue to be conducted with relative ease. An understanding of the cognitive orientations surrounding any behavior set can contribute to an overall understanding of the behavior set, and we will, therefore, consider the belief system within which the current conduct of criminological research makes sense.

TWO FORMS OF LEGALISM

While the law has traditionally been the starting point for modern criminologists, there have been two general approaches to its role in determining the content of research: social legalism and strict legalism. When taken as categories of research input, these terms have a meaning opposite those normally given them in discussion of research output.

When concerned with violence, criminologists have characteristically focused upon those forms which are most feared by the public and most frequently prosecuted by the justice system. The relationship between these two factors—public fear and enforcement practices—is an ambiguous one. While it is generally held by both the public and many criminologists that the former determines the latter, the writer has suggested elsewhere that social-learning principles support an opposite interpretation (Michalowski 1976). That is, there may be validity to Stephens' statement that "murder may be a serious crime because men are hanged for it." Regardless of the direction, however, there appears to be a strong relationship between public fear of certain crimes and law-enforcement practices, and these two factors have delineated the content of a substantial proportion of criminological literature.

The researchers who are representative of social legalism, such as Tappan (1947, 1960), Burgess (1950), and Reckless (1973), would agree that this is as it should be. The appropriate focus of criminological research, they would say, is behavior prohibited by the law and the frequent target of measures designed to enforce that law. From the point of view of research input, such writers are social legalists because the focus of research should be determined

266 / LEGALITY, MORALITY, AND ETHICS

not only by the bare specifications of the law, but also by those social processes that determine which illegal behaviors receive the most frequent and most stringent enforcement. Tappan (1947) went so far as to suggest that the study of "the criminal," if it were to be methodologically adequate, must be limited to those actually convicted of criminal offenses. While not all criminologists operating from a social-legalist perspective would agree with Tappan's relatively narrow description of subject matter, they do share the common assumption that behaviors which are neither the target of serious law-enforcement efforts nor organized public resentment are of less sociological importance than behaviors more aggressively controlled.

The merits of this approach lie in its ability to describe an unambiguous subject matter, the units of which are far more readily available for study than the processes which led to their creation. Its weakness is that it subordinates the study of crime as a social phenomenon to a complex of antecedent political and social processes, making it difficult to approach these processes as subject matter for research. This perspective may be adequate for the study of crime as a social-psychological phenomenon—crime as what people believe it to be. It is not adequate, however, for the study of crime as a product of a politically created and bureaucratically enforced social structure.

Unlike social legalism, strict legalism accepts as relevant any behavior prohibited by law, regardless of the severity or frequency of the sanctions applied. The early studies of white-collar crime (Sutherland 1940, 1941; Hartung 1950; Clinard 1952) were instrumental in fostering this perspective. I term this perspective strict legalism because it takes the law at face value when seeking input for criminological research. The effects of this perspective upon criminology were twofold. It facilitated the expansion of criminology beyond those behaviors which were of greatest concern to the police and the public, and it contributed to the acceptance of the criminal justice process as appropriate subject matter for research (see Figure 2). In many respects the latter effect is a function of the former. Early research forays beyond conventional justice system concerns, and the debates they caused [for example, see Sutherland's (1945) response to critiques of White Collar Crime] demonstrated the significance of differential enforcement in the production of what we refer to as the crime problem. This, in turn, served to demystify the criminal justice process somewhat and to sensitize criminologists to its importance as a focus of study.

Acceptance of the criminal justice process as a focus for research gained substantial momentum with its development as a research discipline distinct from purely sociological criminology. This concern with the justice process soon outdistanced the initial effect

FIGURE 2

Criminalization as a Societal Process and its Relationship to Criminology

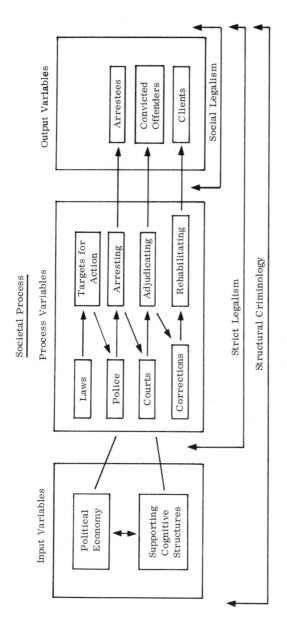

Note: While the total number of variables within each category is larger and the interconnectedness both within and between categories is more complex than shown here, this simplified diagram is presented to illustrate the general orientations of different approaches to criminology.

Source: Compiled by the author.

of strict legalism—the expansion of criminological research into all areas of prohibited behavior. As a result, criminological research remained primarily, although no longer exclusively, concerned with those offenses most frequently and severely prosecuted. However, there was an additional emphasis upon the processes involved in the control of such offenses.

Contemporarily, most criminologists can easily approach both the process and the output of the criminal justice system as appropriate subjects for research. However, while strict legalism expanded the subject matter of criminology and contributed to the acceptance of process as a research topic, its impact stopped short of propelling criminologists into examining those factors which serve as inputs to the criminal justice system, or even giving extensive consideration to criminal offenses other than those most frequently prosecuted. Part of the explanation for this, it appears, is located in the fact that criminologists share with the general public and the criminal justice system certain cognitive orientations toward the nature of the social world, in general, and the nature of crime, in particular.

The remainder of this discussion will examine two forms of criminal violence which have received noticeably different treatment from the public, the criminal justice system, and criminologists. These two forms of violence—the conventional homicide and the negligent traffic death—will be compared in an attempt to identify the specific cognitive orientations which support this differential treatment.

The conduct of this inquiry is based upon two assumptions which should be made explicit. First, it is valid to distinguish between events as social objects to which individuals respond in certain ways and events as physical realities, at least within a given linguistic framework. As social objects, deaths due to homicide can be distinguished from deaths due to traffic negligence according to the responses evoked by each. As physical realities—states of cellular decomposition signifying death—they are not distinguishable. The second assumption is that cognitive orientations, of themselves, are not sufficient causes of differential responses to social objects. While important in the production of individual responses to social facts, they are both reflections of and supports for the structural arrangements of the society in which they are located. They are part of the belief system through which individuals make sense of the events which occur within given structural arrangements.

TWO FORMS OF VIOLENCE

Narrowly defined, criminal violence is any harm-producing act prohibited by criminal law. Certain acts which fall under this definition are perceived as grave transgressions of the social order

while others are considered relatively minor harms. Our comparison of criminal homicides and traffic deaths resulting from driver
negligence provides a good case in point. In both cases the offender
is liable for prosecution under the criminal law, and both result in a
substantial number of wrongful deaths yearly. However, both public
opinion and governmental action demonstrate that homicide is considered the more serious form of violence.

Since the mid-1960s, opinion polls have consistently shown
that the public considers crime in general and crimes of violence in
particular among the top three problems facing the nation. Traffic
fatalities, on the other hand, have never evoked such public concern,
even though the statistical chances of dying as the result of some
other driver's negligence are slightly greater. It is interesting to
note that while this concern with "law and order" has been translated
into a significant political issue in the last four presidential campaigns,
at no time has the problem of traffic deaths received such attention.

While there has been little public opposition to, and considerable public demand for, increased spending on police protection,
some of the most vocal responses in the area of traffic safety (Ralph
Nader not withstanding) have been in opposition to measures designed
to reduce traffic death tolls—e.g., seat belts and seat belt warning
systems, head restraints, mandatory seat belt usage laws, and so on.
Some may disagree as to how crime-control money should be spent,
but few would suggest that measures to reduce violent crimes should
not be undertaken. On the other hand, editorial comments and letters
opposing current and proposed traffic safety measures as an infringe-
ment upon basic individual rights are not at all uncommon.

The expenditures of public order-systems in an attempt to
lessen violent deaths reflect similar priorities. From 1955 to 1965,
state and local expendituresfor police protection more than doubled,
and projected budgets correctly predicted that they would double again
by 1975 (Kakalik and Wildhorn 1971: 25). There is no evidence of
similar increases at state and local levels for traffic-safety measures,
although the increases in traffic deaths more than kept pace with increases in crime until the oil crisis and the imposition of the national
55-mile-per-hour speed limit.

The same pattern is found at the national level. The Law
Enforcement Assistance Administration received approximately $790
million for 1974 while the National Highway Traffic Safety Administration received approximately 190 million (Bureau of the Budget 1973).
Furthermore, since 1972, the NHTSA's budget has risen 44 percent
while the budget for LEAA has grown by 108 percent.

While it would be incorrect to claim that traffic deaths are
accepted with complete equanimity, public opinion and public expenditures indicate that criminal homicide is considered the more serious
form of violence. Certainly there are reasons for these differences,

and those between other forms of criminal violence. This raises
two important questions for criminological research: (1) What are
the factors which support differential perception and treatment of
various forms of violence? (2) Do those factors which support differential perception and treatment of various forms of violence by the
public and law-enforcement institutions, also constitute sufficient
justification for their differential treatment by criminologists?

EVALUATING VIOLENCE: PHYSICAL CRITERIA

As a generic category of actions, criminal violence encom-
passes many different forms. That certain forms of violence cause
no public outcry, that their perpetrators are not considered truly
criminal, and that they result in only minor penalties is a consequence
of the social meanings ascribed to them. This meaning results from
a process of evaluation through which each form of violence is measured in terms of some criteria of seriousness.

What factors are evaluated to determine the seriousness of
the various forms of criminal violence? Four categories of physical
criteria, which can be utilized in evaluating the seriousness of violence, are suggested here:

1. The severity of physical harm caused by one form in comparison to another.
2. The frequency of one form in comparison to another.
3. The characteristics of the perpetrators generally associated with one form versus another.
4. The characteristics of the victims generally associated
with one form versus another.

The last two are included as physical criteria because, although
the response to them may be determined by social values, factors
such as age, sex, race and income earned, of themselves, fit the
definition of physical realities as outlined above. When applied to
our comparison case, how effective are these factors in explaining
the differential response to these two forms of violence?

Severity of Harm

When comparing negligent traffic deaths and homicides, the
severity of physical harm is equal. Physical death is absolute:
there are no degrees of death. The victim of a drunken driver is
equally as dead as the victim of a murder. The same equality holds

true for any injury less than death. In terms of physical harm to the victim, whether an individual receives a broken arm from being struck by a speeding driver or from being assaulted in an alley, the amount of pain, time lost from work, and possible physical limitation on future activities are relatively equal.

Evaluation based upon severity of harm alone provides little explanation of the differential response to these two forms of violence since each form can result in an equally broad range of physical harms. If severity of harm was a primary criterion, the negligent accident resulting in death, for example, would be considered more serious than the assault resulting in only injury. Yet, the penalties prescribed for these acts and the public's perception of them (Rossi et al. 1974) demonstrates that severity of harm is not a primary reason why one is perceived as more serious than the other.[2]

Frequency

The relative frequency of these two forms of criminal violence also provides little clue as to why one is considered more serious than the other. The negligent traffic death, which is considered the less serious form of violence, is the more frequent. The National Safety Council (1971) estimates that nearly half of those who die in traffic accidents are innocent victims. In raw figures, this represented approximately 20,000 deaths in 1971. In that same year, homicides accounted for 17,627 deaths—12 percent less than just the innocent victims of traffic negligence.[3] At least for our two comparison cases, frequency does not explain the difference in perceived severity.

Characteristics of the Harmers

It has been argued by some (Monkkenen 1973) that the importance attached to various criminal acts is primarily a function of the social characteristics associated with the typical offender for that act. Thus, common-law crimes of violence are feared more than other crimes because historically they have been linked to the less integrated and more transient members of society—the "dangerous classes." It is not physical alone harm that determines the degree of public apprehension, but rather the more general fear of the dangerous classes which gives common law crimes of violence a seriousness not associated with other crimes.

According to this criterion, criminal homicide would be perceived as the more serious crime if those responsible for homicides are more frequently members of groups having a lower socioeconomic status than those responsible for traffic deaths. Murderers should be disproportionately from lower-SES groups while traffic death offenders should be more evenly distributed throughout the social scale.

The writer's research on traffic deaths, however, offers no empirical support for this contention. Traffic-death offenders were found to be nearly identical, in terms of SES, to conventional violent offenders (Michalowski 1973, 1975). Specifically, the traffic-death offenders significantly often are young, black males, of low income, residing in areas characterized by high rates of interpersonal violence, with prior records for crimes of violence. Thus, the actual characteristics of the harmers offers little explanation as to why homicides are more fearful than traffic deaths.

There is reason to believe, despite empirical evidence to the contrary, that it is assumed that traffic-death offenders are substantially different in social characteristics from murderers. This assumption, even if incorrect, could explain the greater seriousness attached to murder. However, if this is the case, there is a need to consider what has led to an assumption which cannot be empirically confirmed.

Characteristics of the Victims

From the earliest times, legal codes have made distinctions concerning the severity of an act based upon the characteristics of the person harmed. Ancient codes such as the Hammarabian, Justinian, and Mycenaean all acknowledge, in some way, that crimes committed upon an elite or a freeman were more serious than the same crimes committed against a commoner or a slave. With the exception of special laws governing the killing of political figures and officers of the law, our own legal codes do not explicitly make such distinctions. However, an unwritten distinction still remains as part of our practice. That is, the severity of an act of violence, at least when measured by either public response or penalties assessed, appears to vary somewhat with the status of the person victimized.

The notoriety given to, and the public outrage caused by, violence committed against public figures—the assassination of Dr. King, the robbery of Senator Stennis, or the murder of Sharon Tate—are contemporary cases in point. The rule of thumb is that acts of violence committed against public figures or those of high status are considered more severe disruptions of social order than similar acts committed against either persons of low status or those who are publicly obscure.

If the characteristics of the harmed explained the different perception of murders and traffic deaths, one would expect to find that murder victims are generally of higher status or greater public exposure than the victims of negligent traffic fatalities. This is not the case, however. Sociologically, there is no distinction between the victims of homicides and the victims of negligent traffic accidents; as groups they are nearly identical in social characteristics (Michalowski 1973).

Although distinctions concerning the characteristics of the harmed do affect the perception of <u>individual</u> acts, there are few, if any, forms of violence limited to a single type of victim. For inter-category comparisons, the characteristics of the victim are not particularly relevant. It is limited in its explanatory power to the differential perception of specific acts rather than categories of acts.

EVALUATING VIOLENCE: INTERPRETIVE CRITERIA

The physical criteria for evaluating forms of violence offer little explanation as to why homicides are perceived as more serious crimes than negligent traffic deaths. In each case, the physical criteria do not support the conventional response. From what, then, are these responses constructed if not the physical differences between the acts being compared?

Part of the explanation, it seems, is associated with five perceived dimensions of human behavior: inevitability, controllability, intent, deviance, and social utility. These dimensions are components of a larger belief system which provides a basis for interpreting and assigning meaning to human behavior. In short, they are cognitive orientations which reflect beliefs about the nature of humans and their environment, through which we attempt to categorize experience in a meaningful and systematic way.

It is only after experiences have been categorized—that is, assigned a social reality—that a "meaningful" response can be made. Because these cognitive orientations are part of the "rules" for categorization, they have a compelling quality not exerted by the physical criteria. By directing the interpretive process, they, in effect, determine the eventual response. The following discussion attempts to show how these cognitive orientations influence the interpretation of homicides and negligent traffic deaths, and direct our subsequent response to them.

Inevitability

Inevitability is the quality of being unavoidable. Most traffic fatalities are perceived as "accidents" while homicides are not. The term "accident" implies, among other things, an unavoidable con-currence of circumstances. Since this concurrence is unavoidable, the behaviors of individual participants are considered largely irrele-vant to the outcome. Because human behavior cannot be a focus for explanation, "accidents," as one category of inevitable occurrences, can be understood only as resulting from "fate" or "chance," making them inappropriate as topics for behavioral science.

Unlike "accidents," homicides are seen as resulting from deliberate human behavior, and therefore "fate" is not a satisfactory explanation. The reason for this distinction may be that the rela-tionship between a human act and a resulting death is obvious and direct in the case of homicide, while it is obscured by a more com-plex causal sequence in the case of a traffic fatality. Where causal sequences are obscured by complexity, the cognitive orientation of inevitability facilitates categorizing these events as "accidents."

Certainly, many forms of death which were once seen as the work of fate or the direct and unopposable intervention of some "god"—plagues, heart attacks, and so on—ceased to be "inevitable" as an understanding of the causal sequence which produced these events developed. However, once the cognitive orientation of inevitability has been used to categorize an event, there is resistance to recate-gorization even in the face of new evidence. As can be seen from the responses to new explanations which characterized the development of physical sciences, there is substantial resistance within existing thought systems to the emergence of new roles for categorizing ex-perience (Kuhn 1962: 67-90).

Many traffic researchers have long conducted their investiga-tions on the basis that the causal sequence leading to traffic accidents is not intrinsically different from that leading to other everyday events (Haddon 1964). However, outside of traffic research, and certainly among many criminologists there still exists the distinction that traffic fatalities are, in the main, accidents while more conventional forms of violence are purposeful sociological events. This distinc-tion extends beyond traffic deaths. Mine disasters, industrial acci-dents, and increasing rates of respiratory diseases, for example, are seldom examined as harms which may result from violations of law.

Controllability

Controllability is the quality of being manipulatable. While inevitability suggests the operation of fate, chance, or some other invisible mover in the production of events, humans have often sought, despite the seeming illogic, to influence the course of such events.

Efforts to control events or conditions perceived as resulting from fate-like forces have generally remained in the area of "magic" until technological or ideational changes culminated in a recategorization of these events. What is important for our consideration here is the target of these control efforts rather than simply their existence.

Rational manipulation of human behavior is of little use in controlling events which do not arise from such behavior. Such events can be controlled, if at all, only through some supernatural manipulation of forces which exist outside the realm of everyday human activities. When human behavior, on the other hand, is seen as the cause of the event, manipulation of that behavior will be viewed as potentially affecting the course of events. Where it is not, control efforts must be directed toward other factors. The folk song which begins:

> "I don't care if it rains or freezes, as long as I got my
> plastic Jesus 'sitting on the dashboard of my car"

may have far more than humorous implications.

Traffic fatalities, which are presumed to arise from a "fateful" concurrence of circumstances, are not controllable through manipulation of human behavior. Homicides which are assumed to arise from willful acts of individuals are controllable. Thus, it is reasonable that the public should demand strong measures to control homicide, the statistically lesser occurrence, and respond either indifferently or in opposition to measures to reduce traffic fatalities.

This orientation has had its effect upon criminologists both perceptually and pragmatically. To the degree that criminologists share the everyday reality that traffic fatalities are uncontrollable, at least in terms of manipulating human behavior, it is not meaningful to apply their skills as social scientists to the study of that behavior. Pragmatically, conventional perception influences the availability of support for such research, thereby directing researchers through the relative availability of research monies into those areas which most fit the everyday understanding of what is and is not controllable. There is little reason to invest considerable energy and money toward ameliorating what is perceived as relatively uncontrollable. This holds true for a number of other form of violence as well as traffic accidents.

Intent

Intent is a basic orientation in categorizing any harm-producing event in our society. That we maintain a decreasing scale of punishments for wrongful death, based upon the degree of specific <u>mens rea</u> involved, is forthright proof that the intent to cause harm is more important than the harm itself in determining the social meaning of a wrongful death. The more absolute the intent to cause harm, the more severe will be the societal response toward the harm producer.

The reasons for this are twofold. First, based on the assumption that humans are free moral agents capable of making choices, the willful intent to cause harm justifies strong moral outrage among the righteous. Second, intended acts can be controlled. Since they are assumed to result from deliberate choice, making it impossible (specific deterrence), or unattractive (general deterrence), for an individual to make a wrong moral choice should effectively reduce the incidence of such acts.

On the other hand, the unintended consequences of human acts—called "accidents"—cannot be similarly controlled. Our philosophy of human thought and action forges a strong inverse relationship between intent and controllability, thereby making it both legitimate and purposeful to direct stringent social control measures only against those who intend harmful outcomes.

Traffic fatalities, even clearly negligent vehicular homicides, do not directly involve specific intent to cause harm. Individuals may speed, drive while intoxicated, or violate some other traffic law with full intent to do so, but it is safe to say that, with the exception of vehicular suicide, drivers seldom premeditate accidents. Since the harm produced by a fatal traffic accident was not specifically intended, the societal response is low key. Thus, the penalties for homicide by vehicle are less severe, and the demands for strict application of these penalties are less vocal, than for any other form of wrongful death despite the equivalence of the physical harm with that of conventional homicides.

Deviance

Deviance is behavior which violates the conduct norms of a group, or at the societal level, of that group with sufficient power to define normative conduct for all the various subgroups within the society (Quinney 1970). "Normal" behavior is seldom viewed as problematic by society, while "deviant" behavior is almost always considered a problem. However, it is not all behavior in violation of stated conduct norms which is viewed as socially problematic— only those behaviors in violation of the operative behavioral norms established within the group or society. Many forms of behavior, formally defined as deviant, may actually be quite acceptable within the group or society defining them as deviant (Dinitz et al. 1969: 10-11).

The degree to which any deviant behavior is common within a group must influence the strength of that group's reaction against such behavior. If, as Erikson (1966) suggests, the enforcement of conduct norms functions to define the boundaries between legitimate and unacceptable behavior within a group, no society can afford to enforce stated conduct norms which would result in labeling the majority, or even a significant minority, of its population as deviant. Numerous patterns of behavior, in contradiction to stated norms, become regularized within any group and even contribute to the functioning of that group. That is, "normal" deviance becomes acceptable and little stigma is attached to it despite formal legal norms and statements to the contrary.

Action against a behavior, and not simply its proscription, is the true measure of the degree to which any behavior is viewed as problematic by a group. The traffic death is perceived as less of a problem than murder because the context in which it occurs is the more normal. Like white-collar crime, traffic deaths occur during the performance of normal, everyday activities (Sutherland 1949).

In 1971, over 80 percent of all American households possessed at least one car, and over half of the nation's population were licensed automobile drivers (Automobile Manufacturers Association 1970). This leaves very few people of legal driving age and who are physically capable who do not drive. In addition, the violation of traffic regulations is only slightly less common than driving itself. Despite its proscription, the negligent operation of an automobile—the behavior from which traffic fatalities generally arise—is a common, acceptable, and therefore normal behavior in our society. This results in an inability to perceive automotive negligence as criminal behavior and a reluctance to initiate strong social-control measures against it.

Murder is most commonly the culmination of some altercation or verbal hostility, just as the traffic fatality is frequently a consequence of the negligent operation of a motor vehicle. The hostilities leading to murder, however, are perceived as abnormal, particularly by those with the power to define law, while the antecedents to traffic fatalities are not. Therefore, murder is socially perceived and defined as a far more serious and threatening problem. Interestingly, the behaviors leading to murder, particularly the verbal exchanges between victim and perpetrator, are not necessarily illegal, while the negligent driving which results in a traffic fatality is always illegal.

In attempting to study crime as social deviance, criminologists have had to take their direction from those definitions of deviance which are operative in society. While this is to some extent unavoidable, it is unfortunate that for the most part these definitions of deviance have served to define research input rather than being the focus of study themselves. Although considerable energy has been devoted to identifying what forms of deviance individuals perceive as most serious, much less consideration has been given to why they are perceived this way. Individuals appear to uniformly define interpersonal violence as among the most serious forms of deviance and it is sometimes considered a truism that this reflects a basic human fear of physical injury and death. However, the salience of this fear as a modern concern may reflect structural factors as much as, or possibly more than, human nature. Modern political states have appropriated to themselves the task of protecting individuals from interpersonal violence. The net effect may be to render individuals psychologically, and perhaps pragmatically, more vulnerable to the threat of interpersonal violence because they perceive a lack of any immediate means of protection. Another consideration is that the response to the possibility of physical injury and death is not uniform. Under certain social definitions, the risk of injury or death may be desirable to other social consequences. In time of war, for example, individuals may choose such risk rather than the social stigma associated with not choosing them. What are the structural and social forces which combine to create this differential response? Why is dying in the war against communism more glorious than dying in the "war against crime"?

Questions such as these, and even better ones, would result from incorporating the definitions of deviance and their sources into the field of criminological research. As it is now, criminologists, for the most part, study the consequences of these definitions, not their sources.

Social Utility

When comparing behaviors which may have undesirable consequences, it is important to consider the relative social utility of behavior sets as well as their degree of perceived deviance. In a society oriented toward efficiency, speed, and technological advancement, the motor vehicle is a transportation godsend, and is likely to remain so until viable alternatives are developed.

Over 90 percent of all intercity transportation is by motor vehicle (Automobile Manufacturers Association 1970). This represents a critical flow of people, materials, and machinery which is necessary to keep a technocracy in operation. In addition, the automotive industry itself is a critical component of the American economy. The motor vehicle, perceived as a positive good in itself, is a crucial element in achieving other socially defined goals. For this reason, motor vehicles and their consequences are accepted with tolerance. On the other hand, a society which desires social and domestic tranquillity will view social hostility, the antecedent of murder, as making no utilitarian contribution whatsoever. This further directs social-control efforts away from traffic fatalities and towards homicide, even when the undesirable violent consequences of the former may exceed the latter. This analysis would also apply to many other forms of socially utilitarian activities, the conduct of which include violations of law resulting in physical harm. In fact, it would incorporate the entire range of economically productive activities and, if our response to white-collar crime is at all indicative, it would suggest that social utility may be one of the most important orientations in determining what is and is not categorized as criminal violence.

THE CRIMINOLOGIST'S DILEMMA

The seriousness ascribed to any form of violence reflects a complex of cognitive orientations which provide the rules for understanding these events. As with most rules for analysis, they require certain assumptions to be made. While these orientations have been discussed up to this point as discrete elements of thought, it is important to recognize that they interact and combine to create an overall, everyday reality through which we make sense of our experience.

Criminologists have characteristically studied those behaviors whose interpretations as serious acts of deviance were supported by this everyday reality. This selection of subject matter, however, brings with it an acceptance of the cognitive orientations and their constituent assumptions from which everyday reality is constructed.

The criminologist's dilemma is (or should be) whether or not these cognitive orientations should determine the substance of scientific inquiry. That is, should criminologists accept the everyday assumptions about the nature of social reality as valid parameters for the study of that reality.

It is not possible to answer a question of what should be without reference to one's own belief system. This study's answer to the criminologist's dilemma is no for the following, and admittedly value-based, reasons which are offered as an alternative to the everyday reality that many criminologists appear to share with much of the rest of society.

First, as phenomenologists have emphasized, everyday reality is a taken-for-granted reality. If social scientists begin their inquiries with an uncritical acceptance of the cognitive orientations from which social reality is constructed, their work can only be a reflection of everyday reality rather than an analysis of it in any meaningful sense. This does not mean that assumptions should never enter into the research process—that would be an impossible goal. However, in the study of violence for example, the decision to accept certain types of harms as more serious than others, because they are defined as such in the everyday reality, should be a conscious one. It should not be by default. We must constantly ask, when seeking topics of inquiry, not only what is the social meaning of a particular behavior, but, also, why does it have that meaning?

Second, everyday reality is a reflection of and a support for structural arrangements. The cognitive orientations for evaluating violence discussed above are very adequate to the needs of a capitalist social structure. A strong orientation towards intent, for example, both reflects and supports the concept of individual responsibility. This, in turn, provides an adequate basis for over-rewarding some and under-rewarding others while at the same time offering both the over-rewarded and the under-rewarded a means of making sense of their condition. Similarly, a strong orientation towards social utility, defined in monetary terms, serves to minimize the harms committed in the production of economic capital, and enables substitution of the harms caused by structurally more insignificant individuals as a focus for public sentiment. As examples, these cognitive orientations demonstrate the types of relationships which can exist between everyday reality and social structure.

Capitalist arrangements characterize the structure of American society. Regardless of a researcher's orientation, the relationship between this structure and the everyday reality supportive of it should be a part, rather than a determinant, of the subject matter of criminological research.

Considering that the maintenance of the dominant social structure benefits certain social groups more than others, the concept of justice as part of the subject matter of criminology fairly demands that the relationship between social structure, the definition of crimes, and the enforcement of laws be included as part of the subject matter of criminological research. One need not conclude on an a priori basis that justice does not exist in order to examine the structural relationships governing criminal justice in a capitalist or any other society. In fact, justice is too important a concern in the social life of any society for the burden of proof to rest solely with those who seek to demonstrate that it does not exist.

Criminology has the potential of serving as an ongoing critique of the state of justice in society. To actualize this, however, it must incorporate the structural arrangements and the everyday realities supportive of them into its ordinary subject matter. This, in turn, can only be accomplished by going beyond the cognitive orientations by which we normally evaluate violence and other forms of criminal behavior.

Third, criminology need not be limited by the needs of the criminal justice system. It may be impossible or impractical to design and operate a public-order system in America without reference to inevitability, controllability, intent, deviance, and social utility. However, if criminology is to truly examine these phenomena, it must examine the underlying basis of needs such as these, as well as acknowledging their existence.

CONCLUSION

Various forms of violence have received differential treatment from law enforcement, the public, and criminologists. Part of the explanation for this differential treatment is the adherence to cognitive orientations through which we evaluate various forms of violence and assign them meaning within our everyday reality. It has been the aim here to demonstrate that these cognitive orientations should not serve as basis for differential treatment of violence by those seeking to understand crime as a social phenomenon. I have presented this discussion, not with certainty of its absolute rightness, but with the hope that it will stimulate others to consider the importance of creating a criminology adequate to the examination of crime as a phenomenon embedded in the very nature of social structure and supported by cognitive orientations beneficial to the maintenance of that structure.

NOTES

1. For a more detailed discussion of the incompatibilities between positivism and structural criminology see Taylor et al. (1973: 31-66) and Grabiner (1973).

2. Rossi et al. in examining the perceived seriousness of crimes found that respondents ranked assault with a gun on a stranger eighteenth in seriousness, but gave killing a pedestrian while speeding a ranking of forty-sixth.

3. These figures do not include an additional 15,000 persons who died as the result of their own negligence.

REFERENCES

Automobile Manufacturer's Association. 1970. Automobile Facts and Figures. Detroit, Michigan: Automobile Manufacturers Association, Inc.

Bureau of the Budget. 1973. Special Analysis, Budget of the United States Government: Fiscal Year 1974. Washington, D.C.: U.S. Government Printing Office.

Burgess, E. W. 1950. Comment. American Sociological Review 56 (July): 32-33.

Clinard, M. B. 1952. The Black Market. New York: Holt, Rinehart and Winston.

Clinard, M. B. and R. Quinney. 1973. Criminal Behavior Systems. New York: Holt, Rinehart and Winston.

Dinitz, S., R. R. Dynes, and A. C. Clark. 1969. Deviance: Studies in the Process of Stigmatization and Societal Reaction. New York: Oxford University Press.

Erikson, K. 1966. Wayward Puritans. New York: John Wiley and Sons, Inc.

Haddon, W. 1964. Accident Research. New York: Harper & Row.

Hartung, F. E. 1950. White collar offenses in the wholesale meat industry in Detroit. American Journal of Sociology 56 (July): 25-34.

Kakalik, J. S. and S. Wildhorn. 1972. The Private Police Industry: Its Nature and Extent. Washington, D.C.: U.S. Government Printing Office.

Kuhn, T. S. 1962. The Structure of Scientific Revolutions. Chicago: The University of Chicago Press.

——. 1973. Vehicular negligence: the social and criminal patterns of auto traffic fatalities. Ph.D. diss. Ohio State University.

Michalowski, R. J. 1975. Violence on the road: the crime of vehicular homicide. Journal of Research in Crime and Delinquency 12, 1 (January): 30-43.

——. 1976. Repression and criminal justice in capitalist America. Sociological Inquiry 46.

Monkkenen, E. 1973. Crime and poverty in a 19th century city: the "dangerous classes" of Columbia, Ohio 1860-1885. Ph.D. diss. University of Minnesota.

National Safety Council. 1971. Accidents Facts. Chicago: National Safety Council.

Platt, A. 1974. Prospects for a radical criminology in the United States. Crime and Social Justice 1, 1 (Spring): 2-10.

President's Commission on Law Enforcement and the Administration of Justice. 1967. Task Force Report: Crime and Its Impact. Washington, D.C.: U.S. Government Printing Office.

Quinney, R. 1974. Criminal Justice in America. Boston: Little, Brown and Co.

Reckless, W. C. 1973. The Crime Problem. New York: Appleton-Century Crofts.

Reid, S. T. 1976. Crime and Criminology: Hinsdale, Ill.: The Dryden Press.

Rossi, P. H. et al. 1974. The seriousness of crimes: normative structure and individual differences. American Sociological Review 39 (April): 224-37.

Schwendinger, H. and J. Schwendinger. 1970. Defenders of order or guardians of human rights. Issues in Criminology 5, 2 (Summer).

Sutherland, E. H. 1940. White collar criminality. American Sociological Review 5: 1-12.

———. 1945. Is "white-collar crime" crime? American Sociological Review 10: 132-39.

Tappan, P. W. 1947. Who is the criminal? American Sociological Review 12 (February): 96-102.

———. 1960. Crime, Justice and Correction. New York: McGraw Hill.

19

ISSUES FACING THE CRIMINOLOGY RESEARCHER WORKING IN THE CRIMINAL JUSTICE SYSTEM

Richard Dembo

Recent years have witnessed a growing recognition that the criminal justice system not only fails to rehabilitate the offender, but contributes to the development of criminal careers among a large proportion of the individuals it processes (Jones 1965, President's Commission 1968, Morris and Hawkins 1970, Jacob 1973, National Advisory Commission 1973, Howard 1974: 223-32). Various points of view have been put forth to account for the crisis in courts and corrections, ranging from suggestions to decriminalize certain behavior presently regarded as being in violation of the law to increasing the use of punishment as a means of coping with the epidemic increase in crime (cf. Morris and Hawkins 1970, Antilla 1972: 287-90, National Commission on Marijuana and Drug Abuse 1973). These contrasting views of how the law and correctional systems should be constituted underscore an important aspect of the public debate which affects the criminology researcher. Whether working for a federal, state, or local agency mandated to deal with law-violating behavior, or using clients of these organizations to pursue scientific interests, the criminology researcher is faced with several critical ethical issues which have been neglected in the wider controversy concerning the future of the criminal justice system.

Based upon the author's research experience in the criminal justice field and a review of the relevant literature, it is the purpose of the present chapter to detail several dimensions of conflict between the criminology researcher working in corrections, or other parts of the criminal justice system, and the employers and/or sponsors of this work. In the context of this discussion, it will be possible to show how these issues touch on some basic problems affecting the progress of the criminal justice system and the maturation of the field of criminology.

MODELS OF INQUIRY AND CRIMINOLOGY

Traditional social science and criminology have sought to develop methods of inquiry and theoretical systems that are not value-laden. Tracing from the thoughts of Max Weber (1949), and finding recent, professional influence in the work of Parsons (1951, 1954), Merton (1957) and Wolfgang (1963: 155-62), the concept of value-free social science has come under increasing attack, as social scientists have found it impossible to divorce their ethical premises from the formulation of the issues they research (Polanyi 1962, Myrdal 1969). This is particularly the case for areas involving social concerns which are, themselves, value based.

Indeed, the view that social science research can be conducted in an atmosphere that is devoid of the orientations of the researcher is, itself, a biased one (Gouldner 1970, Becker 1970). Theoretical models presume particular views of the phenomena the social scientist sets out to study. Notions of what ought to be, as well as what exists, are involved in the premises of various social science paradigms.

The criminologist's predominant concern has been to uncover patterns of "deviant" behavior existing in the society. This naive empiricist position regards the knower and the known as fundamentally separate, and sees both parties as being increasingly united by various techniques of observation and methods of analysis which are systematically accumulated. It entails acceptance of an orderly universe which exists outside the researcher, one which is never critically examined (Blumer 1969).

The fundamental intellectual failure of this positivistic view of nature lies in its treatment of the individual as an object, its negation of the moral element that underlies so much of human activity, especially that which has been defined as criminal, and its inability to see beyond its own limitations (Quinney 1974). The researcher is so preoccupied with finding out what exists that he neglects to consider whether the particular issue he is examining is worthwhile to pursue in the first place.

Notwithstanding the limitations of positivism, this model of inquiry in criminology has found widespread support among bureaucratic managers of criminal justice and correctional agencies. An important reason for this acceptance is that the positivistic model takes a very conservative view of the social world. It regards existing forms of social organization and behavior as given and seeks to understand them in their own terms. In particular, criminal behavior is accepted as a social problem, and not problematic in terms of how the law is created and enforced. This narrow-minded focus on the phenomenon of crime fits in well with the interests of criminal justice and correctional officials. Wanting to perpetuate their positions and bureaus, these administrators are concerned over the demystification resulting from research of current theories, policies and practices supporting their organizations. While fiscal and political pressures have forced criminal justice and correctional departments to be more accountable for their activities, the heads of these agencies do not want to have research pursued which could lead to a questioning of the value of their organizations. Accordingly, interest in social-science research usually centers on the acquisition of information that can permit the reinforcement of vulnerable parts of a given agency, answering public criticism or enabling criminal justice and correctional departments to be more efficient in their operation. It is beyond the capability of this line of research work to illuminate weaknesses in the criminal justice system and to provide guidelines to devise a system that can be more humane (Quinney 1970).

CONSTRAINTS OF EMPLOYMENT AND THE FINANCING OF RESEARCH

Regardless of the orientations of the criminology researcher to the issues under investigation, there are the interests of the employer or sponsors which provide conditions limiting the lines along which work can be pursued. These influences are rarely felt in a direct manner. Rather, they are indirectly encouraged in terms of the research priorities which provide a frame of reference for one's efforts; or, in the case of the funding of research, they are sensed as areas of inquiry that stand a realistic chance of receiving a grant.

Employment Constraints

Concerned with the efficient operation of their organizations, managers of the various components of the criminal justice system give high priority to the orderly processing and surveillance of their clients with a minimum of intrusion and expense. These interests lend themselves to head counting which, even today, constitutes a large bulk of the so-called research activities carried out by these agencies.

Because the research needs of criminal justice and correctional agencies are usually of a more immediate kind—such as resolving a problem in their operation or answering public criticism—programmatic studies are seldom pursued. When long-term projects are undertaken, they are often hampered by the pragmatic, narrow-minded interests of the officials of these organizations.

Basic research is a luxury in criminal justice and corrections. When it is engaged in, it runs the risk of being affected by a limited view of the clients who are the individual organization's mandated responsibility. This narrow focus, which looks at clients in terms of how they can be made to fit into the criminal justice system, rather than the more sensible view of examining the system of services in terms of making it more useful to clients, has served to perpetuate the antiquated state of the treatment arts as practiced by these organizations (Mitford 1973, Takagi 1973: 313-19).

An important reason that basic research is discouraged in criminal justice and correctional agencies is, as was alluded to earlier, the potential threat that findings may pose to these organizations. To be worthwhile in its own terms, basic research requires freedom in the definition of its agenda and in the analysis and interpretation of its results. This research process can produce conclusions which suggest the need for fundamental changes in the activities of the organizations that were studied. Concerned with this possible outcome, agency officials and personnel are often reluctant to cooperate in these research efforts.

Researchers who uncover findings that do not support the interests and beliefs of their agency sponsors or employers may face a difficult situation. Their competence may be questioned because of their alleged failure to ask the "right" or "important" questions. Further, the investigators may see their research results ignored or selectively reinterpreted by agency officials. This can occur in several ways, three of which are illustrative of this process.

In the first case, the specific findings of the research are not questioned. However, the relevance of the results are taken to task by claims that changes in the agency's operations have addressed or will resolve the issues uncovered by the study. A second, related, agency response is to question the merit of the research on the grounds that the investigators lack a comprehensive knowledge of the history, philosophy, and current activities of the agency. According to the thrust of this argument, the research is slowed for failing to properly define its problem areas. A third way of neutralizing the findings of a given inquiry is to assert that the results obtained reflect the fact that the personnel who were the study's focus were not performing their jobs properly. Presumably, if these individuals were more skilled, not overworked, and exemplified the goals of the agency more clearly, the research would have come up with more complimentary conclusions. Associated with this third way of dealing with negative research findings is the attempt to rationalize them as constituting administrative concerns, and, therefore, not meriting their release to the public.

These ways in which agency officials relate to research findings that conflict with their interests may be consciously chosen. In many cases, however, they are unconsciously pursued, reflecting sincere attempts to protect the particular views that criminal justice and correctional officials have of their organizations and their own motives.

The Funding of Research

The pursuit of a study of any reasonable scope is expensive and time consuming and requires personnel. These realities have forced the criminologist to a greater reliance on various patrons for his work. In the last two decades, government has become the major provider of research monies in the criminal justice and correctional fields. Government sponsorship has had consequences for the theoretical and empirical interests of the criminologist. Drawing upon Galliher and McCartney's (1973: 77-90) analysis of published delinquency research from 1940 to 1970, government funding of research has led to a focus on defective individual theories of crime and delinquency. Studies whose results might raise questions that challenge the existing social structure are often regarded as too controversial to support. Further, researchers have increasingly emphasized the statistical examination of official police and court records in their work, using the individual as the primary unit of analysis. In summarizing their results, Galliher and McCartney (1973: 88) make the following pointed assessment:

> Most governments can be expected to find comfort in an orientation that proclaims a controlled and contained mankind and deemphasizes freedom. When combined with scientific empiricism, hard positivism becomes especially attractive to government. Hard positivists, maintaining that man is controlled, strive to isolate the specific mechanisms of control. This view of man is appealing when dealing with criminals since it suggests that research can isolate the variables necessary for controlling crime.

In this regard, it is understandable, although particularly distressing, that so much of the research financed by the Law Enforcement Assistance Administration (LEAA) of the Department of Justice (1970) and the National Institute of Mental Health (NIMH), through its Center for Studies of Crime and Delinquency (1971), is designed to increase the managerial efficiency of the criminal justice system and to develop more sophisticated police techniques. There appears to be relatively little interest in supporting research that can help in understanding what it means to grow up in a high-crime area, what it means to be processed by the criminal justice system, and the problems facing the ex-convict in contemporary society. These issues, which raise alternative views about the way in which crime is treated in America, are given little encouragement by these powerful grant-giving bodies.

THE CRIMINOLOGIST'S PROFESSIONALISM AND COMMITMENT TO A BETTER SOCIETY

Another dilemma involves the conflict over the criminology researchers' professional status and the pursuit of their responsibility to help create a better society. This issue is most frequently encountered in instances in which the criminologist comes across cases of incompetence or failure to provide claimed services which, if corrected, could improve the operation of the particular organization in question. It is appreciated that personnel may be widely diffused within institutions and that abuses or inadequacies may take place that are unknown to centrally located administrators. It is, also, an understandable reaction of administrators that, when such deficiencies are discovered, their first response is to come to the defense of their agency and then consider the remediation of the matters that have been uncovered. Pitted against more powerful institutional forces, the criminology researcher may feel inclined to withdraw from the situation, rather than pursue the issue either through the agency concerned, a higher public level represented by the organization for whom he or she works, or through the mass media. On the other hand, it can be argued that neglecting to pursue the correction of any aspects of agency performance that hinder its capability to provide services to its charges only serves to continue these unacceptable activities. The criminologist can be forgiven for being ignorant about how to redress the conditions that may have been found, and for being concerned about the career consequences of running head-on with powerful bureaucratic organizations seeking to protect themselves. However, failure to act responsibly under these circumstances cannot be excused.[1]

One way in which administrators attempt to deal with the potential conflict between the researcher's sense of social responsibility and the wish to protect the operations of their agencies is to define any matters concerning the activities of the organization as managerial concerns, and outside the province of legitimate research interest. This tactic acts to limit the thrust of research to the exploration of issues that are tangential to the way in which the agency actually works and affects the lives of its clients, which may have been one reason for conducting the research in the first place. In this posture, criminologists fulfill the role of hired-hand experts, enhancing the credentials of the organization for whom they works, or are sponsored or funded by without being able to take comfort in the fact that what they do has any relevance to the experience of the agency. In this manner, criminal justice organizations assure the continued dominance of the uninformed premises that have misguided their operation for so long.

Criminologists have contributed to their hired-hand posture within the criminal justice system. Concerned with status and academic respectability, the criminology researcher has too often accepted these "benefits" at the expense of intellectual integrity. The cost of this compromise has not only been personal. Collectively, it has resulted in making the field of criminology less challenging and has reduced the discipline's ability to make a more informed contribution to society.

CONCLUSIONS

The criminal justice system is in a state of crisis, and the field of criminology at a crossroads. They cannot resolve their difficulties without a more critical view of their premises and goals. As part of this process, the criminologists working in correctional or other criminal justice agencies face increasingly important intellectual and ethical issues surrounding their work that demand attention. Criminologists, and the professional bodies to which they belong, would do well to develop codes of ethics that legitimate the questioning by criminological research of the assumptions of existing correctional programs and criminal justice agencies, with a view toward making them more relevant to the needs of American society.

In this regard, the criminologist has a responsibility to make research findings public—even when it may not be in the interests of the agency sponsors or employers to do so. Criminologists should view their commitment to the profession and the enhancement of the character of American life, as more important than their loyalty to a given organization. It is only in this way that the debate over the criminal justice system can be fully informed. When necessary, the criminologist should take an activist role in pressing for needed reforms in criminal justice or correctional agencies.

While the integrity of the field of criminology rests on the ethically informed behavior of its practitioners, the professional bodies to which they belong need to be supportive. These associations should support researchers when they seek to convince employers and/or sponsors that the priorities of investigation should be dictated on the basis of improving the prospects of rehabilitation. They should also encourage researchers to let their sense of social responsibility guide their research, even if it means requiring employers or sponsors to improve their services. What is being asked is that societies of criminology be less concerned with increasing the professional status of their membership than with directing their energies to improve the quality of life in America. To urge criminology researchers to give first priority to their social responsibilities is the best way to insure the progress of the criminal justice system and of the discipline to which they have committed themselves.[2]

NOTES

1. In this context, it is interesting to note that Brodsky (1972) has urged psychologists working in penitentiary and reformatory settings to take a more activist role in pursuing correctional reform.

2. I would like to thank Michael Agar, Harriet Bloch, Robinson Smith, and Torrington Watkins for their reactions to earlier versions of this paper.

REFERENCES

Antilla, I. 1972. Punishment versus treatment—is there a third alternative? Abstracts on Criminology and Penology 12: 287-90.

Becker, H. S. 1970. Sociological Work. Chicago: Aldine.

Blumer, H. 1969. Symbolic Interactionism: Perspective and Method. Englewood Cliffs, N.J.: Prentice-Hall.

Brodsky, S. L. 1972. Psychologists in the Criminal Justice System. Marysville, Ohio: American Association of Correctional Psychologists.

Galliher, J. F. and J. L. McCartney. 1973. The influence of funding agencies on juvenile delinquency research. Social Problems 21 (Summar): 77-90.

Gouldner, A. W. 1970. The Coming Crisis of Western Sociology. New York: Basic Books.

Howard, Jr., J. W. 1974. Law enforcement in an urban society. American Psychologist 29 (April): 223-32.

Jacob, H. 1973. Urban Justice. Englewood Cliffs, N.J.: Prentice-Hall.

Jones, H. 1965. The Courts, The Public and The Law Explosion. Englewood Cliffs, N.J.: Prentice-Hall.

Law Enforcement Assistance Administration. 1970. Grants and Contracts: Fiscal Year 1970. Washington, D.C.: Department of Justice.

Merton, R. K. 1957. Social Theory and Social Structure, Second Ed., Rev. Glencoe, Ill.: Free Press.

Mitford, J. 1973. Kind and Usual Punishment: The Prison Business. New York: Alfred A. Knopf.

Morris, N. and G. Hawkins. 1970. The Honest Politician's Guide to Crime Control. Chicago: University of Chicago Press.

Myrdal, G. 1969. Objectivity in Social Research. New York: Pantheon.

National Advisory Commission on Criminal Justice Standards and Goals. 1973. National Strategy to Reduce Crime. Washington, D.C.: U.S. Government Printing Office.

National Commission on Marijuana and Drug Abuse, Second Report. 1973. Drug Use in America: Problem in Perspective. Washington, D.C.: U.S. Government Printing Office.

National Institute of Mental Health, Center for Studies of Crime and Delinquency. 1971. Active Training Grants. Rockville, Md. Mimeographed.

Parsons, T. 1954. Essays in Sociological Theory, Pure and Applied, Second Ed. Glencoe, Ill.: Free Press.

——. 1951. The Social System. Glencoe, Ill.: Free Press.

Polanyi, M. 1962. Personal Knowledge: Towards a Post-Critical Philosophy. New York: Harper Torchbooks.

President's Commission on Law Enforcement and Administration of Justice. 1968. The Challenge of Crime in a Free Society. New York: Avon.

——. 1970. The Social Reality of Crime. Boston: Little, Brown and Co.

Quinney, R. 1974. Critique of Legal Order. Boston: Little, Brown and Co.

Takagi, P. 1973. Administration and Professional Conflicts in Modern Corrections. Journal of Criminal Law and Criminology 64 (September): 313-19.

Weber, M. 1949. The Methodology of the Social Sciences, trans. E. A. Shils and H. A. Finch. Glencoe, Ill.: Free Press.

Wolfgang, M. E. 1963. Criminology and the criminologist. Journal of Criminal Law, Criminology and Police Science 54 (June): 155-62.

20

THIEVERY AS A PROFESSION: A FOOTNOTE ON THE HISTORY OF A CURIOUS IDEA

Jack Kamerman

INTRODUCTION

Sociologists, in their approaches to criminal and noncriminal occupations, imply a relationship between criminality and the moral order (see, for example, Erikson 1966: 19-23). This chapter explores one version of that relationship—the notion of thievery as a "profession."

In his now-classic study, The Professional Thief (1956), Sutherland suggested that "full-time" thievery might well be viewed as a profession, not simply in the common sense of the term ("I am a cooper by profession"), but in the sociological sense. He did not suggest a metaphorical usage; rather, he matched the characteristics of "professional" thievery (Sutherland 1956: 215-17) with the ideal type of profession developed by Carr-Saunders and Wilson (1964: 284-87) and found a match on all characteristics but one: "ethical standards which minimize the pecuniary motive" (Sutherland 1956: 216; His thief informant, Conwell, used "professional" to distinguish that brand of thievery from the amateur brand and not as an occupational status ranking.) He further qualified this categorization by saying that, since the body of traditional knowledge passed along to young thieves was done by "apprenticeship methods rather than through a professional school . . . professional theft should not be regarded as a learned profession. It is probably more nearly on the level of professional athletics, so far as learning is concerned" (Sutherland 1956: 217).

In sum, Sutherland regarded thievery as a profession in the sociological sense, having matched all but one of the defining characteristics embodied in the ideal type developed by Carr-Saunders and Wilson.[1] He did not regard it as a learned profession. Learned, however, seems an accompanying, rather than a defining, characteristic of professions. Consequently, to regard it as resembling professional athletics in this respect in no way dislodges it from the category of profession.

It is argued in this paper that designating thievery as a profession was an eminently bad choice according to current thinking in the sociology of professions and the particular definitions Sutherland worked with in 1937. Moreover, like the proverbial bad penny, this elevation of thievery's place on the status ladder of occupations frequently turns up in contemporary criminological writings. Some suggestions will be offered to explain the acceptance of the notion of thievery as a profession both by examining the consequences of adopting that perspective and, more directly, by examining some possible reasons for its adoption. Finally, an alternative approach to the confluence of the sociology of occupations and criminology, delineated by Ritzer (1972) and more recently exemplified implicitly by Kockars (1974) will be discussed.

This critique is in no way meant to depreciate the seminal contribution in this area of criminology, or sociology in general for that matter, made by Sutherland in The Professional Thief. It is merely a footnote on the history of a curious idea.

THIEVERY AS A PROFESSION

The major source of difficulty in Sutherland's use of Carr-Saunders' and Wilson's ideal type lay in his apparent misinterpretation of technique, one of a profession's defining characteristics. By technique, Carr-Saunders and Wilson meant "specialized intellectual techniques . . . founded on the knowledge acquired by the study of a natural science . . . or based upon the study of human institutions" (Carr-Saunders and Wilson 1974: 284-85). They considered possession of a technique to be the single most important characteristic of a profession because each of the other characteristics flowed from it.

Ernest Greenwood similarly sees skill grounded in theory as the crucial characteristic differentiating professions from non-professions. After pointing out that tool-and-die making may involve more intricate skills than the activities of certain professions, he says:

> The crucial distinction in this: the skills that characterize a profession flow from and are supported by a fund of knowledge that has been organized into an internally consistent system, called a body of theory. A profession's underlying body of theory is a system of abstract propositions that describe in general terms the classes of phenomena comprising the profession's focus of interest. Theory serves as a base in terms of which the professional rationalizes his operations in concrete situations.

> Acquisition of the professional skill requires a prior or
> simultaneous mastery of the theory underlying that skill.
> Preparation for a profession, therefore, involves con-
> siderable preoccupation with systematic theory, a feature
> virtually absent in the training of the non-professional.
> And so treatises are written on legal theory, musical
> theory, social work theory, the theory of the drama, and
> so on; but no books appear on the theory of punchpressing
> or pipefitting or bricklaying (Greenwood 1966: 11).[2]

Yet in spite of these difficulties, the idea (albeit in a somewhat
diluted form) persists. Don C. Gibbons, for example, begins his
discussion of "property offender careers" by suggesting that "although
some might quarrel with the designation of professional attached to
these lawbreakers, such criminals do exhibit a long period of training, complex occupational skills, and a shared set of occupationally
oriented attitudes—elements usually regarded as central to professional status" (Gibbons 1973: 262). He cites Everett Hughes' concept
of profession for support (Hughes 1958: 33) although he recognizes
that Highes' chapter on license and mandate presents "some problems." And, while later referring to the professional thief as a
"skilled worker" (Gibbons 1973: 267), he again returns to the theme
of theft as a profession in his discussion of the "semiprofessional
property criminal role career":

> They [semiprofessional property offenders] employ crime
> skills which are relatively simple and uncomplicated.
> For example, strong-arm robbery does not involve much
> detailed planning and careful execution of the crime, but
> rather application of crude physical force in order to re-
> lieve a victim of his money. This is referred to as semi-
> professional crime, because even though technical skill
> is not characteristic of these offenders, most of them
> attempt to carry on crime as an occupation (1973: 273).

Gibbons obviously does not mean professional in a defensible sense,
that is, as an activity practices as an occupation, or else why refer
to strong-arm robbers as specifically semi-professional? They
also work full-time. Instead, he uses the term in much the same
way as certain sociologists studying occupations who refer to medicine and law as professions and nursing and social work as semi-
professions, that is, as different occupational status levels.

As a final example, William Chambliss, in his commentary
on Harry King's autobiographical <u>Box Man, A Professional Thief's
Journey</u> (Chambliss 1972) picks up the theme of theft as a profession

some 35 years after the publication of Sutherland's book. He expends several pages developing the similarities between "the thief and the most revered professions" (: 171-79). The thief (like the doctor), for example, "spends long and arduous hours learning his craft . . . the thief also <u>feels an obligation</u> to pass on this information and train others" (Chambliss 1972: 171-79; emphasis added).

CONSEQUENCES OF VIEWING THIEVERY AS A PROFESSION

The adoption of particular intellectual postures influences what is seen and isn't seen, what is emphasized and deemphasized, and so on. Viewing thievery as a profession, or at the very least as sharing some characteristics in common with professions (see Vollmer and Mills 1966: 28-29) has tended to produce certain consequences in the study of thievery. Pointing to these connections has no necessary effect on the validity of these ideas; however, it is hoped that it will help to expose the network of choices that develops after a particular perspective is adopted. The major consequences are:

1. a concentration on the complexity of skills and training required to become a "professional" thief;
2. a buttressing of the ideological claims of thieves;
3. support of the self-ratings of thieves;
4. an emphasis on the moral code of thieves;
5. a tendency to "normalize" criminal activity;
6. a blocking out of the similarities between thievery and occupations at status levels other than profession; and
7. an emphasis on the "useful" functions of criminal activity.

Running through the autobiographical accounts of thieves and the editorial commentary of sociologists on them (for example, Chambliss 1972, Sutherland 1956), as well as other criminological works (Einstadter 1969, Shover 1973, Gibbons 1973), are the themes of the sophistication and specialization of the skills required to become a thief (or "good" burglar as Shover would have it) and the necessity of tutelage in the form of an extended apprenticeship during which those complex skills are acquired. The skills range from manual and technical skills—in the case of the box man—to the art of impression management—in the case of the con man (Clinard and Quinney 1973: 250-51). Concentration on the complexity of these skills follows from the process of "naming" thieves professionals (see Strauss 1969: 15-25 on naming as an act of placement). The ideology of professional thieves is frequently detailed, although the distinction between the use of an idea ideologically and the validity of that notion is sometimes blurred. Clinard and Quinney (1973: 250) point out that seeing all people as dishonest is part of the occupational ideology of "professional" thieves. They quickly add that "the victim of the con game, after all, has been willing to participate in a crime in order to make money." Yet these authors never succumb to the temptation of an extended discourse on the corruption of all people. The same cannot be said for Chambliss. He adopts the thief's ideology as his picture of the world (1972: 171-75). "The thief shares with the business man a commitment to violation of certain laws whenever necessary. . . . [The laws are different] but the principle remains the same; the thief and the businessman systematically and consistently violate the law" (: 172). The point, again, is simply that seeing the thief as a professional has, as one of its consequences, tended to concentrate on professional ideology as an object of study and, in the case of some, to accept it as the true version of the world.[3]

One of the claims which Sutherland and Chambliss accepted was their thieves' self-ratings. First, both thieves thought of their work as an "occupation," a quasi-legitimate gainful pursuit. In addition, both thought of themselves as "professionals." The two editors accepted their respondents' ranking of illegal occupations without commenting on the possible biases in those rankings. For example, Harry King was a box man and that might explain why he ranks box men at the top of the hierarchy of thieves (Chambliss 1972: 70).

Another consequence of conceptualizing thievery as a profession is the tendency to emphasize the thieves' code of ethics. This emphasis derives from defining thievery as a profession as opposed to some other occupational ranking. A code of ethics is one of the crucial characteristics of a profession; studies of the ethical codes of professionals swell the literature. On the other hand, a code of ethics is a trace element in the ideal type of other occupational rankings—skilled workers, for example; and certainly few studies have focused on those codes. The studies under examination not only detailed the "honor code" among thieves, but, in some recent analyses, lamented its supposed passing.[4] This emphasis has the further consequence of generating sympathy in the plight of the old craftsman displaced by the young hustler who has no respect for elder statesmen and their honorable ways.[5] As Harry King so succinctly put it, "Professional theft is just like the rest of the world: kind of falling apart" (Chambliss 1972: 70).

Intimately tied to this sentimental confection is the "normalization" of criminal activity embedded in the writings examined. To begin with, the notion of occupation itself suggests respectability because it implies work, and work, in American society, is considered intrinsically good. Chambliss spends the bulk of his commentary drawing parallels between legal and illegal occupations (1972: 167-79). Clinard and Quinney (1973: 256-58) make similar comparisons. Frequently, the parallels are well drawn. Often, however, they neglect to mention the basic difference that colors much of the activities involved in illegal occupations—their illegality. For those sociologists with a labeling bias, this inattention to the importance of differing reactions to the occupational behavior, which flows from the definition of some behavior as legal and some as illegal, is particularly ironic.[6]

The notion that criminals are just like everybody else in the sense that their criminality is just like non-criminal behavior may result in part, as Klockars (1974: 136) points out, from the fact that they are only asked to define that relationship to outsiders. It is certainly likely that their explanations to outsiders are to some extent situational—they have more to do with the specific social situation in which these explanations are given (an interview by, or conversation with, outsiders) than with their more general belief or their existence as a prerequisite for carrying on criminal activity.[7] Whether or not it is true that professional criminals believe their activity to be just like any non-criminal business enterprise is not as important as the apparent acceptance by sociologists of that piece of occupational ideology and the consequent aiding and abetting of the "normalization" of their criminal activity. The situational attractiveness of this notion makes suspect any claim by criminals to straights that "we're just like everybody else—for example, prostitutes have orgasms, attachments, and hearts of gold (Bryan 1965). Also, because of this fixation on professions, the parallels between illegal and legal occupations of different rankings have generally been neglected.[8] Finally, there is an emphasis on the "useful" functions of criminal activity. Prostitutes are not so much "hookers" as practitioners of a venerable service profession who prevent rapes, salvage the integrity of families, and act as lay therapists. This, of course, is the mirror fallacy of the position which sees activity defined as criminal or deviant as "pathological."[9]

These, then, are the consequences of viewing thievery as a profession. Some of the reasons such a perspective might be adopted are suggested by the implications of these consequences.

WHY SEE THIEVERY AS A PROFESSION?

Reasons can be grouped under two headings: extrasociological and sociological.

Extrasociological

The sociologists considered in this paper exhibit what Alvin Gouldner has called, "sympathy with the underdog" (Gouldner 1968).

Gouldner (: 606) characterizes liberalism as an "official ideology of wide sectors of the American University Community as well as broader strata of American life":

> The new underdog propounded by Becker, is, then, a standpoint that possesses a remarkably convenient combination of properties; it enables the sociologist to befriend the very small underdogs in local settings, to reject the standpoing of the 'middle dog' respectables and notables who manage local caretaking establishments, while at the same time, to make and remain friends with the really top dogs in Washington agencies or New York foundations. While Becker adopts a posture as the intrepid preacher of a new underdog sociology, he has really given birth to something rather different: to the first version of new Establishment sociology, to a sociology compatible with the new character os social reform in the United States today. It is a sociology of and for the new welfare state. It is a sociology of young men with friends in Washington. It is a sociology that succeeds in solving the oldest problem in personal politics: how to maintain one's integrity without sacrificing one's career, or how to remain a liberal although well-heeled (Gouldner 1968: 602).

There is a parallel development in the writings of some criminologists who have wholeheartedly adopted the underdog's viewpoint (for example, Chambliss).[10] Chambliss makes King into a folk hero much in the spirit of the Boy Scouts greeting Al Capone as he entered his box in a Chicago ball field.[11]

There is another concomitant of this middle-class sociology: the Puritan belief in the excitement which inheres in evil. Puritanism is a value complex that has thrived throughout the history of the United States.[12] From a Puritan viewpoint, evil is always more interesting, colorful, and seductive than good, the popular cultural romance that middle-class America has had with outlaw motorcycle gangs further evidences this notion. It is only a Puritanical mind, after all, that could produce the category of literature known as "dirty books." I think this is what underlies Matza's remark, "We do not for a moment wish that we could rid ourselves of deviant phenomena. We are intrigued by them. They are an intrinsic, ineradicable, and vital part of human society" (Matza 1969: 17). Matza fails, however, to mention the extent to which his observations are culture bound.

Sociological

There are also sociological reasons for seeing thievery as a profession. Professionalization, in much recent thinking, is conceptualized as a continuum; it may be fruitful to try to locate an occupation on this continuum if for nothing else than to characterize it by its deficiencies in matching this model. Sutherland's study was good shock therapy for a criminology which had been virtually blind to the intricate and to some extent symbiotic ties between the legal and illegal worlds. (Much as White Collar Crime was some years later.) In addition, criminal activity does in fact have important functions in a society and the literature under scrutiny has helped to expose these functions. It was unfortunate, however, for the future progress of this work that Sutherland chose a professional model against which to match thievery. It would have been enough to simply establish that parallels existed between legal and illegal occupations. Then analysts of illegal occupations might have allowed these occupations to seek their own level.

AN ALTERNATIVE RELATIONSHIP BETWEEN THE SOCIOLOGY OF OCCUPATION AND CRIMINOLOGY

Ritzer (1972: 274-300), following Everett Hughes, suggests that many, but not all, of the problems facing people in deviant occupations are similar to those facing people in non-deviant occupations. His analysis does not seem, however, sufficiently refined. For example, while he does recognize that an occupational hierarchy exists in deviant occupations located in formal organizations, he balances this contribution by lumping together all "free deviant occupations" as "low-status occupations."[13] In fact, while the hierarchy may not extend to professionals (the thesis of the earlier sections of this paper), there are graduations among free deviant occupations which run, for example, from unskilled worker through skilled worker to salesperson.[14] Con men are similar to salespeople while box men are closer to skilled workers. They are, of course, different in some ways, in that they must content with the law as a dominant feature of their occupational activity.

Carl Klockars' study (1974) exemplifies the approach that is suggested here by pointing to the similarities in occupational level between the professional fence and the small entrepreneur while also pointing to the consequences that flow from its illegality. Klockars also, in general, avoids the difficulties that other students of professional crime fell into. Perhaps Klockars focused on the relationship between the consequences that flow from an occupation's level and its illegality in his case study of Vincent Swaggi because Vincent was in fact both a fence and "legitimate businessman" (Klockars 1974: 77). The juxtaposition of the two was almost unavoidable. The advantages of locating an illegal occupation at the appropriate occupational level are borne out by Kockars' astute analysis.

In summary, only after attempts to elevate thieves to the level of professionals have been abandoned can criminologists and occupational sociologists begin to exploit each others' findings and abandon the polemics that have characterized their association until now.

NOTES

1. Even this deficiency—that is, ethical standards minimizing the pecuniary motive—was neutralized by Chic Conwell who pointed out that "the medical and legal professions would have very few members if that were used as a criterion of membership" (Sutherland 1956: 216). If it is used as a criterion for classifying an occupation along the continuum of professionalization, however, it is more successful (cf. Ritzer 1972: 58-59).

2. More recently, Freidson has defined profession "primarily as a special status in the division of labor supported by official and sometime public belief that it is worthy of such status. . . ."—a definition which would also exclude thievery (Freidson 1970: 187). The point here is not to make an exhaustive examination of the merits of various approaches to the definition of profession offered by sociologists over the past 40 years; rather, it is to point to the obvious fact, using definitions by way of example, that thievery cannot be construed as a profession using any sociological definition of profession.

I wish also to point briefly to the poor fit of thievery to the other characteristics Sutherland used to judge it a profession. Immunity from punishment hardly amounts to license from the state to steal. That this immunity is informal and partial should be enough to differentiate it from the license granted to practice medicine, for example. Thieves also have no mandate (cf. Hughes 1958: 78-87 for a full discussion of license and mandate). These differences are central to Freidson's conception of the legitimacy of an occupation's claim to professional status. Informal tolerance should in no way be lumped together with formal sanction. The use of marijuana may be tolerated and in many ways be similar to the use of alcohol, but you can be arrested and sent to prison for using one and, in general, not be so "reacted to" for using the other. Labeling theorists should be particularly sensitive to these reactive differences.

3. Contrast this with Skolnick's portrait of the working personality of the policeman (1966: 42-70). It is seen as a function of the elements of the work setting of police. Chambliss makes no such point; instead, he sees his respondent's version of straight citizens not as a function of the ones he met in his work, but rather as an accurate portrayal of the rampant dishonesty in the straight world in general.

4. For citations of recent studies, see Shover (1973: 512).

5. This interestingly parallels the argument of some recent popular writings which claim the disillusionment of some older Mafia "dons" in their young American-born underlings and the consequent importation of young Italians who understand honor, respect, and loyalty.

6. See Ritzer (1972: 274-300) for a treatment which strikes a balance in pointing to the similarities and differences between illegal occupations and their legal analogues.

7. For an example of this view, see Sykes and Matza (1957).

8. With some notable exceptions: Ritzer (1972: 274-300), Goffman (1972), and Cressey (1969: 112-19)—although in this last the parallels are merely drawn and not explored. Some effects of adopting this alternative posture are discussed in the last section of this chapter.

9. Compare Mills (1942) and Becker (1963: 7) for criticism of the "square-john" version of this fallacy.

10. It will be remembered that Sutherland, in contrast, was professionally skeptical of Conwell's story, characterizing some of his remarks as "sketchy and rationalistic interpretation" (Sutherland 1956: 231) and showing parts of the manuscript to other thieves for corroboration. His error seemed more intellectual and less ideological, that is, exploring the extensions of the idea of thievery as a profession. Compare this with Chambliss' uncritical and passionate defense of his "friend," Harry King.

11. I do not believe that this is a necessary consequence of taking the interactionist and ethnomethodological positions of either

trying to see things from the point of view of others or respecting the intelligence and analytic capacities of one's respondents. It is just another example of garden variety "bad" sociology.

12. This idea was suggested by a Canadian Broadcasting Company documentary on American westerns titled "Let's Shoot the Devil." Its narration pointed out that in classic westerns the "good girl" was blond and bland while the "bad girl" black-haired, seductive, and fascinating. The Devil, himself, is often depicted in literature, opera, and so on as a suave, engaging gentleman, although in the western he is the sly stranger dressed in black (the "bad guy").

13. "Since free deviant occupations are similar to low-status occupations, individuals in them have very restricted career patterns" (Ritzer 1972: 292).

14. As was mentioned, he recognizes these distinctions in deviant occupations which exist in formal organizations—"However, it is true that there are deviant occupations within the Mafia which parallel the occupations discussed earlier in this book. Thus we will assume that, for example, an individual in a foreman-level occupation within the Mafia faces the same kinds of problems as an industrial foreman, or that the low-status employee in the Mafia is similar in many ways to the low-status worker in straight organizations" (Ritzer 1972: 290).

REFERENCES

Becker, Howard S. 1963. Outsiders, Studies in the Sociology of Deviance. New York: The Free Press of Glencoe.

Bryan, James H. 1965. Apprenticeships in prostitution. Social Problems 12 (Spring): 287-97.

Carr-Saunders, A. M. and P. A. Wilson. 1964. The Professions. London: Frank Cass & Co., Ltd.

Chambliss, W., ed. 1972. Box Man: A Professional Thief's Journey. New York: Harper & Row.

Clinard, M. B. and R. Quinney. 1973. Criminal Behavior Systems. A Typology, Second Ed. New York: Holt, Rinehart and Winston.

Cressey, D. R. 1969. Theft of the Nation. The Structure and Operations of Organized Crime in America. New York: Harper & Row.

Einstadter, W. J. 1969. The social organizations of armed robbery. Social Problems 17 (Summer): 64-83.

Erikson, K. T. 1966. Wayward Puritans: A Study in the Sociology of Deviance. New York: John Wiley & Sons, Inc.

Freidson, E. 1970. Profession of Medicine. A Study of the Sociology of Applied Knowledge. New York: Dodd, Mead & Co.

Gibbons, D. C. 1973. Society, Crime, and Criminal Careers, Second Ed. Englewood Cliffs, N.J.: Prentice-Hall.

Goffman, E. 1962. On cooling the mark out: some aspects of adaptation to failure. In Human Behavior and Social Processes: An Interactionist Approach, ed. A. M. Rose. Boston: Houghton Mifflin Company.

Gouldner, A. W. 1971. The sociologist as partisan: sociology and the welfare state. In The Sociological Perspective, Second Ed., ed. S. G. McNall. Boston: Little, Brown and Company.

Greenwood, E. 1966. The elements of professionalization. In Professionalization, eds. H. M. Vollmer and D. L. Mills. Englewood Cliffs, N.J.: Prentice-Hall.

Hughes, E. C. 1958. Men and Their Work. Glencoe, Ill.: The Free Press.

Klockars, C. B. 1974. The Professional Fence. New York: The Free Press.

Matza, D. 1969. Becoming Deviant. Englewood Cliffs, N.J.: Prentice-Hall.

Mills, C. W. 1942. The professional ideology of social pathologists. American Journal of Sociology 49 (September): 165-80.

Ritzer, G. 1972. Man and His Work. Conflict and Change. New York: Appleton-Century-Crofts.

Shover, N. 1973. The social organization of burglary. Social Problems 20 (Spring): 499-514.

Skolnick, J. H. 1966. Justice Without Trial: Law Enforcement in Democratic Society. New York: John Wiley & Sons, Inc.

Strauss, A. L. 1969. Mirrors and Masks. The Search for Identity. San Francisco: The Sociology Press.

Sutherland, E. H., ed. 1956. The Professional Thief. Chicago: The University of Chicago Press.

Sykes, G. M. and D. Matza. 1957. Techniques of neutralization: a theory of delinquency. American Sociological Review 22: 667-70.

Vollmer, H. M. and D. L. Mills, eds. 1966. Professionalization. Englewood Cliffs, N.J.: Prentice-Hall.

ABOUT THE EDITORS

NICHOLAS N. KITTRIE is dean and professor of criminal and comparative law at The American University Law School. Former counsel to the United States Senate Judiciary Committee, Dr. Kittrie is also past president of the American Society of Criminology. His current research areas are: political crime and terrorism, biomedical ethics, and moral issues in technological development.

JACKWELL SUSMAN teaches and conducts research at The American University. He is a member of numerous professional societies, and has written and published extensively. He is also a poet, actor, and student of oriental philosophies and martial arts.

RELATED TITLES
Published by
Praeger Special Studies

BARGAINING FOR JUSTICE: Case Disposition
and Reform in the Criminal Courts

Suzann R. Thomas Buckle
Leonard G. Buckle

DRUGS, CRIME, AND POLITICS

edited by
Arnold S. Trebach

THE NEW AND THE OLD CRIMINOLOGY

edited by
Edith Elizabeth Flynn
John P. Conrad

REFORM IN CORRECTIONS: Problems
and Issues

edited by
Harry E. Allen
Nancy J. Beran

TOWARD A JUST AND EFFECTIVE
SENTENCING SYSTEM: Agenda for
Legislative Reform

Pierce O'Donnell
Michael J. Churgin
Dennis E. Curtis